S0-BGG-645

MARK TWAIN ON MAN AND BEAST

MARK TWAIN
ON
MAN AND BEAST

by
Janet Smith

WITHDRAWN
Pierce Library
Eastern Oregon University
From EOU Library
La Grande, OR 97850

LAWRENCE HILL & CO.

NEW YORK   WESTPORT

Copyright © 1972 Janet Smith
All rights reserved
ISBN clothbound edition: 0-88208-007-5
ISBN paperback edition: 0-88208-008-3
Library of Congress catalogue
card number: 72-78319

First edition September 1972

Manufactured in the United States of America
1 2 3 4 5 6 7 8 9 10 11 12

Design by Andrea Marquez

This book is
dedicated, with love,
to
Nathan Katz.

ACKNOWLEDGMENTS

I am indebted in many ways to my friend Robert Smith, and to Frederick Anderson, editor of The Mark Twain Papers. But neither of them is responsible for my opinions.

I am grateful to Harper and Row for permission to reprint the following: "The Bee" from *What Is Man? and Other Essays* (1917); "The President and the Nature Fakir," "The President and the Cow," "Jim Wolf and the Wasps," and "Jim Wolf and More Wasps" from *Mark Twain in Eruption* (1940); "The Lowest Animal," "The Goat and the Tortoise," "Noah's Ark," and "A Cat-Tale" from *Letters from the Earth* (1962); "This Friend of Satan" from *The Mysterious Stranger* (1916).

I also appreciate use of the following material originally published by the University of California Press; reprinted by permission of The Regents of the University of California: "Sailor Dog" and "Swinks and Sooflaskies" from *Which Was the Dream?* (1967); "The Admiral and the Cat" from *Mark Twain's Fables of Man* (1972).

TABLE OF CONTENTS

MARK TWAIN ON MAN AND BEAST

INTRODUCTION

He was a good enough sort of cretur, and hadn't no harm in him, and was just a genius, as the papers said, which wasn't his fault. We can't all be sound; we've got to be the way we're made.

—*Tom Sawyer Abroad*

For short, we can call the forty-four selections in this book animal stories. But as the reader will see, that doesn't really describe them. It helps, but not very much, to add that some of them are parables, like Aesop's. It helps a little more to add that they include poetry written in prose, alleged lectures that are very funny, and alleged fun that is so savage there's no laughing at it. In short, what we have here are forty-four of Mark Twain's highly emotional comments on life, distinguished from his other comments only because in each of them birds or beasts or fish or insects play a part. And so do people. Sometimes his animals are instantly recognizable as people; his coyote is every poor, wretched, scavenging human failure anybody has ever met. But none of this (except for the bit called "Reptiles") is done in Aesop's simple fashion. Morals there are aplenty, but not for Mark Twain the simple moral of the dog in the manger—in which, of course, the dog isn't doggish. For although Mark Twain's coyote may be human, he is also every inch a coyote, and his look, sound, smell, and habits are observed with precision and sympathy.

If Mark Twain had extended to people the kind of tolerance

he extended to every other species, he would have been a saint, and possibly a dull one. But, although he loved some people, his own species filled him with horror. He said so frequently and eloquently enough, but many readers have made the mistake of imagining that this was only his fun, or some sort of literary exaggeration. "I never could tell a lie that anybody would doubt," he once said, "nor a truth that anybody would believe." The truth was that the damned human race, as he called us, appalled him so deeply that, just to stay sane, it was necessary for him constantly to unpack his heart, either in his art or to his long-suffering family and friends, of the poisonous stuff—shock, despair, contempt, or rage—that bubbled everlastingly within him. It was just as he wrote his friend William Dean Howells: "I have been reading the morning paper. I do it every morning—well knowing that I shall find in it the usual depravities and basenesses and hypocrisies and cruelties that make up civilization, and cause me to put in the rest of the day pleading for the damnation of the human race."

And so many of these animal stories are simply outbursts at people; "The Lowest Animal" is typical of that sort. And some, like "Noah's Ark," are outbursts at God. And some are stories, and some are portraits like flashes of lightning, and some are simple nonsense. The same is true of the miniature stories—snapshots or wisecracks, most of them with their own bird or beast or bug—that follow the selections. It is improbable that everyone will like them all.

But I do. That, necessarily, was my standard of selection. Out of all the Mark Twain that could, by any definition, be called an animal story, I discarded nine because they seemed to me inferior. I made no effort to concentrate on the obscure, although eleven of these selections are not in print elsewhere. A good many others are available only in little-known or scholarly works, so that only the most fanatical of Mark Twain fans may have run across them. On the other hand, I could not dream of excluding the great familiar classics—familiar at least to schoolchildren, who read them in anthologies, although not, perhaps,

to grown-ups—such as "Baker's Blue Jays" and "The Celebrated Jumping Frog."

In the notes that precede each section of this book I have
tried to provide a condensed biography of Mark Twain. Necessarily, it is cut up—one part of Mark Twain's life in one note,
another in another. The chronological outline at the back of the
book will help put the bits together. There is, unfortunately, a
dearth of good biographies of Mark Twain in the bookstores. If
things were as I think they should be, this would not be the
case, for one of the greatest biographies of any American is of
Mark Twain; this three-volume work by his friend and secretary, Albert Bigelow Paine, has long been out of print and is
still considered, by some literary authorities, hopelessly old-
fashioned.

But times are changing. I don't know when or how, but undoubtedly the great Paine work will come back into print.
Moreover, teams of scholars, working under the direction of
Mark Twain's current literary executor, Frederick Anderson,
and sponsored by the Modern Language Association, have em-
barked on a mighty project: to publish the whole vast treasury
of still-unpublished Mark Twain that has long been stored at
various universities. "Sailor Dog," "The Admiral and the Cat,"
and "Swinks and Sooflaskies," all in this book, come from such
recent scholarly volumes of hitherto unpublished Mark Twain.
In time there will even appear his full *Autobiography,* only part
of which has been published. This massive manuscript is not
chronological and indeed is no more an "autobiography" than
the many volumes, thinly disguised as travel books or essays, in
which Mark Twain told the tale of his inner life. The latter—
which I have rifled freely for this anthology—are Mark Twain's
"personal books," according to his friend, the great nineteenth-
century critic William Dean Howells. They are, said Howells,
"of an immediate and most informal hospitality which admits
you at once to the author's confidence, and makes you frankly
welcome. . . . He takes no trouble in the matter and asks you
to take none. All that he requires is that you will have common

sense, and be able to tell a joke when you see it." [1] This seems a modest demand, but part of the difficulty in the Mark Twain criticism is that so many critics have been deficient in common sense or unduly solemn.

All the same, times are changing. Educated people—I don't know why or how—have a new feeling for Mark Twain. (The comparatively uneducated never deserted him.) With them are the scholars who are investing such enormous efforts to bring out his work complete and as he intended it.

So much for the public and the scholars. But for literary critics times have changed very little. For fifty years they have strongly objected to Mark Twain, both the man and the writer. But before I trace this critical tradition, I had better make plain the difference, which many people may not have considered, between scholars and critics.

Roughly, scholars are concerned with facts and critics with opinions. Of course there is overlapping; there are opinionated scholars—I am one myself—and many critics are more or less scholarly. The difficulty here is the ground that the critics try to cover. Typically, they include as their field, not only American literature, past and present, but world literature too. Moreover, many of these literary men double as experts on political, economic, and social questions. Considering the amount of petty— and important—detail in all these fields, who is gifted enough to master all of it?

The result has been that what critics could not master they were rather tempted to denigrate. And that is a dangerous line to take. To scorn another man's opinion is harmless, but once the lowly fact is despised, the very foundations of criticism are affected, so that it gradually becomes more and more inaccurate, reckless, and even corrupt. Something of this is illustrated by the Mark Twain criticism. Something of it also appears in the fact that a few of our most powerful critics have objected strongly to the publication of the scholarly editions of Mark Twain now coming out. And not only to the editions of Mark Twain. The Modern Language Association, an important organization for literary scholars, is also sponsoring scholarly editions of all the American writers that it considers classic. This project has been bitterly attacked by critics, led by the late Edmund Wilson, and including thirteen out of fourteen people whose support he enlisted. Not all the thirteen were full-time professional critics; indeed one of them (President Kennedy) was a politician: some others, such as W. H. Auden, Robert Lowell, R. P. Blackmur, and Mark Van Doren double as poets or scholars. But on this occasion they were all acting as critics in that they were expressing opinion on a literary subject rather than governing the country, writing poetry, or dealing with fact. And all, said Wilson, "expressed cordial agreement" with his attack on the scholarly editions.[2]

The critics' position does seem a little like coming out against motherhood or peace. What's the matter with scholarship, especially since, in this case, nobody denies that the scholars concerned are engaged in bringing out the full, correct text of important American writers?

Briefly, Mr. Wilson, who in 1968 called the whole series of books "ill-judged and quite sterile," [3] has said that the scholarly editions are too confusing for the ordinary reader. (In them, author's corrections are indicated, there are detailed notes, and, where necessary, more than one version of the text.) Also, for his taste, they are dull. Moreover, although Mr. Wilson said that he did want complete texts of all our important writers, he didn't want it so complete that it included works he considered inferior. In the case of Mark Twain he announced that Clemens' long-buried short novel, *3,000 Years Among the Microbes,* which was first published in 1967 and from which comes the selection "Swinks and Sooflaskies," should never have been published at all because it was "rambling and labored and boring." [4] I, on the other hand, consider it second only to *Tom Sawyer Abroad,* one of Mark Twain's two most neglected masterpieces. But about taste, let us hope, there will always be disputing.

The heart of Mr. Wilson's argument is a defense of the ordinary reader. What such readers need, he says—what we all need—is a cheap, well-printed, straightforward edition of all

our so-called classics. I don't know who could disagree with
him. But the choice is not between a scholarly edition and a
popular one. On the contrary, the second depends on the
first—at least, this is so in the case of Mark Twain. Before popular editions of Mark Twain, complete and as written, can be
ours to enjoy, years of scholarship must be devoted to the complicated task of establishing which of the many versions of
Mark Twain's work is as he wrote it or (sometimes he wrote
many versions) which is closest to expressing what he intended.

The conflict between critics and scholars, who are sometimes
called "academics," has never been an equal one. Characteristi-
cally, even our foremost scholars have labored in comparative
obscurity, while our foremost critics have been very powerful
indeed. According to critic Alfred Kazin, literary criticism has
been "the great American lay philosophy . . . . the secret intermediary . . . between literature and society." [5]

Unfortunately this intermediary has become so powerful that
a great many people accept, sometimes at third or fourth hand,
the judgment of critics as to what they should and shouldn't
like. The result is that they become ashamed of their own taste.
But in Mark Twain's case, masses of readers have had the courage of their convictions. For example, the early thirties were a
low point in Mark Twain's critical reputation: "There is . . . no
one of his books," said Granville Hicks in 1933, "that is wholly
satisfactory." [6] And yet Charles Compton's 1934 survey of what
was popular with library readers placed Mark Twain first on
the list.[7]

This brings me to the fact that occasionally in my prefatory
notes for these selections I have provided scraps of critics' comments on them that are always niggling and peevish and sometimes malicious. This is odd, of course, because most editors
dealing, as I am, with a writer they revere note only critical
praise of him. I took the other road for two reasons. The first is
that since 1920 there has been little praise of Mark Twain (from
critics as opposed to scholars) worth mentioning.[8] And the second reason is that I wished to provide, by illustration, some hint

of the prolonged hostility and contempt Mark Twain has aroused in professional critics.

Mark Twain died in 1910, beloved and admired at home and abroad. Ten years later came Van Wyck Brooks's *The Ordeal of Mark Twain.* This was—and is—the great classical attack on Clemens, an attack that was to influence the Mark Twain criticism until today. For example, in 1967 appeared Justin Kaplan's semi-biographical critical study, *Mr. Clemens and Mark Twain,* which won a Pulitzer Prize and a National Book Award. Mostly it provoked critical raptures, but Edmund Wilson pointed out, "The conception of Mark Twain . . . upon which the whole book is based, is by no means a novel one. It was first introduced by Van Wyck Brooks as long ago as 1920." [9] What was fresh in Mr. Kaplan's book were new bits of Mark Twain scholarship, but even those were so handled as to fit into the old Brooksian legend of a vulgar man, living in a vulgar country, at a vulgar time.

Vulgarity of some kind—vulgarity broadly interpreted—has been the key complaint against Clemens. ("There are no people," he once wrote, "who are quite so vulgar as the over-refined ones.") And there have been countless other charges against him. Among other things, he has been portrayed as neurotically attached to his mother and his wife, as a social climber, as money-hungry, as incapable of satire but horridly cynical, and as incapable of appreciating that his profession was a sacred vocation. For "Poets and novelists and critics," according to Van Wyck Brooks, "are the pathfinders of society; to them belongs the vision without which the people perish." [10] In this sort of thing he was borrowing from the English Matthew Arnold, who also thought literary critics led society because they were able "to make the best ideas prevail." [11] Other critics enthusiastically embraced this view of their profession. Mark Twain, on the contrary, saw creative writers as craftsmen serving the public, and his view of critics may partly account for their view of him: "I believe," he said in his *Autobiography,* "that the trade of critic, in literature, music, and the drama, is the most degraded of all trades, and that it has no real value—certainly no large value."

For decades after Brooks's attack came geysers of stuff following his line. So low did Mark Twain sink, and so quickly, that by 1927 a teacher of speech in the Iowa State Teachers College was correcting Mark Twain's use of dialect in *Huckleberry Finn.* "It was unfortunate," she said, "that he should have made pretensions of skill where he was but a learner." [12] And this in the teeth of Mark Twain's warning, which prefaces *Huck:*

> In this book a number of dialects are used, to wit: The Missouri Negro dialect; the extremist form of the backwoods Southwestern dialect; the ordinary "Pike County" dialect; and four modified varieties of this last. The shadings have not been done in a haphazard fashion, or by guesswork; but painstakingly, and with the trustworthy guidance and support of personal familiarity with these several forms of speech.
>
> I make this explanation for the reason that without it many readers would suppose that all these characters were trying to talk alike and not succeeding.

There was, in fact, nothing too absurd to say in denigration of Mark Twain once Brooks's book had been greeted as a masterpiece. In 1924, the critics O'Higgins and Reede attributed Mark Twain's shortcomings to the fact that he had been a premature baby, and hence had become "as profound a biological failure as America has produced." [13] Nor was it only nonentities who joined the crusade to discover all that was wrong with Mark Twain. Writers as famous and respected as Lewis Mumford took notice of his "fundamental barbarism," [14] and Theodore Dreiser referred to him as "our simple and almost boobish genius." [15] By the sixties psychoanalytic and symbolic interpretations had become more subtle. Leslie Fiedler found that "his buffoonery is obviously a camouflage for insecurity, the insecurity of a man with genteel ideals and bad manners. . . ." [16] And Dwight Macdonald offered a judgment on his prose that the reader may test for himself as he reads this anthology: "The texture is coarse . . ." said Macdonald; "Individual phrases are rarely memorable." [17]

Most discouraging of all, to people who are fond of the lowly fact, is that the inaccuracy of Brooks's work on Mark Twain is not even considered a major defect. "As time has gone on," said Lewis Leary in 1962, "Brooks has been corrected, point by point, by people who have more carefully investigated the historical background of Samuel Clemens." [18] But the critical attitude toward mere truthfulness is illustrated in a grandiloquent remark from Alfred Kazin that Leary then quotes: "Brooks's conception of the Gilded Age was not false, but was a great literary myth . . . one of those primary hypotheses by literary men that give design to history and awaken its imagination." [19]

That, today, is the critical position. For, true or false, Brooks's work illustrated what he and so many others firmly believed: that the America of Mark Twain's literary day (from the end of the Civil War until 1910) strangled art and hence destroyed Mark Twain as an artist.

True or false . . . there have been those who regarded that difference as all important. At any rate, Brooks's story was false, although it still lives and prospers. ("A lie told well," Mark Twain once said, "is immortal.") It has even been exported, for, since Brooks, European critics (except the Russians, who deeply admire Mark Twain) have followed the line laid down by the Americans. Thus, in 1941 the English critic, V. S. Pritchett, referred to Mark Twain as a "low comedian" but praised *Huckleberry Finn*. He added: "Knowing Mark Twain's life, knowing the hell of vulgarity from which the book has ascended, one dreads as one turns from page to page the seemingly inevitable flop." [20] (In this one case, according to Pritchett, the flop doesn't come.)

I do not hope to establish, by my abbreviated account of Mark Twain's life, all that it was, but I do hope to indicate it was not quite a "hell of vulgarity." I hope also to show that *Huckleberry Finn* isn't the only Mark Twain worth reading. But most of all I hope to give pleasure to people who are interested in other animal species and their relationship to man.

Pierce Library
Eastern Oregon University
1410 L Avenue
La Grande, OR 97850

FRIENDS AND RELATIONS

He who Doubts from what he sees
Will ne'er Believe, do what you Please.

WILLIAM BLAKE, "Auguries of Innocence"

There may seem to be many Mark Twains in this book, but of course there is only one man in many circumstances. He explained all that when he explained that all our lives are the result of circumstance and temperament. "Circumstance," he said, "is man's master—and when Circumstance commands, he must obey; he may argue the matter—that is his privilege . . . but it won't do any good. . . ."

On the other hand: "Circumstance is powerful, but it cannot work alone. . . . Its partner is man's *temperament*—his natural disposition. His temperament . . . is *born* in him, and he has no authority over it, neither is he responsible for its acts. He cannot change it, nothing can change it, nothing can modify it—except temporarily. But it won't stay modified. It is permanent, like the color of the man's eyes. . . . Blue eyes are gray in certain unusual lights; but they resume their natural color when that stress is removed."

Mark Twain knew his own temperament. One of his darkest hours came in the last year of his life, when his youngest daughter, Jean, then twenty-nine, was found dead in the bathtub the day before Christmas. As he took to his pen to pour out his anguish, he wrote: "Shall I ever be cheerful again, happy again? Yes. And soon. For I know my temperament."

He was right. It was certainly not a gloomy temperament that led Mark Twain to curse God and man so often and so earnestly. It was an apple—the bitter fruit of the knowledge of good and evil. Adam and Eve had nibbled it, and the overwhelming majority of their descendants have done the same. But Mark Twain ate it, core and all. It deeply colored his art, but it did not affect his temperament.

Among other things, he was mercurial. No man ever experienced purer bliss or more terrible despair. And, as there are animal stories in this section written at his most joyous, there are some written in his blackest time. Oddly, it is by no means easy to guess, from reading, which is which. For example, "The Long Low Dog," "Augustin Daly's Back Door," and "Bird of Birds" are all from *Following the Equator*, the book written at the time of his most terrible grief, and yet they are quite as gay as the five selections from *Roughing It*, written in the best of good years. The notion of many critics that Mark Twain wrote bitterly of life only when his own affairs went wrong is nonsense.

There is a double joy behind *Roughing It*: the wild fun of living through the events recorded, and the even greater happiness that belonged to the later period when he wrote the book and these words to a friend in Scotland: ". . . if there is one individual creature on all this footstool who is more thoroughly and uniformily and unceasingly *happy* than I am I defy the world to produce him and *prove* him."

That period was the early 1870's when Mark Twain was newly married and living in the East—first in Buffalo and then, for many years, in a suburb of Hartford, Connecticut. Then, while he was writing *Roughing It*, he was the most happily married lover on earth and the father of his first baby girl (two more came later). Thanks to the phenomenal success of *Two Innocents Abroad* (1869), he was rich enough to live and write as he pleased—and he pleased to live high and to write as nobody else had done before. *The Innocents Abroad* had also made him an international celebrity; European tourists made journeys to stare at his home as they did to Niagara Falls. Finally, there were his friends. All his life he attracted them—attracted the miners and politicians of the Far West just as he did England's Prince of Wales and assorted nobility; there was never a man whom so many people loved to be with. But the early Hartford years were especially gay and happy. They were such days, wrote his friend Howells many years later, "as the aging sun no longer shines on in his rounds. There was constant running in and out of friendly houses where the lively hosts and guests called one another by their Christian names or nicknames, and no such vain ceremony as knocking or ringing at doors." [1]

Howells also described how Clemens looked then. He wore, against all convention, "a sealskin coat, with the fur out, in the satisfaction of a caprice, or the love of strong effect which he was apt to indulge through life. . . . With his crest of dense red hair, and the wide sweep of his flaming mustache, Clemens was not discordantly clothed in that sealskin coat. . . . He had always a relish for personal effect, which expressed itself in the white suit[s] . . . which he wore in his last years. . . . That was not vanity in him, but a keen feeling for costume which the severity of our modern tailoring forbids men. . . ." [2] A century later, of course, many men felt that way about their clothes.

Such was Mark Twain when he wrote *Roughing It*. But that earlier period when he lived it (1861–1866) was almost as joyful in a different way. We behold him, in those days, in his late twenties. He has already been a skilled printer, a skilled steamboat pilot, an unskilled Confederate soldier—he is a deserter from a Confederate regiment of frightened boys in which he had served two weeks. He has come West with his older brother, Orion, who is an abolitionist appointed by the Lincoln administration to the post of Secretary of the Nevada Territory. Out there, and on the way out there, and in Hawaii, where he was sent by a Western newspaper, Mark Twain lived *Roughing It*. Not all the details are truthful. "I don't know anything," Mark Twain once said, "that mars good literature so completely as too much truth." But the person who tells the story was a real person; he was Samuel Langhorne Clemens (not yet Mark Twain), the reckless, impulsive, foulmouthed and witty descendant of an old Southern family. He has come West in a mail coach drawn by teams of handsome horses and wild Mexican mules, bringing with him an unabridged dictionary, for which he paid ruinous overweight, and a noble but eccentric older brother, whom he protected and raged at all his life. He also brought a defective seven-shooter, twelve pounds of clothing, and almost as much tobacco.

He had come, so he said, to "have all kinds of adventures and maybe get hanged or scalped . . . and write home and tell . . . all about it, and be a hero"; and above all for the prizes he was born seeking: "a long, strange journey" and a "curious new world." And if ever these were his, it was when he perched atop a flying mail coach in his underwear while "the spinning ground and the waltzing trees appeared to give us a mute hurrah as we went by, and then slack up and look after us with interest, or envy, or something; and as we lay and smoked the pipe of peace and compared all this luxury with the years of tiresome city life that had gone before it, we felt that there was only one complete and satisfying happiness in the world and we had found it."

It wasn't all joy when he got there, of course,[3] but that was what Mark Twain was like, sometimes, when he was young. The moral was drawn by that stern critic, Van Wyck Brooks, years later: "He was out for a good time, oblivious of everything else . . . a moralist would have said that the devil had already marked him out for destruction." [4]

The Mark Twain in *Following the Equator* has turned sixty; he's lost a fortune (for a writer) in the depression of 1893; he owns nothing but his debts and his copyrights and he's "lecturing" around the world to pay his creditors. Mark Twain set out on that journey exhausted and dreading it. As usual, thanks to temperament, he enjoyed himself. He also paid his debts. But to the world the great bonus of that trip is *Following the Equator*, the book that tells about it all, and about so many other things.

Notes for *Following the Equator* were made on the spot, but the book was written the next year, in London, in Mark Twain's blackest hour. For that year (1896) his beloved daughter Susy died suddenly, at twenty-four; no other private trouble in all his life was so hard to bear as that.

A few years before he'd written a riddle: "Why is that we rejoice at a birth and grieve at a funeral? It is because we are not the person involved." He wasn't trying to be funny. Consistently, Mark Twain sang the praises of death: "the only immortal who treats us all alike, whose pity and whose peace and whose refuge are for all. . . ." Just as consistently, he always declared that he would not, if he could, bring back a loved one. He felt like that when his adored wife died, after a long illness, and his epileptic daughter, Jean, and some dear friends. But with Susy it was different. Sometimes, especially to comfort her mother, he would try to remember that death was the only peace. "Be comforted, my darling," he wrote his wife when the thing happened, "we shall have *our* release in time. Be comforted, remembering how much hardship, grief, pain, she is spared; and that her heart can never be broken, now, for the loss of a child. . . . How lovely is death; and how niggardly it is doled out."

But he himself was never resigned to Susy's death. Of that he said what he never said of any other death: "If by asking I could bring her back, I could stoop to that treachery, so weak am I. . . ." [5]

This is the story of Susy's death.

When the Clemenses set off around the world, Susy stayed behind because she dreaded sea travel, but when the trip was over she was to join her parents and sister Clara in London. They were awaiting her there when a letter came saying she was slightly unwell. A cable next day said it was serious, but not dangerous. Her mother sailed for New York. Three days later—before her mother reached her—Susy was dead of spinal meningitis.

Except for her mother, this shy, beautiful, tormented daughter was the person Mark Twain loved most. For years after her death he worked overtime, "not for print . . ." as he wrote his friend William Dean Howells, "for much of it fails to suit me" but to drown "the deadness which invaded me when Susy died." For although Van Wyck Brooks alleged that Mark Twain's heart was not in his work, but only in "his power and his fame," [6] the fact is that work was his joy in good times, his solace in bad. The year after Susy's death he wrote Howells that he was not miserable; that he was "worse than that—indifferent. Indifferent to nearly everything but work. I like that; I enjoy it, and stick to it. I do it without purpose and without ambition; merely for the love of it."

There are no sermons, no blasphemies, no deep bitterness (except perhaps for "Sailor Dog") in this section of the book; there are only Mark Twain's accounts of his friends and relations in the animal kingdom. Geographically, perhaps it's a little confusing, because there's no telling when old friends will pop into his head. In Germany he remembered a blue jay he'd known in California, in California a camel he'd met in Syria. But for a century now the world has had no trouble following the free and easy way Mark Twain's mind worked. On the contrary, modern critics excepted, the world has rejoiced in the fact that, as Howells said, "He saunters out into the trim world of letters, and lounges across its neatly kept paths, and walks about on the grass at will, in spite of all the signs that have been put up since the beginning of literature, warning people of dangers and penalties for the slightest trespass." [7]

BIRD OF BIRDS

India, said Mark Twain, four years before his death, was "the only foreign land I ever daydream about or deeply long to see again." The fact is surprising since he met the Bird of Birds his very first night in India, and suffered all the other sounds described in this story. His sufferings are not playfully exaggerated; on the contrary, they are made light of, for the truth is that Mark Twain was not quite normal about sounds. Even a ticking clock disturbed him and there were none in his house. Various other sounds, according to his daughter Clara, drove him "to the borders of hysteria," making him suffer so acutely that "he would almost lose control of himself if he could neither get out of reach nor cause them to stop." [1] That was why the same man who could not endure to see a horse touched with a whip once begged a friend to shoot a barking dog; his own hands were shaking so that he couldn't aim.

Barking dogs and certain kinds of music were the worst. If the Bird of Birds had barked, Mark Twain would never have pursued the acquaintance.

This selection comes from *Following the Equator*.

> Some natives—I don't remember how many—went into my bedroom, now, and put things to rights and arranged the mosquito-bar, and I went to bed to nurse my cough. It was about nine in the evening. What a state of things! For three hours the yelling and shouting of natives in the hall continued, along with the velvety patter of their swift bare feet—what a racket it was! They were yelling orders and messages down three flights. Why, in the matter of noise it amounted to a riot, an insurrection, a revolution. And then there were other noises mixed up with these and at intervals tremendously accenting them—roofs falling in, I judged, windows smashing, persons being murdered, crows squawking, and deriding, and cursing, canaries screeching, monkeys jabbering, macaws blaspheming, and every now and then fiendish bursts of laughter and explosions of dynamite. By mid-

night I had suffered all the different kinds of shocks there are, and knew that I could never more be disturbed by them, either isolated or in combination. Then came peace—stillness deep and solemn—and lasted till five.

Then it all broke loose again. And who restarted it? The Bird of Birds—the Indian crow. I came to know him well, by and by, and be infatuated with him. I suppose he is the hardest lot that wears feathers. Yes, and the cheerfulest, and the best satisfied with himself. He never arrived at what he is by any careless process, or any sudden one; he is a work of art, and "art is long"; he is the product of immemorial ages, and of deep calculation; one can't make a bird like that in a day. He has been reincarnated more times than Shiva; and he has kept a sample of each incarnation, and fused it into his constitution. In the course of his evolutionary promotions, his sublime march toward ultimate perfection, he has been a gambler, a low comedian, a dissolute priest, a fussy woman, a blackguard, a scoffer, a liar, a thief, a spy, an informer, a trading politician, a swindler, a professional hypocrite, a patriot for cash, a reformer, a lecturer, a lawyer, a conspirator, a rebel, a royalist, a democrat, a practicer and propagator of irreverence, a meddler, an intruder, a busybody, an infidel, and a wallower in sin for the mere love of it. The strange result, the incredible result, of this patient accumulation of all damnable traits is that he does not know what care is, he does not know what sorrow is, he does not know what remorse is; his life is one long thundering ecstasy of happiness, and he will go to his death untroubled, knowing that he will soon turn up again as an author or something, and be even more intolerably capable and comfortable than ever he was before.

In his straddling wide forward-step, and his springy sidewise series of hops, and his impudent air, and his cunning way of canting his head to one side upon occasion, he reminds one of the American blackbird. But the sharp resemblances stop there. He is much bigger than the blackbird; and he lacks the blackbird's trim and slender and beautiful build and shapely beak; and of course his sober garb of gray and rusty black is a poor and humble thing compared with the splendid luster of the blackbird's metallic sables and shifting and flashing bronze glories. The blackbird is a perfect gentleman, in deportment and attire, and is not noisy, I believe, except when holding religious services and political conventions in a tree; but this Indian sham-Quaker is just a rowdy, and is always noisy when awake—always chaffing, scolding, scoffing, laughing, ripping, and cursing, and carrying on about something or other. I never saw such a bird for delivering opinions. Nothing escapes him; he notices everything that happens, and brings out his opinion about it, particularly if it is a matter that is none of his business. And it is never a mild opinion, but always violent—violent and profane—the presence of ladies does not affect him. His opinions are not the outcome of reflection, for he never thinks about anything, but heaves out the opinion that is on top of his mind, and which is often an opinion about some quite different thing and does not fit the case. But that is his way; his main idea is to get out an opinion, and if he stopped to think he would lose chances.

I suppose he has no enemies among men. The whites and Mohammedans never seemed to molest him; and the Hindoos, because of their religion, never take the life of any creature, but spare even the snakes and tigers and fleas and rats. If I sat on one end of the balcony, the crows would gather on the railing at the other end and talk about me; and edge closer, little by little, till I could almost reach them; and they would sit there, in the most unabashed way, and talk about my clothes, and my hair, and my complexion, and probable character and vocation and politics, and how I came to be in India, and what I had been doing, and how many days I had got for it, and how I had happened to go unhanged so long, and when would it probably come off, and might there be more of my sort where I came from, and when would *they* be hanged—and so on, and so on, until I could no longer endure the embarrassment of it; then I would shoo them away, and they would circle around in the air a little while, laughing and deriding and mocking, and presently settle on the rail and do it all over again.

From Mark Twain's *Autobiography*: I can call back the prairie, and its loneliness and peace, and a vast hawk hanging motionless in the sky, with his wings spread wide and the blue of the vault showing through the fringe of their end-feathers.

THE TARANTULAS AND THE BRIGADE

At least some—perhaps all—of this story is true. The Brigade was fourteen big-city Republican ward heelers who had performed political services for Nevada's Territorial Governor, James Nye (formerly Police Commissioner of New York City), and had followed him to Nevada.

As for "Mrs. O'Flannigan," she was really a Mrs. Murphy, and in 1861, with Nevada prices wildly inflated, her ten-dollar weekly rate for board and room was much cheaper than it seems. It was what attracted Sam Clemens and his brother Orion, newly arrived to Nevada and almost as poor as The Brigade. Sam had still some of his pilot's pay left, but he'd spent most of it on their coach fare west. Orion was trying to live on his salary as Territorial Secretary: $1,800 a year. Nobody, including the federal government, had counted on that kind of honesty, which was downright eccentric in Nevada then. But when Governor Nye tried to force poor Orion into shady doings that would have increased his income, his brother Sam called on his Excellency and told him to stop it. Mark Twain's friendship with Nye began that day.

The tarantula's bite is not dangerous. And yet Bob H——was Mark Twain's friend Bob Howland, who was one day to win renown as the most fearless marshal in the West. That was when a band of tough characters set out to take over the Aurora mining camp and Howland's final message to Nye became famous through the West: "All quiet in Aurora. Five men will be hung in an hour." [1] They were. And Mark Twain was one day to write of Bob Howland that he could quell an armed desperado with his eye. But as this story makes clear, tarantulas can be more terrible than desperadoes.

The "office hours" of a Nevada "Zephyr," according to Mark Twain, were from two in the afternoon till two in the morning. It could demolish flimsy houses and roll up tin roofs "like sheet music."

The story comes from *Roughing It*.

It was a jolly company, the fourteen. They were principally voluntary camp-followers of the Governor, who had joined his reti-

nue by their own election at New York and San Francisco, and
came along, feeling that in the scuffle for little territorial crumbs
and offices they could not make their condition more precarious
than it was, and might reasonably expect to make it better. They
were popularly known as the "Irish Brigade," though there were
only four or five Irishmen among all the Governor's retainers.
His good-natured Excellency was much annoyed at the gossip
his henchmen created—especially when there arose a rumor that
they were paid assassins of his, brought along to quietly reduce
the Democratic vote when desirable!

Mrs. O'Flannigan was boarding and lodging them at ten dollars a week apiece, and they were cheerfully giving their notes
for it. They were perfectly satisfied, but Bridget presently found
that notes that could not be discounted were but a feeble constitution for a Carson [City] boardinghouse. So she began to harry
the Governor to find employment for the "Brigade." Her im-
portunities and theirs together drove him to a gentle desperation
at last, and he finally summoned the Brigade to the presence.
Then, said he:

"Gentlemen, I have planned a lucrative and useful service for
you—a service which will provide you with recreation amid
noble landscapes, and afford you never-ceasing opportunities
for enriching your minds by observation and study. I want you
to survey a railroad from Carson City westward to a certain
point! When the legislature meets I will have the necessary bill
passed and the remuneration arranged."

"What, a railroad over the Sierra Nevada Mountains?"

"Well, then, survey it eastward to a certain point!"

He converted them into surveyors, chain-bearers, and so on,
and turned them loose in the desert. It was "recreation" with a
vengeance! Recreation on foot, lugging chains through sand and
sagebrush, under a sultry sun and among cattle bones, coyotes,
and tarantulas. "Romantic adventure" could go no further.
They surveyed very slowly, very deliberately, very carefully.
They returned every night during the first week, dusty, footsore,
tired, and hungry, but very jolly. They brought in great store of
prodigious hairy spiders—tarantulas—and imprisoned them in
covered tumblers upstairs in the "ranch." After the first week,
they had to camp on the field, for they were getting well east-

ward. They made a good many inquiries as to the location of that indefinite "certain point," but got no information. At last, to a peculiarly urgent inquiry of "How far eastward?" Governor Nye telegraphed back:

"To the Atlantic Ocean, blast you!—and then bridge it and go on!"

This brought back the dusty toilers, who sent in a report and ceased from their labors. The Governor was always comfortable about it; he said Mrs. O'Flannigan would hold him for the Brigade's board anyhow, and he intended to get what entertainment he could out of the boys; he said, with his old-time pleasant twinkle, that he meant to survey them into Utah and then telegraph Brigham [Young] to hang them for trespass!

The surveyors brought back more tarantulas with them, and so we had quite a menagerie arranged along the shelves of the room. Some of these spiders could straddle over a common saucer with their hairy, muscular legs, and when their feelings were hurt, or their dignity offended, they were the wickedest-looking desperadoes the animal world can furnish. If their glass prison-houses were touched ever so lightly they were up and spoiling for a fight in a minute. Starchy?—proud? Indeed, they would take up a straw and pick their teeth like a member of Congress. There was as usual a furious "zephyr" blowing the first night of the Brigade's return, and about midnight the roof of an adjoining stable blew off, and a corner of it came crashing through the side of our ranch. There was a simultaneous awakening, and a tumultuous muster of the Brigade in the dark, and a general tumbling and sprawling over each other in the narrow aisle between the bed rows. In the midst of the turmoil, Bob H—— sprung up out of a sound sleep, and knocked down a shelf with his head. Instantly he shouted:

"Turn out, boys—the tarantulas is loose!"

No warning ever sounded so dreadful. Nobody tried, any longer, to leave the room, lest he might step on a tarantula. Every man groped for a trunk or a bed, and jumped on it. Then followed the strangest silence—a silence of grisly suspense it was, too—waiting, expectancy, fear. It was as dark as pitch, and one had to imagine the spectacle of those fourteen scant-clad men roosting gingerly on trunks and beds, for not a thing could be seen. Then came occasional little interruptions of the silence, and one could recognize a man and tell his locality by his voice, or locate any other sound a sufferer made by his gropings or changes of position. The occasional voices were not given to much speaking—you simply heard a gentle ejaculation of "Ow!" followed by a solid thump, and you knew the gentleman had felt a hairy blanket or something touch his bare skin and had skipped from a bed to the floor. Another silence. Presently you would hear a gasping voice say:

"Su-su-something's crawling up the back of my neck!"

Every now and then you could hear a little subdued scramble and a sorrowful "O Lord!" and then you knew that somebody was getting away from something he took for a tarantula, and not losing any time about it, either. Directly a voice in the corner rang out wild and clear:

"I've got him! I've got him!" (Pause, and probable change of circumstances.) "No, he's got me! Oh, ain't they *never* going to fetch a lantern!"

The lantern came at that moment, in the hands of Mrs. O'Flannigan, whose anxiety to know the amount of damage done by the assaulting roof had not prevented her waiting a judicious interval, after getting out of bed and lighting up, to see if the wind was done now, upstairs, or had a larger contract.

The landscape presented when the lantern flashed into the room was picturesque, and might have been funny to some people, but was not to us. Although we were perched so strangely upon boxes, trunks, and beds, and so strangely attired, too, we were too earnestly distressed and too genuinely miserable to see any fun about it, and there was not the semblance of a smile anywhere visible. I know I am not capable of suffering more than I did during those few minutes of suspense in the dark, surrounded by those creeping, bloody-minded tarantulas. I had skipped from bed to bed and from box to box in a cold agony, and every time I touched anything that was fuzzy I fancied I felt the fangs. I had rather go to war than live that episode over again. Nobody was hurt. The man who thought a tarantula had "got him" was mistaken—only a crack in a box had caught his finger. Not one of those escaped tarantulas was ever seen again. There were ten or twelve of them. We took candles and hunted the place high and low for them, but with no success. Did we go back to bed then? We did nothing of the kind. Money could not have persuaded us to do it. We sat up the rest of the night playing cribbage and keeping a sharp lookout for the enemy.

From _Tom Sawyer Abroad_—in a balloon: . . . at daybreak it cleared, and the world looked mighty soft and gray and pretty, and them forests and fields so good to see again, and the horses and cattle standing sober and thinking.

SAILOR DOG

This is the fragment of a fragment: _The Enchanted Sea-Wilderness_, unfinished, but released by The Mark Twain Papers in 1967 and published in _Which Was the Dream?_, an anthology of hitherto unpublished Mark Twain.[1]

. . . when we were lying at the dock the day we sailed, a lovely big beautiful dog came aboard and went racing around with his nose down hunting for somebody that had been there—his owner, I reckon—and the crew caught him and shut him up below, and we sailed in an hour. He was a darling, that dog. He was full of play, and fun, and affection and good nature, the dearest and sweetest disposition that ever was. Inside of two days he was the pet of the whole crew. We bedded him like the aristocracy, and there wasn't a man but would divide his dinner with him, and he was ever so loving and grateful. And smart, too; smart and willing. He elected of his own notion to stand watch and watch with us. He was in the larboard watch, and he would turn out at eight bells without anybody having to tell him it was "Yo-ho, the larboard watch!" And he would tug at the ropes and help make sail or take it in, and seemed to know all about it, just like any old veteran. The crew were proud of him— well, of course they would be.

And so, as I was saying, we got becalmed when we were out about two months. It was warm that night, and still and drowsy and lazy; and the sails hung idle, and the deck watch and the lookout and everybody else was sound asleep, including the dog, for it was his trick below and he had turned in at midnight. Well, along about an hour after midnight there was a tremendous scratching and barking at the captain's door, and he jumped out of his bunk, and that dog was just wild with excitement, and rushed off, and just as good as *told* the captain to come along and come *quick*. You see, the ship was afire down in the hold, and he had discovered it. Down the captain plunged, and the dog rushed off waking up the others.

Dear, dear, it was the closest fit! The fire was crowding a pile of the powder-kegs close, and in another minute or two it would have had them and we should have been blown into the sky. The captain snatched the pile of kegs out of reach in half a second, and we were safe; because the bulk of the powder was away up forward. And by this time we all came tearing down—white?— oh, white as ghosts when we saw what a close shave we had had. Well, then we started in and began to hug the dog. And wasn't he a proud dog?—and happy?—why, if he had had speech he couldn't have expressed it any better. The captain snarled at us and said:

"You may well hug him, you worthless hounds! he saved my life, not you, you lazy rips. I've never cared for dogs before, but next time I hear people talking against them I'll put in a word for this one, anyway."

Overboard went that little batch of powder-kegs, and then we flew around getting food and water and compass and sextant and chart and things for the boat; and the dog helped, just like anybody else. He did a grown man's work carrying things to the boat, and then went dancing around *superintending* whilst we launched her. Bright?—oh, you can't think how bright he was, and intelligent.

When everybody was in the boat but the captain, and the flames were soaring up and lighting the whole ocean, he tied the dog to the foot of the mainmast and then got in himself and took the tiller and said—

"All ready. Give way!"

We were all struck dumb, for a second, then all shouted at once—

"Oh, *Captain!*—going to leave the dog?"

He roared out in a fury—

"Didn't you hear the order? Give way!"

Well, the tears began to run down our faces; and we said,

"Why, he saved our *lives*—we *can't* leave him. Please, Captain! please let him come."

"What, in this little tub of a boat? You don't know what you are talking about. He'd be more in the way than a family of children; and he can eat as much as a family of children, too. Now, men, you know *me*"—and he pulled an old pepper-box revolver and pointed it—"give *way!*"

Well, it was pitiful, the way that poor dog acted. At first he was dancing and capering· and barking, happy and proud and gay; but when he saw us going away he stopped and stood still, gazing; it seemed as if he was trying to believe it, and couldn't. And dear, dear, how noble and handsome he was, in that red glare. He was a huge big Saint Bernard, with that gentle good face and that soft loving eye that they've got.

Well, pretty soon when he saw that he *was* left, he seemed to go kind of crazy; and he rose on his hind legs in the strong light, and strained and lunged and tugged at his rope, and begged and moaned and yelped—why it was as plain as if he was *saying*, Oh, *don't* leave me, *please* don't leave me, *I* haven't done any harm. And then presently the fire swept down on him and swallowed him up, and he sent up two or three awful shrieks, and it was all over. And the men sat there crying like children.

From *A Connecticut Yankee in King Arthur's Court*: . . . we dreamed along through glades in a mist of green light that got its tint from the sundrenched roof of leaves overhead, and by our feet the clearest and coldest of runlets went frisking and gossiping over its reefs and making a sort of whispering music comfortable to hear; and at times we left the world behind and entered into the solemn great deeps and rich gloom of the forest, where furtive wild things whisked and scurried by and were gone before you could even get your eye on the place where the noise was; and where only the earliest birds were turning out and getting to business with a song here and a quarrel yonder and a mysterious far-off hammering and drumming for worms on a tree trunk away somewhere in the impenetrable remotenesses of the woods.

THE BEE

"The Bee" was written about 1902 and published for the first time
in 1917, by Harper & Brothers, in *What Is Man? and Other Essays*.
Maeterlinck's *Life of the Bee* appeared in 1901.

It was Maeterlinck who introduced me to the bee. I mean, in the
psychical and in the poetical way. I had had a business introduction earlier. It was when I was a boy. It is strange that I should
remember a formality like that so long; it must be nearly sixty
years.

Bee scientists always speak of the bee as she. It is because all
the important bees are of that sex. In the hive there is one married bee, called the queen; she has fifty thousand children; of
these, about one hundred are sons; the rest are daughters. Some
of the daughters are young maids, some are old maids, and all
are virgins and remain so.

Every spring the queen comes out of the hive and flies away
with one of her sons and marries him. The honeymoon lasts only
an hour or two; then the queen divorces her husband and returns home competent to lay two million eggs. This will be
enough to last the year, but not more than enough, because hundreds of bees get drowned every day, and other hundreds are
eaten by birds, and it is the queen's business to keep the population up to standard—say, fifty thousand. She must always have
that many children on hand and efficient during the busy season, which is summer, or winter would catch the community
short of food. She lays from two thousand to three thousand
eggs a day, according to the demand; and she must exercise
judgment, and not lay more than are needed in a slim flower-
harvest, nor fewer than are required in a prodigal one, or the
board of directors will dethrone her and elect a queen that has
more sense.

There are always a few royal heirs in stock and ready to take
her place—ready and more than anxious to do it, although she is

their own mother. These girls are kept by themselves, and are regally fed and tended from birth. No other bees get such fine food as they get, or live such a high and luxurious life. By consequence they are larger and longer and sleeker than their working sisters. And they have a curved sting, shaped like a simitar, while the others have a straight one.

A common bee will sting anyone or anybody, but a royalty stings royalties only. A common bee will sting and kill another common bee, for cause, but when it is necessary to kill the queen other ways are employed. When a queen has grown old and slack and does not lay eggs enough, one of her royal daughters is allowed to come to attack her, the rest of the bees looking on at the duel and seeing fair play. It is a duel with the curved stings. If one of the fighters gets hard-pressed and gives it up and runs, she is brought back and must try again—once, maybe twice; then, if she runs yet once more for her life, judicial death is her portion; her children pack themselves into a ball around her person and hold her in that compact grip two or three days, until she starves to death or is suffocated. Meantime the victor bee is receiving royal honors and performing the one royal function—laying eggs.

As regards the ethics of the judicial assassination of the queen, that is a matter of politics, and will be discussed later, in its proper place.

During substantially the whole of her short life of five or six years the queen lives in the Egyptian darkness and stately seclusion of the royal apartments, with none about her but plebeian servants, who give her empty lip-affection in place of the love which her heart hungers for; who spy upon her in the interest of her waiting heirs, and report and exaggerate her defects and deficiencies to them; who fawn upon her and flatter her to her face and slander her behind her back; who grovel before her in the day of her power and forsake her in her age and weakness. There she sits, friendless, upon her throne through the long night of her life, cut off from the consoling sympathies and sweet companionship and loving endearments which she craves, by the gilded barriers of her awful rank; a forlorn exile in her own house and home, weary object of formal ceremonies and machine-made worship, winged child of the sun, native to the free air and the blue skies and the flowery fields, doomed by the splendid accident of her birth to trade this priceless heritage for a black captivity, a tinsel grandeur, and a loveless life, with shame and insult at the end and a cruel death—and condemned by the human instinct in her to hold the bargain valuable!

Huber, Lubbock, Maeterlinck—in fact, all the great authorities—are agreed in denying that the bee is a member of the human family. I do not know why they have done this, but I think it is from dishonest motives. Why, the innumerable facts brought to light by their own painstaking and exhaustive experiments prove that if there is a master fool in the world, it is the bee. That seems to settle it.

But that is the way of the scientist. He will spend thirty years in building up a mountain range of facts with the intent to prove a certain theory; then he is so happy in his achievement that as a rule he overlooks the main chief fact of all—that his accumulation proves an entirely different thing. When you point out this miscarriage to him, he does not answer your letters; when you call to convince him, the servant prevaricates and you do not get in. Scientists have odious manners, except when you prop up their theory; then you can borrow money of them.

To be strictly fair, I will concede that now and then one of them will answer your letter, but when they do they avoid the issue—you cannot pin them down. When I discovered that the bee was human, I wrote about it to all those scientists whom I have just mentioned. For evasions, I have seen nothing to equal the answers I got.

After the queen, the personage next in importance in the hive is the virgin. The virgins are fifty thousand or one hundred thousand in number, and they are the workers, the laborers. No work is done, in the hive or out of it, save by them. The males do not work, the queen does no work, unless laying eggs is work, but it does not seem so to me. There are only two million of them, anyway, and all of five months to finish the contract in. The distribution of work in a hive is as cleverly and elaborately specialized as it is in a vast American machine-shop or factory. A bee that has been trained to one of the many and various industries of the concern doesn't know how to exercise any other, and would be offended if asked to take a hand in anything outside of her profession. She is as human as a cook; and if you should ask the cook to wait on the table, you know what would happen.

Cooks will play the piano if you like, but they draw the line there. In my time I have asked a cook to chop wood, and I know about these things. Even the hired girl has her frontiers; true, they are vague, they are ill-defined, even flexible, but they are there. This is not conjecture; it is founded on the absolute. And then the butler. You ask the butler to wash the dog. It is just as I say; there is much to be learned in these ways, without going to books. Books are very well, but books do not cover the whole domain of aesthetic human culture. Pride of profession is one of the boniest bones of existence, if not the boniest. Without doubt it is so in the hive.

From Roughing It: Yes, take it all around, there is quite a good deal of information in the book. I regret this very much, but really it could not be helped: information appears to stew out of me naturally, like the precious attar of roses out of the otter.

THE LONG LOW DOG

Mark Twain was not anti-dog, but because his best friends were cats, and because he so disliked barking, he was sometimes reserved with dogs he didn't know.

This train is bound for Bombay. The natives were "packed and crammed into the cars that held each about fifty." But "where the sacred white people were," his own accommodations, for once suited Mark Twain perfectly. "Yet the cost of it—well, economy could no further go. . . . It was built of the plainest and cheapest partially smoothed boards. . . . The floor was bare. . . . On each side of the car . . . was a broad, leather-covered sofa. . . . Over each sofa hung, by straps, a wide, flat, leather-covered shelf—to sleep on. In the daytime you can hitch it up against the wall . . . and then you have a big unencumbered and most comfortable room to spread out in. No car in any country is quite its equal for comfort . . . and even when there are four [in it] there is but little sense of impaired privacy."

Which was just as well, considering the company he had.

The story comes from *Following the Equator*.

In the train, during a part of the return journey from Baroda, we had the company of a gentleman who had with him a remarkable-looking dog. I had not seen one of its kind before, as far as I could remember; though of course I might have seen one and not noticed it, for I am not acquainted with dogs, but only with cats. This dog's coat was smooth and shiny and black, and I think it had tan trimmings around the edges of the dog, and perhaps underneath. It was a long, low dog, with very short, strange legs—legs that curved inboard, something like parentheses turned the wrong way) (. Indeed, it was made on the plan of a bench for length and lowness. It seemed to be satisfied, but I thought the plan poor, and structurally weak, on account of the distance between the forward supports and those abaft. With age the dog's back was likely to sag; and it seemed to me that it would have been a stronger and more practicable dog if it had had some more legs. It had not begun to sag yet, but the shape of the legs showed that the undue weight imposed upon them was beginning to tell. It had a long nose, and floppy ears that hung down, and a resigned expression of countenance. I did not like to ask what kind of a dog it was, or how it came to be deformed, for it was plain that the gentleman was very fond of it, and naturally he could be sensitive about it. From delicacy I thought it best not to seem to notice it too much. No doubt a man with a dog like that feels just as a person does who has a child that is out of true. The gentleman was not merely fond of the dog, he was also proud of it—just the same, again, as a mother feels about her child when it is an idiot. I could see that he was proud of it, notwithstanding it was such a long dog and looked so resigned and pious. It had been all over the world with him, and had been pilgriming like that for years and years. It had traveled fifty thousand miles by sea and rail, and had ridden in front of him on his horse eight thousand. It had a silver medal from the Geographical Society of Great Britain for its travels, and I saw it. It had won prizes in dog shows, both in India and in England—I saw them. He said its pedigree was on record in the Kennel Club, and that it was a well-known dog. He said a great many people in London could recognize it the moment they saw it. I did not say anything, but I did not think it anything strange; I should know that dog again, myself, yet I am not careful about noticing dogs. He said that when he walked along in London, people often stopped and looked at the dog. Of course I did not say anything, for I did not want to hurt his feelings, but I could have explained to him that if you take a great long low dog like that and waddle it along the street anywhere in the world and not charge anything, people will stop and look. He was gratified because the dog took prizes. But that was nothing; if I were built like that I could take prizes myself. I wished I knew what kind of a dog it was, and what it was for, but I could not very well ask, for that would show that I did not know. Not that I want a dog like that, but only to know the secret of its birth.

I think he was going to hunt elephants with it, because I know, from remarks dropped by him, that he has hunted large game in India and Africa, and likes it. But I think that if he tries to hunt elephants with it, he is going to be disappointed. I do not believe that it is suited for elephants. It lacks energy, it lacks force of character, it lacks bitterness. These things all show in the meekness and resignation of its expression. It would not attack an elephant, I am sure of it. It might not run if it saw one coming, but it looked to me like a dog that would sit down and pray.

I wish he had told me what breed it was, if there are others; but I shall know the dog next time, and then if I can bring myself to it I will put delicacy aside and ask.

From _Following The Equator_: In that garden I also saw the wild Australian dog—the dingo. He was a beautiful creature—shapely, graceful, a little wolfish in some of his aspects, but with a most friendly eye and sociable disposition. . . . It may be that he is the oldest dog in the universe; his origin, his descent . . . are as unknown and untraceable as are the camel's. He is the most precious dog in the world, for he does not bark. But in an evil hour he got to raiding the sheep-runs to appease his hunger, and that sealed his doom . . . He has been sentenced to extermination, and the sentence will be carried out. This is all right, and not objectionable. The world was made for man—the white man.

AUGUSTIN DALY'S BACK DOOR

This story is also from *Following the Equator*; Mark Twain's body is still on that Bombay train, but his mind is not. The long, low dog has reminded him of another dog. Augustin Daly was an important theatrical personality last century.

It was years and years ago. I had received a note from Mr. Augustin Daly of the Fifth Avenue Theater, asking me to call the next time I should be in New York. I was writing plays, in those days, and he was admiring them and trying to get me a chance to get them played in Siberia. I took the first train—the early one—the one that leaves Hartford at 8:29 in the morning. At New Haven I bought a paper, and found it filled with glaring display-lines about a "bench-show" there. I had often heard of bench-shows, but had never felt any interest in them, because I supposed they were lectures that were not well attended. It turned out, now, that it was not that, but a dog show. There was a double-leaded column about the king-feature of this one, which was called a Saint Bernard, and was worth $10,000, and was known to be the largest and finest of his species in the world. I read all this with interest, because out of my schoolboy readings I dimly remembered how the priests and pilgrims of Saint Bernard used to go out in the storms and dig these dogs out of the snowdrifts when lost and exhausted, and give them brandy and save their lives, and drag them to the monastery and restore them with gruel.

Also, there was a picture of this prize-dog in the paper, a noble great creature with a benignant countenance, standing by a table. He was placed in that way so that one could get a right idea of his great dimensions. You could see that he was just a shade higher than the table—indeed, a huge fellow for a dog. Then there was a description which went into the details. It gave his enormous weight—150½ pounds; and his length—4 feet 2 inches, from stem to stern-post; and his height—3 feet 1 inch, to

the top of his back. The pictures and the figures so impressed
me, that I could see the beautiful colossus before me, and I kept
on thinking about him for the next two hours; then I reached
New York, and he dropped out of my mind.

In the swirl and tumult of the hotel lobby I ran across Mr.
Daly's comedian, the late James Lewis, of beloved memory, and
I casually mentioned that I was going to call upon Mr. Daly in
the evening at eight. He looked surprised, and said he reckoned
not. For answer I handed him Mr. Daly's note. Its substance
was: "Come to my private den, over the theater, where we cannot be interrupted. And come by the back way, not the front.
No. 642 Sixth Avenue is a cigar shop; pass through it and you
are in a paved court, with hugh buildings all around; enter the
second door on the left, and come upstairs."

"Is this all?"

"Yes," I said.

"Well, you'll never get in."

"Why?"

"Because you won't. Or if you do you can draw on me for a
hundred dollars; for you will be the first man that has accomplished it in twenty-five years. I can't think what Mr. Daly can
have been absorbed in. He has forgotten a most important detail, and he will feel humiliated in the morning when he finds
that you tried to get in and couldn't."

"Why, what is the trouble?"

"I'll tell you. You see—"

At that point we were swept apart by the crowd, somebody
detained me with a moment's talk, and we did not get together
again. But it did not matter; I believed he was joking, anyway.

At eight in the evening I passed through the cigar shop and
into the court and knocked at the second door.

"Come in!"

I entered. It was a small room, carpetless, dusty, with a naked
deal table, and two cheap wooden chairs for furniture. A giant
Irishman was standing there, with shirt collar and vest unbut-
toned, and no coat on. I put my hat on the table, and was about
to say something, when the Irishman took the innings himself.
And not with marked courtesy of tone:

"Well, sor, what will *you* have?"

I was a little disconcerted, and my easy confidence suffered a shrinkage. The man stood as motionless as Gibraltar, and kept his unblinking eye upon me. It was very embarrassing, very humiliating. I stammered at a false start or two; then:

"I have just run down from—"

"Av ye plaze, ye'll not smoke here, ye understand."

I laid my cigar on the window ledge; chased my flighty thoughts a moment, then said in a placating manner:

"I—I have come to see Mr. Daly."

"Oh, ye *have,* have ye?"

"Yes."

"Well, ye'll not see him."

"But he *asked* me to come."

"Oh, he *did,* did he?"

"Yes, he sent me this note, and—"

"Lemme see it."

For a moment I fancied there would be a change in the atmosphere, now; but this idea was premature. The big man was examining the note searchingly under the gas jet. A glance showed me that he had it upside down—disheartening evidence that he could not read.

"Is ut his own hand-write?"

"Yes—he wrote it himself."

"He did, did he?"

"Yes."

"H'm. Well, then, why ud he write it like that?"

"How do you mean?"

"I mane, why wudn't he put his name to ut?"

"His name *is* to it. *That's* not it—you are looking at *my* name."

I thought that that was a home shot, but he did not betray that he had been hit. He said:

"It's not an aisy one to spell; how do you pronounce ut?"

"Mark Twain."

"H'm. H'm. Mike Train. H'm. I don't remember ut. What is it ye want to see him about?"

"It isn't I that want to see *him,* he wants to see *me.*"

"Oh, he does, does he?"

"Yes."

"What does he want to see ye about?"

"I don't know."

"Ye don't *know!* And ye confess it, becod! Well, I can tell ye wan thing—ye'll not see him. Are ye in the business?"

"What business?"

"The show business."

A fatal question. I recognized that I was defeated. If I answered no, he would cut the matter short and wave me to the door without the grace of a word—I saw it in his uncompromising eye; if I said I was a lecturer, he would despise me, and dismiss me with opprobrious words; if I said I was a dramatist, he would throw me out of the window. I saw that my case was hopeless, so I chose the course which seemed least humiliating: I would pocket my shame and glide out without answering. The silence was growing lengthy.

"I'll ask ye again. Are ye in the show business yerself?"

"Yes!"

I said it with splendid confidence; for in that moment the very twin of that grand New Haven dog loafed into the room, and I saw that Irishman's eye light eloquently with pride and affection.

"Ye are? And what is it?"

"I've got a bench-show in New Haven."

The weather *did* change then.

"You don't *say,* sir! And that's *your* show, sir! Oh, it's a grand show, it's a wonderful show, sir, and a proud man I am to see your honor this day. And ye'll be an expert, sir, and ye'll know all about dogs—more than ever they know theirselves, I'll take me oath to ut."

I said, with modesty:

"I believe I have some reputation that way. In fact, my business requires it."

"Ye have *some* reputation, your honor! Bdad I believe you! There's not a jintleman in the worrld that can lay over ye in the judgmint of a dog, sir. Now I'll vinture that your honor'll know that dog's dimensions there better than he knows them his own self, and just by the casting of your educated eye upon him. Would you mind giving a guess, if ye'll be so good?"

I knew that upon my answer would depend my fate. If I made this dog bigger than the prize-dog, it would be bad diplomacy, and suspicious; if I fell too far short of the prize-dog, that would be equally damaging. The dog was standing by the table, and I believed I knew the difference between him and the one whose picture I had seen in the newspaper to a shade. I spoke promptly up and said:

"It's no trouble to guess this noble creature's figures: height, three feet; length, four feet and three-quarters of an inch; weight, a hundred and forty-eight and a quarter."

The man snatched his hat from its peg and danced on it with joy, shouting:

"Ye've hardly missed it the hair's breadth, hardly the shade of a shade, your honor! Oh, it's the miraculous eye ye've got, for the judgmint of a dog!"

And still pouring out his admiration of my capacities, he snatched off his vest and scoured off one of the wooden chairs with it, and scrubbed it and polished it, and said:

"There, sit down, your honor, I'm ashamed of meself that I forgot ye were standing all this time; and do put on your hat, ye mustn't take cold, it's a drafty place; and here is your cigar, sir, a-getting cold, I'll give ye a light. There. The place is all yours, sir, and if ye'll just put your feet on the table and make yourself at home, I'll stir around and get a candle and light ye up the ould crazy stairs and see that ye don't come to anny harm, for be this time Mr. Daly'll be that impatient to see your honor that he'll be taking the roof off."

He conducted me cautiously and tenderly up the stairs, lighting the way and protecting me with friendly warnings, then pushed the door open and bowed me in and went his way, mumbling hearty things about my wonderful eye for points of a dog. Mr. Daly was writing and had his back to me. He glanced over his shoulder presently, then jumped up and said:

"Oh, dear me, I forgot all about giving instructions. I was just writing you to beg a thousand pardons. But how is it you are here? How did you get by that Irishman? You are the first man that's done it in five and twenty years. You didn't bribe him, I know that; there's not money enough in New York to do it. And you didn't persuade him; he is all ice and iron: there isn't a soft place nor a warm one in him anywhere. What is your secret? Look here; you owe me a hundred dollars for unintentionally giving you a chance to perform a miracle—for it *is* a miracle that you've done."

"That is all right," I said, "collect it of Jimmy Lewis."

From **Puddin'head Wilson** : We should be careful to get out of an experience only the wisdom that is in it—and stop there; lest we be like the cat that sits down on a hot stove-lid. She will never sit down on a hot stove-lid again—and that is well; but also she will never sit down on a cold one any more.

THE CHARACTER OF THE COYOTE

It was nineteen days by stagecoach, from Missouri to Nevada, changing teams every ten miles. This is the third day. The story comes from *Roughing It.*

. . . morning came, by and by. It was another glad awakening to fresh breezes, vast expanses of level greensward, bright sunlight, an impressive solitude utterly without visible human beings or human habitations, and an atmosphere of such amazing magnifying properties that trees that seemed close at hand were more than three miles away. We resumed undress uniform, climbed atop of the flying coach, dangled our legs over the side, shouted occasionally at our frantic mules, merely to see them lay their ears back and scamper faster, tied our hats on to keep our hair from blowing away, and leveled an outlook over the world-wide carpet about us for things new and strange to gaze at. Even at this day it thrills me through and through to think of the life, the gladness and the wild sense of freedom that used to make the blood dance in my veins on those fine overland mornings!

Along about an hour after breakfast we saw the first prairie-dog villages, the first antelope, and the first wolf. If I remember rightly, this latter was the regular *coyote* (pronounced ky-*o*-te) of the farther deserts. And if it *was,* he was not a pretty creature, or respectable either, for I got well acquainted with his race afterward, and can speak with confidence. The coyote is a long, slim, sick, and sorry-looking skeleton, with a gray wolf-skin stretched over it, a tolerably bushy tail that forever sags down with a despairing expression of forsakenness and misery, a furtive and evil eye, and a long, sharp face, with slightly lifted lip and exposed teeth. He has a general slinking expression all over. The coyote is a living, breathing allegory of Want. He is *always* hungry. He is always poor, out of luck, and friendless. The meanest creatures despise him, and even the fleas would desert him for a velocipede. He is so spiritless and cowardly that even while his exposed teeth are pretending a threat, the rest of his face is apologizing for it. And he is *so* homely!—so scrawny, and ribby, and coarse-haired, and pitiful. When he sees you he lifts his lip and lets a flash of his teeth out, and then turns a little out of the course he was pursuing, depresses his head a bit, and strikes a long, soft-footed trot through the sagebrush, glancing over his shoulder at you, from time to time, till he is about out of easy pistol range, and then he stops and takes a deliberate survey of you; he will trot fifty yards and stop again—another fifty and stop again; and finally the gray of his gliding body blends with the gray of the sagebrush, and he disappears. All this is when you make no demonstration against him; but if you do, he develops a livelier interest in his journey, and instantly electrifies his heels and puts such a deal of real estate between himself and your weapon that by the time you have raised the hammer you see that you need a minie rifle, and by the time you have got him in line you need a rifled cannon, and by the time you have "drawn a bead" on him you see well enough that nothing but an unusually long-winded streak of lightning could reach him where he is now. But if you start a swift-footed dog after him, you will enjoy it ever so much—especially if it is a dog that has a good opinion of himself, and has been brought up to think he knows something about speed. The coyote will go swinging gently off on that deceitful trot of his, and every little while he will smile a fraudful smile over his shoulder that will fill that dog entirely full of encouragement and worldly ambition, and make him lay his head still lower to the ground, and stretch his neck further to the front, and pant more fiercely, and stick his tail out straighter behind, and move his furious legs with a yet wilder frenzy, and leave a broader and broader, and higher and denser cloud of desert sand smoking behind, and marking his long wake across the level plain! And all this time the dog is only a short twenty feet behind the coyote, and to save the soul of him he cannot understand why it is that he cannot get perceptibly closer; and he begins to get aggravated, and it makes him madder and madder to see how gently the coyote glides along and never pants or sweats or ceases to smile; and he grows still more and more incensed to see how shamefully he has been taken in by an entire stranger, and what an ignoble swindle that long, calm, soft-footed trot is; and next he notices that he is getting fagged, and that the coyote actually has to slacken speed a little to keep from running away from him—and *then* that town-dog is mad in earnest, and he begins to strain and weep and swear, and paw the sand higher than ever, and reach for the coyote with concentrated and desperate energy. This "spurt" finds him six feet behind the gliding enemy, and two miles from his friends. And then, in the instant that a wild new hope is lighting up his face, the coyote turns and smiles blandly upon him once more, and with a something about it which seems to say: "Well, I shall have to tear myself away from you, bub—business is business, and it will not do for me to be fooling along this way all day"— and forthwith there is a rushing sound, and the sudden splitting of a long crack through the atmosphere, and behold that dog is solitary and alone in the midst of a vast solitude!

It makes his head swim. He stops, and looks all around; climbs the nearest sand-mound, and gazes into the distance; shakes his head reflectively, and then, without a word, he turns and jogs along back to his train, and takes up a humble position under the hindmost wagon, and feels unspeakably mean, and looks ashamed, and hangs his tail at half-mast for a week. And for as much as a year after that, whenever there is a great hue and cry after a coyote, that dog will merely glance in that direction without emotion, and apparently observe to himself, "I believe I do not wish any of the pie."

The coyote lives chiefly in the most desolate and forbidding deserts, along with the lizard, the jackass-rabbit, and the raven, and gets an uncertain and precarious living, and earns it. He seems to subsist almost wholly on the carcasses of oxen, mules, and horses that have dropped out of emigrant trains and died, and upon windfalls of carrion, and occasional legacies of offal bequeathed to him by white men who have been opulent enough to have something better to butcher than condemned army bacon. He will eat anything in the world that his first cousins, the desert-frequenting tribes of Indians, will, and they will eat anything they can bite. It is a curious fact that these latter are the only creatures known to history who will eat nitroglycerin and ask for more if they survive.

The coyote of the deserts beyond the Rocky Mountains has a peculiarly hard time of it, owing to the fact that his relations, the Indians, are just as apt to be the first to detect a seductive scent on the desert breeze, and follow the fragrance to the late ox it emanated from, as he is himself; and when this occurs he has to content himself with sitting off at a little distance watching those people strip off and dig out everything edible, and walk off with it. Then he and the waiting ravens explore the skeleton and polish the bones. It is considered that the coyote, and the obscene bird, and the Indian of the desert, testify their blood-kinship with each other in that they live together in the waste places of the earth on terms of perfect confidence and friendship, while hating all other creatures and yearning to assist at their funerals. He does not mind going a hundred miles to breakfast, and a hundred and fifty to dinner, because he is sure to have three or four days between meals, and he can just as well be traveling and looking at the scenery as lying around doing nothing and adding to the burdens of his parents.

We soon learned to recognize the sharp, vicious bark of the coyote as it came across the murky plain at night to disturb our dreams among the mail-sacks; and remembering his forlorn aspect and his hard fortune, made shift to wish him the blessed novelty of a long day's good luck and a limitless larder the morrow.

From _Tom Sawyer Abroad_: By this time monstrous big birds begun to come and settle on the dead animals. . . . you could make them out with the glass while they was still so far away you couldn't see them with your naked eye. Tom said the birds didn't find out the meat was there by the smell; they had to find it out by seeing it. Oh, but ain't that an eye for you!

THE DIGESTION OF A CAMEL

It was in Syria, in 1867, traveling roads "filled with mule-trains and long processions of camels," that Mark Twain decided what a camel looked like, and so the first paragraph of this selection is from *The Innocents Abroad*. But the rest comes from *Roughing It*, because it was on a stagecoach in the American West that he first saw sagebrush and noted, among other things: "Nothing can abide the taste of it but the jackass and his illegitimate child, the mule. But their testimony to its nutritiousness is worth nothing, for they will eat pine-knots or anthracite coal, or . . ." And that reminded him.

. . . we have been trying for some time to think what a camel looks like, and now we have made it out. When he is down on all his knees, flat on his breast to receive his load, he looks something like a goose swimming; and when he is upright he looks like an ostrich with an extra set of legs. Camels are not beautiful, and their long under-lip gives them an exceedingly "gallus" * expression. They have immense flat, forked cushions of feet that make a track in the dust like a pie with a slice cut out of it. They are not particular about their diet. They would eat a tombstone if they could bite it. A thistle grows about here which had needles on it that would pierce through leather, I think; if one touches you, you can find relief in nothing but profanity. The camels eat these. They show by their actions that they enjoy them.

. . . Mules and donkeys and camels have appetites that anything will relieve temporarily, but nothing satisfy. In Syria, once, at the headwaters of the Jordan, a camel took charge of my overcoat while the tents were being pitched, and examined it with a critical eye, all over, with as much interest as if he had an idea of getting one made like it; and then, after he was done figuring on it as an article of apparel, he began to contemplate it as an article of diet. He put his foot on it, and lifted one of the sleeves out with his teeth, and chewed and chewed at it, gradually taking it in, and all the while opening and closing his eyes in a kind of religious ecstasy, as if he had never tasted anything as good as an overcoat before in his life. Then he smacked his lips once or twice, and reached after the other sleeve. Next he tried the velvet collar, and smiled a smile of such contentment that it was plain to see that he regarded that as the daintiest thing

* Excuse the slang—no other word will describe it. [It comes from "gallows" and means lugubrious—ED.]

about an overcoat. The tails went next, along with some percussion-caps and cough-candy, and some fig-paste from Constantinople. And then my newspaper correspondence dropped out, and he took a chance on that—manuscript letters written for the home papers. But he was treading on dangerous ground, now. He began to come across solid wisdom in those documents that was rather weighty on his stomach; and occasionally he would take a joke that would shake him up till it loosened his teeth; it was getting to be perilous times with him, but he held his grip with good courage and hopefully, till at last he began to stumble on statements that not even a camel could swallow with impunity. He began to gag and gasp, and his eyes to stand out, and his forelegs to spread, and in about a quarter of a minute he fell over as stiff as a carpenter's workbench, and died a death of indescribable agony. I went and pulled the manuscript out of his mouth, and found that the sensitive creature had choked to death on one of the mildest and gentlest statements of fact that I ever laid before a trusting public.

From *More Maxims of Mark* : Do not tell fish stories where the people know you; but particularly, don't tell them where they know the fish.

BAKER'S BLUE JAYS

Mark Twain heard this story while hiding from the San Francisco police in 1865. He had attacked those exceedingly corrupt officials in a series of articles that anyone with a taste for vitriolic Mark Twain would give his arm to see. Unfortunately, they had mysteriously disappeared even before Mark Twain's death. We have only the word of those who saw them that they were "the greatest series of daily philippics ever written." [1]

Of course Mark Twain couldn't publish such stuff in the San Francisco *Morning Call*, where he was working as a reporter and hating it. So he sent his articles back to Nevada—to the Virginia City *Enterprise*, the paper where he had acquired the name Mark Twain and had worked so happily for the preceding two years—until some remarks he printed almost involved him in a duel with a rival newspaper editor and he had to leave the state. (The challenge came from Clemens, and, by Nevada law, even challenging to a duel was a felony.)

Enterprise editor Joe Goodman always let Mark Twain say what he pleased and the *Enterprise* printers were used to him. But those letters on corruption in San Francisco were too much even for the printers. In answer to their protests—"You can never afford to publish that!" —editor Goodman is supposed to have replied, "If Mark can stand it, I can." [2]

Mark Twain could stand it, but the San Francisco police couldn't. They sued for libel—a pointless gesture since they couldn't collect on libel printed out of the state. And there matters might have ended if Mark Twain's bantamweight friend, Steve Gillis (a compositor on the *Morning Call*), hadn't beaten up a very large bartender who was a friend of San Francisco Police Chief Martin Burke. The charge against Steve was assault with intent to kill. Mark Twain furnished bail and the two men made themselves scarce in San Francisco.

For the next three months Mark Twain hid out with Steve's gentle brother, Jim, in Jackass Hill, California, where the wilderness had covered an old mining town, but where a few dauntless souls, like Jim, still sought—and sometimes found—pockets of gold. There Mark Twain panned for gold himself and listened to stories. In this story Baker is Jim Gillis, and according to Mark Twain he reeled this tale off, just as it appears here, because he was an untaught genius. But then Jim always believed that Mark Twain would have had a future as a pocket miner.

Friendship misled them both, for there were few things Mark Twain loathed so much as physical labor and whatever Jim's talents, and however he told this tale, it was certainly not as Mark Twain told it, fifteen years later, when some ravens in a Hiedelberg forest reminded him of it. It comes from *A Tramp Abroad*, published in 1880.

> Animals talk to each other, of course. There can be no question about that; but I suppose there are very few people who can understand them. I never knew but one man who could. I knew he could, however, because he told me so himself. He was a middle-aged, simple-hearted miner who had lived in a lonely corner of California, among the woods and mountains, a good many years, and had studied the ways of his only neighbors, the beasts and the birds, until he believed he could accurately translate any remark which they made. This was Jim Baker. According to Jim

Baker, some animals have only a limited education, and use only very simple words, and scarcely ever a comparison or a flowery figure; whereas, certain other animals have a large vocabulary, a fine command of language, and a ready and fluent delivery; consequently these latter talk a great deal; they like it; they are conscious of their talent, and they enjoy "showing off." Baker said that, after long and careful observation, he had come to the conclusion that the blue jays were the best talkers he had found among birds and beasts. Said he:

"There's more *to* a blue jay than any other creature. He has got more moods, and more different kinds of feelings than other creatures; and mind you, whatever a blue jay feels, he can put into language. And no mere commonplace language either, but rattling, out-and-out book-talk—and bristling with metaphor, too—just bristling! And as for command of language—why *you* never see a blue jay get stuck for a word. No man ever did. They just boil out of him! And another thing: I've noticed a good deal, and there's no bird, or cow, or anything that uses as good grammar as a blue jay. You may say a cat uses good grammar. Well, a cat does—but you let a cat get excited, once; you let a cat get to pulling fur with another cat on a shed, nights, and you'll hear grammar that will give you the lockjaw. Ignorant people think it's the *noise* which fighting cats make that is so aggravating, but it ain't so; it's the sickening grammar they use. Now I've never heard a jay use bad grammar but very seldom; and when they do, they are as ashamed as a human; they shut right down and leave.

"You may call a jay a bird. Well, so he is, in a measure—because he's got feathers on him, and don't belong to no church, perhaps; but otherwise he is just as much a human as you be. And I'll tell you for why. A jay's gifts, and instincts, and feelings, and interests, cover the whole ground. A jay hasn't got any more principle than a Congressman. A jay will lie, a jay will steal, a jay will deceive, a jay will betray; and four times out of five, a jay will go back on his solemnest promise. The sacredness of an obligation is a thing which you can't cram into no blue jay's head. Now, on top of all this, there's another thing; a jay can outswear any gentleman in the mines. You think a cat can swear. Well,, a cat can; but you give a blue jay a subject that calls for his reserve powers, and where is your cat? Don't talk to *me*—I know too much about this thing. And there's yet another thing: in the one little particular of scolding—just good, clean, out-and-out scolding—a blue jay can lay over anything, human or divine. Yes, sir, a jay is everything that a man is. A jay can cry, a jay can laugh, a jay can feel shame, a jay can reason and plan and discuss, a jay likes gossip and scandal, a jay has got a sense of humor, a jay knows when he is an ass just as well as you do—maybe better. If a jay ain't human, he'd better take in his sign, that's all. Now I'm going to tell you a perfectly true fact about some blue jays.

"When I first begun to understand jay language correctly, there was a little incident happened here. Seven years ago, the last man in this region but me, moved away. There stands his house—been empty ever since; a log house, with a plank roof—just one big room, and no more; no ceiling—nothing between the rafters and the floor. Well, one Sunday morning I was sitting out here in front of my cabin, with my cat, taking the sun, and looking at the blue hills, and listening to the leaves rustling so lonely in the trees, and thinking of the home away yonder in the States, that I hadn't heard from in thirteen years, when a blue jay lit on that house, with an acorn in his mouth, and says, 'Hello, I reckon I have struck something.' When he spoke, the acorn dropped out of his mouth and rolled down the roof, of course, but he didn't care; his mind was all on the thing he had struck. It was a knot-hole in the roof. He cocked his head to one side, shut one eye, and put the other one to the hole, like a 'possum looking down a jug; then he glanced up with his bright eyes, gave a wink or two with his wings—which signifies gratification, you understand—and says, 'It looks like a hole, it's located like a hole—blamed if I don't believe it *is* a hole!'

"Then he cocked his head down and took another look; he glances up perfectly joyful, this time, winks his wings and his tail both, and says, 'Oh no, this ain't no fat thing, I reckon! If I ain't in luck!—why it's a perfectly elegant hole!' So he flew down and got that acorn, and fetched it up and dropped it in, and was just tilting his head back, with the heavenliest smile on his face, when all of a sudden he was paralyzed into a listening attitude, and that smile faded gradually out of his countenance like breath off'n a razor, and the queerest look of surprise took its place. Then he says, 'Why, I didn't hear it fall!' He cocked his

eye at the hole again, and took a long look; raised up and shook
his head; stepped around to the other side of the hole, and took
another look from that side; shook his head again. He studied
awhile, then he just went into the *details*—walked round and
round the hole, and spied into it from every point of the compass. No use. Now he took a thinking attitude on the comb of
the roof, and scratched the back of his head with his right foot a
minute, and finally says, 'Well, it's too many for *me,* that's certain; must be a mighty long hole; however, I ain't got no time to
fool around here, I got to 'tend to business; I reckon it's all
right—chance it, anyway.'

"So he flew off and fetched another acorn and dropped it in,
and tried to flirt his eye to the hole quick enough to see what become of it, but he was too late. He held his eye there as much as
a minute; then he raised up and sighed, and says, 'Confound it, I
don't seem to understand this thing, no way; however, I'll tackle
her again.' He fetched another acorn, and done his level best to
see what become of it, but he couldn't. He says, 'Well, *I* never
struck no such a hole as this, before; I'm of the opinion it's a to-
tally new kind of a hole.' Then he begun to get mad. He held in
for a spell, walking up and down the comb of the roof and
shaking his head and muttering to himself; but his feelings got
the upper hand of him, presently, and he broke loose and cussed
himself black in the face. I never see a bird take on so about a
little thing. When he got through he walks to the hole and looks
in again for half a minute; then he says, 'Well, you're a long
hole, and a deep hole, and a mighty singular hole altogether—
but I've started in to fill you, and I'm d—d if I *don't* fill you, if it
takes a hundred years!'

"And with that, away he went. You never see a bird work so
since you was born. He laid into his work like a nigger, and the
way he hove acorns into that hole for about two hours and a half
was one of the most exciting and astonishing spectacles I ever
struck. He never stopped to take a look any more—he just hove
'em in and went for more. Well, at last he could hardly flop his
wings, he was so tuckered out. He comes a-drooping down, once
more, sweating like an ice-pitcher, drops his acorn in and says,
'*Now* I guess I've got the bulge on you by this time!' So he bent
down for a look. If you'll believe me, when his head come up
again he was just pale with rage. He says, 'I've shoveled acorns

enough in there to keep the family thirty years, and if I can see a sign of one of 'em I wish I may land in a museum with a belly full of sawdust in two minutes!'

"He just had strength enough to crawl up onto the comb, and lean his back agin the chimbly, and then he collected his impressions, and begun to free his mind. I see in a second that what I had mistook for profanity in the mines was only just the rudiments, as you may say.

"Another jay was going by, and heard him doing his devotions, and stops to inquire what was up. The sufferer told him the whole circumstance, and says, 'Now yonder's the hole, and if you don't believe me go and look for yourself.' So this fellow went and looked, and comes back and says, 'How many did you say you put in there?' 'Not any less than two tons,' says the sufferer. The other jay went and looked again. He couldn't seem to make it out, so he raised a yell, and three more jays come. They all examined the hole, they all made the sufferer tell it over again, then they all discussed it, and got off as many leather-headed opinions about it as an average crowd of humans could have done.

"They called in more jays; then more and more, till pretty soon this whole region 'peared to have a blue flush about it. There must have been five thousand of them; and such another jawing and disputing and ripping and cussing, you never heard. Every jay in the whole lot put his eye to the hole and delivered a more chuckle-headed opinion about the mystery than the jay that went there before him. They examined the house all over, too. The door was standing half open, and at last one old jay happened to go and light on it and look in. Of course that knocked the mystery galley-west in a second. There lay the acorns, scattered all over the floor. He flopped his wings and raised a whoop. 'Come here!' he says, 'come here, everybody; hang'd if this fool hasn't been trying to fill up a house with acorns!' They all came a-swooping down like a blue cloud, and as each fellow lit on the door and took a glance, the whole absurdity of the contract that that first jay had tackled hit him home, and he fell over backwards suffocating with laughter, and the next jay took his place and done the same.

"Well, sir, they roosted around here on the housetop and the trees for an hour, and guffawed over that thing like human beings. It ain't any use to tell me a blue jay hasn't got a sense of humor, because I know better. And memory, too. They brought jays here from all over the United States to look down that hole, every summer for three years. Other birds too. And they could all see the point, except an owl that come from Nova Scotia to visit the Yo Semite, and he took this thing in on his way back. He said he couldn't see anything funny in it. But then he was a good deal disappointed about Yo Semite, too."

From *What Is Man?* : Let us . . . call them the Unrevealed Creatures; so far as we can know, there is no such thing as a dumb beast.

THE CELEBRATED JUMPING FROG OF CALAVERAS COUNTY

THE AMERICAN FROG

This is the frog that made Mark Twain famous and one of the trickiest beasts in literature. *The Private History of the "Jumping Frog" Story* was his creator's gallant effort, thirty-odd years later, to clear up some frog-caused confusion. But by then not even he was sure how many frogs there'd been. His friend Professor Henry Van Dyke, of Princeton, had told him there was only one—a Greek frog two thousand years old. As proof Van Dyke offered to send Clemens the original Greek tale or the English translation. Mark Twain chose English "because Greek makes me tired," and when he received it recognized "every essential" of his Jumping Frog.

What puzzled him was that he had heard about his frog years before from a man who was "telling it to his hearers as a thing . . . which *they had witnessed and would remember.*" Moreover his source was a "dull person" with no interest in stories. "Now then, the interesting question is, *did* the frog story happen in Angel's Camp in the spring of '49, as told in my hearing that day in the fall of 1865? I am perfectly sure that it did. I am also sure that its duplicate happened in Boetia a couple of thousand years ago."

He wanted to believe that, for it was a favorite theory of his that everything that happens has happened before. On the other hand, he noticed that the Greek frog was suspiciously faithful in most details to his own, and in one detail suspiciously unfaithful: he ate gravel. "One can't," he said, "beguile a modern frog with that product." [1]

It turned out that Professor Henry Sidgwick of Cambridge University had written *Greek Prose Composition* as an exercise book—it was in English to be translated into Greek—and had included a condensed version of Mark Twain's "Jumping Frog," changing California to Boetia and shot to gravel. He hadn't identified it, the professor said, because it hadn't occurred to him that anybody would fail to recognize it.

The facts behind the original frog story:

On Jackass Hill, California, where he heard the seed of his blue jay yarn, Mark Twain did pan for gold and learned all there was to be learned about that trade. But practicing was another thing. Thus, while he was at Jackass Hill, a compromise was worked out: in good weather they would work; otherwise—and it was a sleety fall—they would restore their strength in a saloon.

Ben Coon, who told the frog story, was a steady customer there. The story was an old one that had been going the rounds of the camps and was probably true. It was dull enough to be true, and Ben made it duller. Then, with Mark Twain's help, the crowd discovered that the worse Ben was, the better he was, and they enlivened their billiards by chanting snatches of his words. Mark Twain enlivened their working days the same way. His job was carrying the pails of water to wash the dirt that might be pay dirt. He didn't like it. Day after day, the others listened to the drawl: *"I don't see no p'ints about that pan o' dirt that's any better'n any other pan o' dirt."* Ten years later versions of this chorus were being chanted in every country but France, and in every language but French. But thereby hangs another tale.

"The Jumping Frog" was first published in 1865, in a New York magazine, *Saturday Press.*

In compliance with the request of a friend of mine, who wrote me from the East, I called on good-natured, garrulous old Simon Wheeler, and inquired after my friend's friend, Leonidas W. Smiley, as requested to do, and I hereunto append the result. I

have a lurking suspicion that *Leonidas W.* Smiley is a myth; that
my friend never knew such a personage; and that he only conjectured that if I asked old Wheeler about him, it would remind
him of his infamous *Jim* Smiley, and he would go to work and
bore me to death with some exasperating reminiscence of him as
long and as tedious as it should be useless to me. If that was the
design, it succeeded.

I found Simon Wheeler dozing comfortably by the barroom
stove of the dilapidated tavern in the decaying mining camp of
Angel's, and I noticed that he was fat and bald-headed, and had
an expression of winning gentleness and simplicity upon his
tranquil countenance. He roused up, and gave me good-day. I
told him a friend of mine had commissioned me to make some
inquiries about a cherished companion of his boyhood named
Leonidas W. Smiley—*Rev. Leonidas W.* Smiley, a young minister
of the Gospel, who he had heard was at one time a resident of
Angel's Camp. I added that if Mr. Wheeler could tell me anything about this Rev. Leonidas W. Smiley, I would feel under
many obligations to him.

Simon Wheeler backed me into a corner and blockaded me
there with his chair, and then sat down and reeled off the monot-
onous narrative which follows this paragraph. He never smiled,
he never frowned, he never changed his voice from the gentle-
flowing key to which he tuned his initial sentence, he never betrayed the slightest suspicion of enthusiasm; but all through the
interminable narrative there ran a vein of impressive earnestness
and sincerity, which showed me plainly that, so far from his
imagining that there was anything ridiculous or funny about his
story, he regarded it as a really important matter, and admired
its two heroes as men of transcendent genius in *finesse.* I let him
go on in his own way, and never interrupted him once.

"Rev. Leonidas W. H'm, Reverend Le—well, there was a feller here once by the name of *Jim* Smiley, in the winter of '49—or
maybe it was the spring of '50—I don't recollect exactly, somehow, though what makes me think it was one or the other is because I remember the big flume warn't finished when he first
come to the camp; but anyway, he was the curiosest man about
always betting on anything that turned up you ever see, if he
could get anybody to bet on the other side; and if he couldn't

he'd change sides. Any way that suited the other man would suit *him*—any way just so's he got a bet, *he* was satisfied. But still he was lucky, uncommon lucky; he most always come out winner. He was always ready and laying for a chance; there couldn't be no solit'ry thing mentioned but that feller'd offer to bet on it, and take ary side you please, as I was just telling you. If there was a horse race, you'd find him flush or you'd find him busted at the end of it; if there was a dog fight, he'd bet on it; if there was a cat fight, he'd bet on it; if there was a chicken fight, he'd bet on it; why, if there was two birds setting on a fence, he would bet you which one would fly first; or if there was a camp-meeting, he would be there reg'lar to bet on Parson Walker, which he judged to be the best exhorter about here, and so he was, too, and a good man. If he even see a straddle-bug start to go anywheres, he would bet you how long it would take him to get to—to wherever he was going to, and if you took him up, he would foller that straddle-bug to Mexico but what he would find out where he was bound for and how long he was on the road. Lots of the boys here has seen that Smiley, and can tell you about him. Why, it never made no difference to *him*—he'd bet an *any* thing—the dangdest feller. Parson Walker's wife laid very sick once, for a good while, and it seemed as if they warn't going to save her; but one morning he come in, and Smiley up and asked him how she was, and he said she was considable better—thank the Lord for his inf'nite mercy—and coming on so smart that with the blessing of Prov'dence she'd get well yet; and Smiley, before he thought, says: 'Well, I'll resk two-and-a-half she don't anyway,'

"Thish-yer Smiley had a mare—the boys called her the fifteen-minute nag, but that was only in fun, you know, because, of course, she was faster than that—and he used to win money on that horse, for all she was so slow and always had the asthma, or the distemper, or the consumption, or something of that kind. They used to give her two or three hundred yards start, and then pass her under way; but always at the fag end of the race she'd get excited and desperate like, and come cavorting and strad-dling up, and scattering her legs around limber, sometimes in the air, and sometimes out to one side among the fences, and kick-ing up m-o-r-e dust and raising m-o-r-e racket with her coughing and sneezing and blowing her nose—and *always* fetch up at the stand just about a neck ahead, as near as you could cipher it down.

"And he had a little small bull-pup, that to look at him you'd think he warn't worth a cent but to set around and look ornery and lay for a chance to steal something. But as soon as money was up on him he was a different dog; his under-jaw'd begin to stick out like the fo'castle of a steamboat, and his teeth would uncover and shine like the furnaces. And a dog might tackle him and bully-rag him, and bite him, and throw him over his shoulder two or three times, and Andrew Jackson—which was the name of the pup—Andrew Jackson would never let on but what *he* was satisfied, and hadn't expected nothing else—and the bets being doubled and doubled on the other side all the time, till the money was all up; and then all of a sudden he would grab that other dog jest by the j'int of his hind leg and freeze to it—not chaw, you understand, but only just grip and hang on till they throwed up the sponge, if it was a year. Smiley always come out winner on that pup, till he harnessed a dog once that didn't have no hind legs, because they'd been sawed off in a circular saw, and when the thing had gone along far enough, and the money was all up, and he come to make a snatch for his pet holt, he see in a minute how he'd been imposed on, and how the other dog had him in the door, so to speak, and he 'peared surprised, and then he looked sorter discouraged-like and didn't try no more to win the fight, and so he got shucked out bad. He give Smiley a look, as much as to say his heart was broke, and it was *his* fault, for putting up a dog that hadn't no hind legs for him to take holt of, which was his main dependence in a fight, and then he limped off a piece and laid down and died. It was a good pup, was that Andrew Jackson, and would have made a name for his-self if he'd lived, for the stuff was in him and he had genius—I know it, because he hadn't no opportunities to speak of, and it don't stand to reason that a dog could make such a fight as he could under them circumstances if he hadn't no talent. It always makes me feel sorry when I think of that last fight of his'n, and the way it turned out.

"Well, thish-yer Smiley had rat-tarriers, and chicken cocks, and tomcats and all them kind of things, till you couldn't rest, and you couldn't fetch nothing for him to bet on but he'd match you. He ketched a frog one day, and took him home, and said he cal'lated to educate him; and so he never done nothing for three months but set in his back yard and learn that frog to jump. And you bet you he *did* learn him, too. He'd give him a little punch behind, and the next minute you'd see that frog whirling in the air like a doughnut—see him turn one summerset, or maybe a couple, if he got a good start, and come down flat-footed and all right, like a cat. He got him up so in the matter of ketching flies, and kep' him in practice so constant, that he'd nail a fly every time as fur as he could see him. Smiley said all a frog wanted was education, and he could do 'most anything—and I believe him. Why, I've seen him set Dan'l Webster down here on this floor—Dan'l Webster was the name of the frog—and sing out, 'Flies, Dan'l, flies!' and quicker'n you could wink he'd spring straight up and snake a fly off'n the counter there, and flop down on the floor ag'in as solid as a gob of mud, and fall to scratching the side of his head with his hind foot as indifferent as if he hadn't no idea he'd been doin' any more'n any frog might do. You never see a frog so modest and straightfor'ard as he was, for all he was so gifted. And when it come to fair and square jumping on a dead level, he could get over more ground at one straddle than any animal of his breed you ever see. Jumping on a dead level was his strong suit, you understand; and when it come to that, Smiley would ante up money on him as long as he had a red. Smiley was monstrous proud of his frog, and well he might be, for fellers that had traveled and been everywheres all said he laid over any frog that ever *they* see.

"Well, Smiley kep' the beast in a little lattice box, and he used to fetch him downtown sometimes and lay for a bet. One day a feller—a stranger in the camp, he was—come acrost him with his box, and says:

" 'What might it be that you've got in the box?'

"And Smiley says, sorter indifferent-like: 'It might be a parrot, or it might be a canary, maybe, but it ain't—it's only just a frog.'

"And the feller took it, and looked at it careful, and turned it round this way and that, and says: 'H'm—so 'tis. Well, what's *he* good for?'

" 'Well,' Smiley says, easy and careless, 'he's good enough for *one* thing, I should judge—he can outjump any frog in Calaveras county.'

"The feller took the box again, and took another long, particular look, and give it back to Smiley, and says, very deliberate, 'Well,' he says, 'I don't see no p'ints about that frog that's any better'n any other frog.'

" 'Maybe you don't,' Smiley says. 'Maybe you understand frogs and maybe you don't understand 'em; maybe you've had experience, and maybe you ain't only a amature, as it were. Anyways, I've got *my* opinion, and I'll resk forty dollars that he can outjump any frog in Calaveras county.'

"And the feller studied a minute, and then says, kinder sad-like, 'Well, I'm only a stranger here, and I ain't got no frog; but if I had a frog, I'd bet you.'

"And then Smiley says, 'That's all right—that's all right—if you'll hold my box a minute, I'll go and get you a frog.' And so the feller took the box, and put up his forty dollars along with Smiley's, and set down to wait.

"So he set there a good while thinking and thinking to hisself, and then he got the frog out and prized his mouth open and took a teaspoon and filled him full of quail shot—filled him pretty near up to his chin—and set him on the floor. Smiley he went to the swamp and slopped around in the mud for a long time, and finally he ketched a frog, and fetched him in, and give him to this feller, and says:

" 'Now, if you're ready, set him alongside of Dan'l, with his forepaws just even with Dan'l's, and I'll give the word.' Then he says, 'One—two—three—*git!*' and him and the feller touched up the frogs from behind, and the new frog hopped off lively, but Dan'l give a heave, and hysted up his shoulders—so—like a Frenchman, but it warn't no use—he couldn't budge; he was planted as solid as a church, and he couldn't no more stir than if he was anchored out. Smiley was a good deal surprised, and he was disgusted too, but he didn't have no idea what the matter was, of course.

"The feller took the money and started away; and when he was going out at the door, he sorter jerked his thumb over his shoulder—so—at Dan'l, and says again, very deliberate, 'Well,' he says, '*I* don't see no p'ints about that frog that's any better'n any other frog.'

"Smiley he stood scratching his head and looking down at Dan'l a long time, and at last he says, 'I do wonder what in the nation that frog throw'd off for—I wonder if there ain't something the matter with him—he 'pears to look mighty baggy, somehow.' And he ketched Dan'l by the nap of the neck, and hefted him, and says, 'Why, blame my cats if he don't weigh five pound!' and turned him upside down and he belched out a double handful of shot. And then he see how it was, and he was the maddest man—he set the frog down and took out after that feller, but he never ketched him. And—"

(Here Simon Wheeler heard his name called from the front yard, and got up to see what was wanted.) And turning to me as he moved away, he said: "Just set where you are, stranger, and rest easy—I ain't going to be gone a second."

But, by your leave, I did not think that a continuation of the history of the enterprising vagabond *Jim* Smiley would be likely to afford me much information concerning the Rev. *Leonidas W.* Smiley, and so I started away.

At the door I met the sociable Wheeler returning, and he button-holed me and re-commenced:

"Well, thish-yer Smiley had a yaller one-eyed cow that didn't have no tail, only just a short stump like a bannanner, and—"

However, lacking both time and inclination, I did not wait to hear about the afflicted cow, but took my leave.

From *Following the Equator*—In South Africa: *The chameleon in the hotel court.* He is fat and indolent and contemplative; but is business-like and capable when a fly comes about—reaches out a tongue like a teaspoon and takes him in. He gums his tongue first. He is always pious, in his looks . . . He has a froggy head, and a back like a new grave—for shape; and hands like a bird's toes that have been frost-bitten. But his eyes are his exhibition feature. A couple of skinny cones project from the sides of his head, with a wee shiny bead of an eye set in the apex of each; and these cones turn bodily like pivot-guns and point every-which-way, and they are independent of each other. . . . When I am behind him and C[lara] in front of him, he whirls one eye rearwards and the other forwards—which gives him a most Congressional expression (one eye on the constituency and one on the swag).

THE FRENCH FROG

When the celebrated frog appeared there was no French word for humor, and humor was considered un-French. There was also

Franco-American disagreement about what it was. According to Mark Twain, humor was "a fragrance." According to Madame Marie-Thérèse Blanc, his French translator and critic, it was a mixture of "zest, melancholy, charm, brutality, malice, and thoughtfulness" peculiar to English writers. It affected "imagination and sensibilities. When these imaginations are French, it soon exhausts them because they are so refined and exacting and so imbued with good taste."

Madame Blanc also explained that it was "jesting with a serious countenance." A year later Mark Twain wrote his wife: "Got a French version of the Jumping Frog—fun is no name for it. I am going to translate it literally . . . and publish it . . . as the grave effort of a man who does not know but what he is as good a French scholar as there is." He was not a French scholar then, though he read and wrote it easily. But he did become one years later when, for his literary defense of Joan of Arc, he went back to the medieval documents.

Why were the French translations of his work so bad? Why did the French enjoy him so little? The traditional explanation has been that the French could not understand Mark Twain because the translations were so bad. Actually, the situation was reversed, for to translate, it is necessary first to understand. It also helps to understand the artist's background. Mark Twain's prompted Madame Blanc to inquire: "Where do they come from, these simple tales for half-civilized readers?" And to reply: "From the jovial irony, petulance, and animal spirits which suffice to entertain a young people." She also made allowances for the author who was at home "only in the *far-west*. . . . There, a smile on his lips, he wrestles some sort of place for himself from the bandits and Indians." [2]

Later French critics never came up to Madame Blanc's style, but the message was the same. "For a long time," said Eugène Forgues, in 1886, "we have tried to understand and enjoy this sort of writing, but we are still unable even to define the English word 'humor.' " [3]

This retranslation comes from "The Jumping Frog. The original Story in English. The Re-Translation Clawed Back from the French, into a Civilized Language Once More, by Patient and Unremunerated Toil." There is only one retranslation, but there are various versions by Mark Twain of the situation that drove him to the "unremunerated toil." In this one, he has just claimed that his American frog killed an American magazine "with a suddenness beyond praise." But that was merely jesting with a serious countenance. "The Jumping Frog" was first published in the final issue of the dying *Saturday Press*.

Early in '66 the "Jumping Frog" was issued in book form, with other sketches of mine. A year or two later Madame Blanc translated it into French and published it in the *Revue des Deux Mondes,* but the result was not what should have been expected, for the *Revue* struggled along and pulled through, and is alive yet. I think the fault must have been in the translation. I ought to have translated it myself. I think so because I examined into the matter and finally retranslated the sketch from the French back into English, to see what the trouble was; that is, to see just what sort of a focus the French people got upon it. Then the mystery was explained. In French the story is too confused, and chaotic, and unreposeful, and ungrammatical, and insane; consequently it could only cause grief and sickness—it could not kill. A glance at my retranslation will show the reader that this must be true.

(My Retranslation.)

THE FROG JUMPING OF THE COUNTY OF CALAVERAS.

Eh bien! this Smiley nourished some terriers á rats, and some cocks of combat, and some cats, and all sort of things; and with his rage of betting one no had more of repose. He trapped one day a frog and him imported with him (*et l'emporta chez lui*) saying that he pretended to make his education. You me believe if you will, but during three months he not has nothing done but to him apprehend to jump (*apprendre a sauter*) in a court retired of her mansion (*de sa maison*). And I you respond that he have succeeded. He him gives a small blow by behind, and the instant after you shall see the frog turn in the air like a grease-biscuit, make one summersault, sometimes two, when she was well started, and re-fall upon his feet like a cat. He him had accomplished in the art of to gobble the flies (*goberdes mouches*), and him there exercised continually—so well that a fly at the most far that she appeared was a fly lost. Smiley had custom to say that all which lacked to a frog it was the education, but with the education she could do nearly all—and I him believe. *Tenez,* I him have seen pose Daniel Webster there upon this plank— Daniel Webster was the name of the frog—and to him sing, "Some flies, Daniel, some flies!"—in a flash of the eye Daniel had bounded and seized a fly here upon the counter, then jumped anew at the earth, where he rested truly to himself scratch the head with his behind-foot, as if he no had not the least idea of his superiority. Never you not have seen frog as modest, as natural, sweet as she was. And when he himself agitated to jump purely and simply upon plain earth, she does more ground in one jump than any beast of his species than you can know.

To jump plain—this was his strong. When he himself agitated for that Smiley multiplied the bets upon her as long as there to him remained a red. It must to know, Smiley was monstrously proud of his frog, and he of it was right, for some men who were traveled, who had all seen, said that they to him would be injurious to him compare to another frog. Smiley guarded Daniel in a little box latticed which he carried bytimes to the village for some bet.

One day an individual stranger at the camp him arrested with his box and him said:

"What is this that you have then shut up there within?"

Smiley said, with an air indifferent:

"That could be a paroquet, or a syringe (*ou un serin*), but this no is nothing of such, it not is but a frog."

The individual it took, it regarded with care, it turned from one side and from the other, then he said:

"*Tiens!* in effect!—At what is she good?"

"My God!" respond Smiley, always with an air disengaged, "she is good for one thing, to my notice (*à mon avis*), she can batter in jumping (*elle peut batter en sautant*) all frogs of the county of Calaveras."

The individual re-took the box, it examined of new longly, and it rendered to Smiley in saying with an air deliberate:

"*Eh bien!* I no saw not that that frog had nothing of better than each frog." (*Je ne vois pas que cette grenouille ait rien de mieux qu'aucune grenouille*). [If that isn't grammar gone to seed, then I count myself no judge.—M.T.]

"Possible that you not it saw not," said Smiley, "possible that you—you comprehend frogs; possible that you not you there comprehend nothing; possible that you had of the exeprience, and possible that you not be but an amateur. Of all manner (*De toute manière*) I bet forty dollars that she batter in jumping no matter which frog of the county of Calaveras."

The individual reflected a second, and said like sad:

"I not am but a stranger here, I no have not a frog; but if I of it had one, I would embrace the bet."

"Strong, well!" respond Smiley; "nothing of more facility. If you will hold my box a minute, I go you to search a frog (*j'irai vous chercher*)."

Behold, then, the individual, who guards the box, who puts his forty dollars upon those of Smiley, and who attends (*et qui attend*). He attended enough longtimes, reflecting all solely. And figure you that he takes Daniel, him opens the mouth by force and with a teaspoon him fills with shot of the hunt, even him fills just to the chin, then he him puts by the earth. Smiley during these times was at slopping in a swamp. Finally he trapped (*attrape*) a frog, him carried to that individual, and said:

"Now if you be ready, put him all against Daniel, with their before-feet upon the same line, and I give the signal"—then he added: "One, two, three—advance!"

Him and the individual touched their frogs by behind, and the frog new put to jump smartly, but Daniel himself lifted ponderously, exalted the shoulders thus, like a Frenchman—to what good? he could not budge, he is planted solid like a church, he not advance no more than if one him had put at the anchor.

Smiley was surprised and disgusted, but he not himself doubted not of the turn being intended (*mais il ne se doutait pas du tour bien entendu*). The individual empocketed the silver, himself with it went, and of it himself in going is that he no gives not a jerk of thumb over the shoulder—like that—at the poor Daniel, in saying with his air deliberate (*L'individu empoche l'argent s'en va et en s'en allant est ce qu'il ne donne pas un coup de pouce par-dessus l'épaule, comme ça, au pauvre Daniel, en disant de son air délibéré*):

"*Eh bien! I no see not that that frog has nothing of better than another.*"

Smiley himself scratched longtimes the head, the eyes fixed upon Daniel, until that which at last he said:

"I me demand how the devil it makes itself that this beast has refused. Is it that she had something? One would believe that she is stuffed."

He grasped Daniel by the skin of the neck, him lifted and said:

"The wolf me bite if he no weigh not five pounds."

He him reversed and the unhappy belched two handfuls of shot (*et le malheureux,* etc.). When Smiley recognized how it was, he was like mad. He deposited his frog by the earth and ran after that individual, but he not him caught never.

From Mark Twain's *Autobiography* : French is not a familiar tongue to me, and the pronunciation is difficult, and comes out of me encumbered with a Missouri accent; but the cats like it, and when I make impassioned speeches in that language they sit in a row and put up their paws, palm to palm, and frantically give thanks.

MULE RACE

"But let us return to the mule," says Mark Twain in this selection and, promptly, does not return. But let the reader who deplores his digression be thankful that Sir Walter Scott is mentioned only once. For it was here, in the second volume of *Life on the Mississippi,* that Mark Twain damned himself repeatedly by pointing out that Scott, that revered and starchy gentleman so beloved in the slave-holding South, had done "measureless harm" by setting the South "in love with sillinesses and emptinesses," "sham grandeurs," "jejune romanticism," "inflated speech," "bogus decorations," "decayed and degraded systems of government," and "pride and pleasure" in "rank and caste."

And the fact is that, before the Civil War the fashionable Southern sport had not been mule racing, but tournaments copied as faithfully as possible from *Ivanhoe,* with knights in costume wearing the colors of fair ladies.

Mark Twain's most unforgiven remark was that Sir Walter had "so large a hand in making Southern character" that "it seems a little harsh toward a dead man to say that we never should have had any war but for Sir Walter; and yet something of a plausible argument might, perhaps, be made in support of that wild proposition." [1] Instead, a solemn treatiese was published, in 1941, answering Mark Twain by proving that Sir Walter Scott had not really caused the Civil War.[2]

But let us return to the mule.

We assisted—in the French sense—at a mule race, one day. I believe I enjoyed this contest more than any other mule there. I enjoyed it more than I remember having enjoyed any other animal race I ever saw. The grandstand was well filled with the beauty and the chivalry of New Orleans. That phrase is not original with me. It is the Southern reporter's. He has used it for two generations. He uses it twenty times a day, or twenty thousand times a day, or a million times a day—according to the exigencies. He is obliged to use it a million times a day, if he have occasion to speak of respectable men and women that often; for he has no other phrase for such service except that single one. He never tires of it; it always has a fine sound to him. There is a kind of swell, medieval bulliness and tinsel about it that pleases his gaudy, barbaric soul. If he had been in Palestine in the early times, we should have had no references to "much people" out of him. No, he would have said "the beauty and the chivalry of Galilee" assembled to hear the Sermon on the Mount. It is likely that the men and women of the South are sick enough of that phrase by this time, and would like a change, but there is no immediate prospect of their getting it. . . .

The trouble with the Southern reporter is—Women. They unsettle him; they throw him off his balance. He is plain, and sensible, and satisfactory, until woman heaves in sight. Then he goes all to pieces; his mind totters, becomes flowery and idiotic. . . .

But let us return to the mule. Since I left him, I have rummaged around and found a full report of the race. In it I find confirmation of the theory which I broached just now—namely, that the trouble with the Southern reporter is Women: Women, supplemented by Walter Scott and his knights and beauty and chivalry, and so on. This is an excellent report, as long as the women stay out of it. But when they intrude, we have this frantic result:

> It will be probably a long time before the ladies' stand presents such a sea of foamlike loveliness as it did yesterday. The New Orleans women are always charming, but never so much so as at this time of the year, when in their dainty spring costumes they bring with them a breath of balmy freshness and an odor of sanctity unspeakable. The stand was so crowded with them that, walking at their feet and seeing no possibility of approach, many a man appreciated as he never did before the Peri's feeling at the Gates of Paradise, and wondered what was the priceless boon that would admit him to

their sacred presence. Sparkling on their white-robed breasts or shoulders were the colors of their favorite knights, and were it not for the fact that the doughty heroes appeared on unromantic mules, it would have been easy to imagine one of King Arthur's gala-days.

There were thirteen mules in the first heat; all sorts of mules, they were; all sorts of complexions, gaits, dispositions, aspects. Some were handsome creatures, some were not; some were sleek, some hadn't had their fur brushed lately; some were innocently gay and frisky; some were full of malice and all unrighteousness; guessing from looks, some of them thought the matter on hand was war, some thought it was a lark, the rest took it for a religious occasion. And each mule acted according to his convictions. The result was an absence of harmony well compensated by a conspicuous presence of variety—variety of a picturesque and entertaining sort.

All the riders were young gentlemen in fashionable society. If the reader has been wondering why it is that the ladies of New Orleans attend so humble an orgy as a mule race, the thing is explained now. It is a fashion freak; all connected with it are people of fashion.

. . . The mule race is one of the marked occasions of the year. It has brought some pretty fast mules to the front. One of these had to be ruled out, because he was so fast that he turned the thing into a one-mule contest, and robbed it of one of its best features—variety. But every now and then somebody disguises him with a new name and a new complexion, and rings him in again.

The riders dress in full jockey costumes of bright-colored silks, satins, and velvets.

The thirteen mules got away in a body, after a couple of false starts, and scampered off with prodigious spirit. As each mule and each rider had a distinct opinion of his own as to how the race ought to be run, and which side of the track was best in certain circumstances, and how often the track ought to be crossed, and when a collision ought to be accomplished, and when it ought to be avoided, these twenty-six conflicting opinions created a most fantastic and picturesque confusion, and the resulting spectacle was killingly comical.

Mile heat; time, 2:22. Eight of the thirteen mules distanced. I had a bet on a mule which would have won if the procession had been reversed. The second heat was good fun; and so was the "consolation race for beaten mules," which followed later; but the first heat was the best in that respect.

I think that much the most enjoyable of all races is a steamboat race; but, next to that, I prefer the gay and joyous mule-rush. Two red-hot steamboats raging along, neck-and-neck, straining every nerve—that is to say, every rivet in the boilers—quaking and shaking and groaning from stem to stern, spouting white steam from the pipes, pouring black smoke from the chimneys, raining down sparks, parting the river into long breaks of hissing foam—this is sport that makes a body's very liver curl with enjoyment. A horse race is pretty tame and colorless in comparison. Still, a horse race might be well enough, in its way, perhaps, if it were not for the tiresome false starts. But then, nobody is ever killed. At least, nobody was ever killed when I was at a horse race. They have been crippled, it is true; but this is little to the purpose.

From *The Innocents Abroad*—In Syria: We had a fine race, of a mile, with an Arab perched on a camel. Some of the horses were fast, and made very good time, but the camel scampered by them without any great effort. The yelling and shouting, and whipping and galloping, of all parties interested, made it an exhilarating, exciting, and particularly boisterous race.

CAMPING OUT

For a few months in the gold-mad West, Sam Clemens resisted the fever. The Humboldt strike in Nevada was his undoing; it was said to make the Comstock lode—the richest ever seen on earth—look like tin. Here he is on the way to Humboldt, frantic lest he be too late. He has invested the last of his savings in wagons, tools, supplies, and horses.

He chose the horses himself, with the help of Gus (later Judge) Oliver, whom he here calls Oliphant. In Judge Oliver's private account of this expedition, he said that Mark Twain was the life of it (except for spells when he scarcely spoke) and that the cow in this selection was an exaggeration.[1]

In life, the blacksmith, Mr. Ballou, was named Fillon, and he knew something about mining—more, at least, than the two lawyers and ex-pilot Clemens, who accompanied him.

Sam Clemens came back from Humboldt with nothing but some extremely improbable stories. And yet these were mainly true, including this one. It was the probable tales of the richness of the Humboldt strike that were lies.

The story is from *Roughing It*.

Hurry, was the word! We wasted no time. Our party consisted of four persons—a blacksmith sixty years of age, two young lawyers, and myself. We bought a wagon and two miserable old horses. We put eighteen hundred pounds of provisions and mining tools in the wagon and drove out of Carson [City] on a chilly December afternoon. The horses were so weak and old that we soon found that it would be better if one or two of us got out and walked. It was an improvement. Next, we found that it would be better if a third man got out. That was an improvement also. It was at this time that I volunteered to drive, although I had never driven a harnessed horse before, and many a man in such a position would have felt fairly excused from such a responsibility. But in a little while it was found that it would be a fine thing if the driver got out and walked also. It was at this time that I resigned the position of driver, and never resumed it again. Within the hour, we found that it would not only be better, but was absolutely necessary, that we four, taking turns, two at a time, should put our hands against the end of the wagon and push it through the sand, leaving the feeble horses little to do but keep out of the way and hold up the tongue. Perhaps it is well for one to know his fate at first, and get reconciled to it. We had learned ours in one afternoon. It was plain that we had to walk through the sand and shove that wagon and those horses two hundred miles. So we accepted the situation, and from that time forth we never rode. . . .

We made seven miles, and camped in the desert. Young Claggett (now member of Congress from Montana) unharnessed and fed and watered the horses; Oliphant and I cut sagebrush, built the fire, and brought water to cook with; and old Mr. Ballou, the blacksmith, did the cooking. This division of labor, and this appointment, was adhered to throughout the journey. We had no tent, and so we slept under our blankets in the open plain. We were so tired that we slept soundly.

We were fifteen days making the trip—two hundred miles; thirteen, rather, for we lay by a couple of days, in one place, to let the horses rest. We could really have accomplished the journey in ten days if we had towed the horses behind the wagon, but we did not think of that until it was too late, and so went on shoving the horses and the wagon too when we might have saved half the labor. Parties who met us, occasionally, advised us to put the horses *in* the wagon, but Mr. Ballou, through whose iron-clad earnestness no sarcasm could pierce, said that that would not do, because the provisions were exposed and would suffer, the horses being "bituminous from long deprivation." The reader will excuse me from translating. What Mr. Ballou customarily meant, when he used a long word, was a secret between himself and his Maker. He was one of the best and kindest-hearted men that ever graced a humble sphere of life. He was gentleness and simplicity itself—and unselfishness, too. Although he was more than twice as old as the eldest of us, he never gave himself any airs, privileges, or exemptions on that account. He did a *young* man's share of the work; and did his share of conversing and entertaining from the general standpoint of *any* age—not from the arrogant, overawing summit-height of sixty years. His one striking peculiarity was his Partingtonian[2] fashion of loving and using big words *for their own sakes,* and independent of any bearing they might have upon the thought he was purposing to convey. He always let his ponderous syllables fall with an easy unconsciousness that left them wholly without offensiveness. In truth, his air was so natural and so simple that one was always catching himself accepting his stately sentences as meaning something, when they really meant nothing in the world. If a word was long and grand and resonant, that was sufficient to win the old man's love, and he would drop that word into the most out-of-the-way place in a sentence or a subject, and be as pleased with it as if it were perfectly luminous with meaning.

We four always spread our common stock of blankets together on the frozen ground, and slept side by side; and finding that our foolish, long-legged hound pup had a deal of animal heat in him, Oliphant got to admitting him to the bed, between himself and Mr. Ballou, hugging the dog's warm back to his breast and finding great comfort in it. But in the night the pup would get stretchy and brace his feet against the old man's back and shove, grunting complacently the while; and now and then, being warm and snug, grateful and happy, he would paw the old man's back simply in excess of comfort; and at yet other times he would dream of the chase and in his sleep tug at the old man's back hair and bark in his ear. The old gentleman complained mildly about these familiarities, at last, and when he got through with his statement he said that such a dog as that was not a proper animal to admit to bed with tired men, because he was "so meretricious in his movements and so organic in his emotions." We turned the dog out.

From *The Innocents Abroad*—in Palestine: We took our last look at the city, clinging like a whitewashed wasp's nest to the hillside. . . . We dismounted and drove the horses down a bridle-path which I think was fully as crooked as a corkscrew; which I know to be as steep as the downward sweep of a rainbow, and which I believe to be the worst piece of road in the geography, except . . . one or two mountain trails in the Sierra Nevadas.

"My Dear Mother"

Soon after this letter was received, it appeared in the *Keokuk Gate City*, in Keokuk, Iowa. It was "hardly necessary" said the paper's editor, to say how he got it. "Let it suffice that we know it was intended for publication." But it wasn't. The editor also headed it "Model Letter from Nevada," which it certainly wasn't. He undoubtedly got it from Mark Twain's sister-in-law, who lived in Keokuk and who had it from his mother in St. Louis. The family passed all letters around, not only Sam's, but there were none like Sam's, and never will be.

The horrors of the alkali desert were as reported. "Tell everything as it is—no better, and no worse," he had recently been instructed by a mother who was just as capable, and also as incapable, as he of following such instructions.[1] For Jane Clemens, like her son, always fascinated conventional liars by her truthfulness, and then held them spellbound by her fairy tales. In fact, she was the only person on earth Mark Twain really resembled.

The letter is the inside story of "Camping Out." In *Roughing It*, the

dog Curney was omitted. Further facts from Judge Oliver's account of
the journey: Just before the alkali desert, they saw signs of a recent Indian war: charred shacks and lonely graves. When they got through
the desert, they dropped in their tracks at 3 A.M., to be awakened at
noon "by a yelling band of Pirute warriors." In due course Sam "put
his hand on his head . . . and then with his inimitable drawl said:
'Boys, they have left us our scalps. Let's give them all the flour and
sugar they ask for.' And we did give them a good supply, for we were
grateful." [2]

This letter was reprinted from the *Keokuk Gate City*, with editorial
notes by Frederick W. Lorch, in the magazine *American Literature*,
November, 1938. This was part of Mr. Lorch's comment on the poem
that begins the letter: "It is with regard to the sense of the poem, however, in so far as it may be said to have sense, that one may legiti-
mately raise a question. In view of the fact that Sam Clemens had very
recently resigned his lieutenancy in the rebel militia of Missouri, after
a brief inglorious 'campaign,' and that even before he left Missouri for
the West, a number of bloody battles of the Civil War had been
fought, does not his poem betray a levity about a deeply serious national crisis that is not altogether commendable even in a humorist?"

Carson City, January 30, 1862

My Dear Mother:

"How sleep the brave who sink to rest
    Far, far from the battle-field's dreadful array,
With cheerful ease and succulent repast
    Now ask the sun to lend his streaming ray."

Bully, isn't it? I mean the poetry, madam, of course. Doesn't it
make you feel just a little "stuck up" to think that your son is
a—Bard? And I have attained to this proud eminence without
an effort, almost. You see, madam, my method is very simple
and easy—thus: When I wish to write a great poem, I just take a
few lines from Tom, Dick, and Harry, Shakespeare, and other
poets, and by patching them together so as to make them rhyme
occasionally I have accomplished my object. Never mind the
sense—sense, madam, has but little to do with poetry. By this
wonderful method, anybody can be a poet—or a bard—which
sounds better, you know.

But I have other things to talk about, now—so, if you please, we will drop the subject of poetry. You wish to know where I am, and where I have been? And, verily, you shall be satisfied. Behold, I am in the middle of the universe—at the center of gravitation—even Carson City. And I have been to the land that floweth with gold and silver—Humboldt. (Now, do not make any ridiculous attempt, ma, to pronounce the "d," because you can't do it, you know.) I went to the Humboldt with Billy C., and Gus., and old Mr. Fillon.[3] With a two-horse wagon, loaded with eighteen hundred pounds of provisions and blankets—necessaries of life—to which the following luxuries were added: Viz: ten pounds of Kinnikinick, two dogs, Watt's Hymns, fourteen decks of cards, "Dombey and Son," a cribbage board, one small keg of lager beer, and the *"Carmina Sacra."* [4]

At first, Billy drove, and we pushed behind the wagon. Not because we were fond of it, ma—Oh, no—but on Bunker's account. Bunker was the "near" horse, on the larboard side. Named after the Attorney General of this Territory. My horse— you are acquainted with him, by reputation, already—and I am sorry you do not know him personally, ma, for I feel toward him, sometimes, as if he were a blood relation of our family—he is so infernally lazy, you know—my horse, I was going to say— was the "off" horse, on the starboard side. But it was on Bunker's account, principally, that we pushed behind the wagon. For whenever we came to a hard piece of road, that poor, lean, infatuated cuss could fall into a deep reverie about something or other, and stop perfectly still, and it would generally take a vast amount of black-snaking and shoving and profanity to get him started again; and as soon as he was fairly under way, he would take up the thread of his reflections where he left off, and go on thinking, and pondering, and getting himself more and more mixed up and tangled in his subject, until he would get regularly stuck again, and stop to review the question.

And always in the meanest piece of road he could find. In fact, ma, that horse had something on his mind, all the way from here to the Humboldt; and he had not got rid of it when I left there—for when I departed, I saw him standing, solitary and alone, away up on the peak of a mountain, where no horse ever ventured before, with his pensive figure darkly defined against the sky—still thinking about it.

Our dog, Tom, which we borrowed at Chinatown without ask-

ing the owner's permission, was a beautiful hound pup, eight
months old. He was a love of a dog, and much addicted to fleas.
He always slept with Billy and me. Whenever we selected our
camp, and began to cook supper, Tom, aided and abetted by us
three boys, immediately commenced laying his plans to steal a
portion of the latter; and with our assistance, he generally succeeded in inserting his long, handsome nose into every dish before anybody else. This was wrong, ma, and we know it—so, to
atone for it, we made Mr. Fillon's dog stand around whenever
he attempted any such liberties. And when our jolly supper was
swallowed, and the night was on the wane, and we had finished
smoking our pipes, and singing songs, and spinning yarns, and
telling lies, and quoting scripture, and all that sort of thing, and
had begun to look for a soft place on the ground to spread our
blankets on, Tom, with immense sagacity, always assisted in the
search, and then with becoming modesty, rewarded himself by
taking first choice between the blankets. No wonder we loved
the dog.

But, Mr. Fillon's dog, "Curney," we utterly despised. He was
not a long, slender graceful dog like Tom, but a little mean,
white, curly, grinning whelp, no bigger than a cat—with a
wretched envious, snappish, selfish disposition, and a tail like an
all-wool capital O, curled immodestly over his back, and apparently wrenched and twisted to its place so tightly that it seemed
to lift his hind legs off the ground sometimes. And we made Tom
pester him; and bite his tail; and his ears; and stumble over him;
and we heaped trouble and humiliation upon the brute to that
degree that his life became a burden to him. And Billy, hating
the dog, and thirsting for his blood, prophesied that Curney
would come to grief. And Gus and I said Amen. And it came to
pass according to the words of the prophet. Thus.

On the fifth day out, we left the village of Ragtown, and entered upon the Forty-five Mile Desert, where the sand is of unknown depth, and locomotion of every kind is very difficult;
where the road is strewn thickly with skeletons and carcasses of
dead beasts of burden, and charred remains of wagons; and
chains, and bolts and screws, and gun-barrels, and such things
of a like heavy nature as weary, thirsty emigrants, grown desperate, have thrown away, in the grand hope of being able, when
less encumbered, to reach water. We left Ragtown, ma, at nine

o'clock in the morning, and the moment we began to plow
through that horrible sand, Bunker, true to his instincts, fell into
a reverie so dense, so profound, that it required all the black-
snaking and shoving and profanity at our disposal to keep him
on the move five minutes at a time. But we did shove, and whip
and blaspheme all day and all night, without stopping to rest or
eat, scarcely (and alas! we had nothing to drink, then). And long
before daylight we struck the big Alkali Flat—and Curney came
to grief; for the poor devil got *Alkalied*—in the seat of honor.
You see he got tired, traveling all day and all night, nearly—
immensely tired—and sat himself down by the wayside to rest.
And lo! the iron entered his soul. (Poetical figure, ma.) And
when he rose from that fiery seat, he began to turn summersets,
and roll over and over and kick up his heels in the most frantic
manner, and shriek, and yelp and bark, and make desperate
grabs at his tail, which he could not reach on account of his excitement and a tendency to roll over; and he would drag himself
over the ground in a sitting posture (which afforded him small
relief, you know) and then jump up and yelp, and scour away
like the wind; and make a circuit of three hundred yards, for all
the world as if he were on the Pony Express. And we three weary
and worn and thirsty wretches forgot our troubles, and fell upon
the ground and laughed until all life and sense passed out of us,
and the colic came to our relief and brought us to again, while
old Mr. Fillon wiped his spectacles, and put them on, and
looked over them, and under them, in a bewildered way, and
"wondered," every now and then, "what in the h-ll was the matter with Curney."

We thought—yea, we fondly hoped, ma—that Curney's time
had come. But it was otherwise ordained. Mr. Fillon was much
exercised on account of his dog's misery, and, sharing his misery, we recommended a bullet as a speedy remedy, but the old
gentleman put his trust in tallow, and Curney became himself
again, except that he walked behind the wagon for many hours
with humble mien and tail transformed from a brave all-wool
capital O to a limp and all-wool capital J, and gave no sign when
Tom bit his ears or stumbled over him.

We took up our abode at Unionville, in Buena Vista Mining
District, Humboldt county, after pushing that wagon nearly two
hundred miles, and taking eleven days to do it in. And we found

that the "National" lead there was selling at $50 per foot, and assayed $2,496 per ton at the Mint in San Francisco. And the "Alba Nueva," "Peru," . . . and others, were immensely rich leads. And moreover, having winning ways with us, we could get "feet" enough to make us all rich one of these days. . . . in the Santa Clara District . . . Billy put up his shingle as Notary Public, and Gus put up his as Probate Judge, and I mounted my horse (in company with the Captain and the Colonel) and journeyed back to Carson, leaving them making preparations for a prospecting tour;[5] and before I can go to Esmeralda and get back to Humboldt, they will have laid, with the certainty of fate, the foundation of their fortunes. It's a great country, ma.

Now, ma, I could tell you how, on our way back here, the Colonel and the Captain and I got fearfully and desperately lousy; and how I got used to it and didn't mind it, and slept with the Attorney General, who wasn't used to it, and did mind it; but I fear my letter is already too long. Therefore—*sic transit gloria mundi, e pluribus unum forever!* Amen. (Latin, madam—which you don't understand, you know.)

S L C

From *The Innocents Abroad* : When we reached the pier, we found an army of Egyptian boys with donkeys no larger than themselves, waiting for passengers. . . . They were good-natured rascals, and so were the donkeys. We mounted, and the boys ran behind us and kept the donkeys at a furious gallop, as is the fashion at Damascus. I believe I would rather ride a donkey than any beast in the world. He goes briskly, he puts on no airs, he is docile, though opinionated.

THE GENUINE

But for "Curry, *Old* Curry, Old *Abe* Curry," the Nevada Territory might have died, said Mark Twain, "in its tender infancy." Not for lack of legislators, for the federal government was offering three dollars a day for those, and "there were plenty of patriotic souls out of employment." But it ignored the problem of a meeting place and Carson City, Nevada's capital, "blandly denied to give a room rent-free,

or let one to the government on credit." It was old Abe Curry who do-
nated the hall, a mile or so outside town, and threw in pine benches
and clean sawdust, as "carpet and spittoon combined."

Hay *was* two hundred and fifty dollars a ton—in greenbacks worth
forty cents on the dollar. Other parts of this story are exaggerated. It
comes from *Roughing It*.

> I resolved to have a horse to ride. I had never seen such wild,
> free, magnificent horsemanship outside of a circus as these pic-
> turesquely clad Mexicans, Californians, and Mexicanized Amer-
> icans displayed in Carson streets every day. How they rode!
> Leaning just gently forward out of the perpendicular, easy and
> nonchalant, with broad slouch-hat brim blown square up in
> front, and long *riata* swinging above the head, they swept
> through the town like the wind! The next minute they were only
> a sailing puff of dust on the far desert. If they trotted, they sat up
> gallantly and gracefully, and seemed part of the horse; did not
> go jiggering up and down after the silly Miss Nancy fashion of
> the riding-schools. I had quickly learned to tell a horse from a
> cow, and was full of anxiety to learn more. I was resolved to buy
> a horse.
>
> While the thought was rankling in my mind, the auctioneer
> came scurrying through the plaza on a black beast that had as
> many humps and corners on him as a dromedary, and was nec-
> essarily uncomely; but he was "going, going, at twenty-two!—
> horse, saddle and bridle at twenty-two dollars, gentlemen!" and
> I could hardly resist.
>
> A man whom I did not know (he turned out to be the auction-
> eer's brother) noticed the wistful look in my eye, and observed
> that that was a very remarkable horse to be going at such a
> price; and added that the saddle alone was worth the money. It
> was a Spanish saddle, with ponderous *tapidaros,* and furnished
> with the ungainly sole-leather covering with the unspellable
> name. I said I had half a notion to bid. Then this keen-eyed per-
> son appeared to me to be "taking my measure"; but I dismissed
> the suspicion when he spoke, for his manner was full of guileless
> candor and truthfulness. Said he:
>
> "I know that horse—know him well. You are a stranger, I take
> it, and so you might think he was an American horse, maybe,
> but I assure you he is not. He is nothing of the kind; but—ex-

cuse my speaking in a low voice, other people being near—he is, without the shadow of a doubt, a Genuine Mexican Plug!"

I did not know what a Genuine Mexican Plug was, but there was something about this man's way of saying it, that made me swear inwardly that I would own a Genuine Mexican Plug, or die.

"Has he any other—er—advantages?" I inquired, suppressing what eagerness I could.

He hooked his forefinger in the pocket of my army shirt, led me to one side, and breathed in my ear impressively these words:

"He can outbuck anything in America!"

"Going, going, going—at *twent-ty*-four dollars and a half, gen —" "Twenty-seven!" I shouted, in a frenzy.

"And sold!" said the auctioneer, and passed over the Genuine Mexican Plug to me.

I could scarcely contain my exultation. I paid the money, and put the animal in a neighboring livery stable to dine and rest himself.

In the afternoon I brought the creature into the plaza, and certain citizens held him by the head, and others by the tail, while I mounted him. As soon as they let go, he placed all his feet in a bunch together, lowered his back, and then suddenly arched it upward, and shot me straight into the air a matter of three or four feet! I came as straight down again, lit in the saddle, went instantly up again, came down almost on the high pommel, shot up again, and came down on the horse's neck—all in the space of three or four seconds. Then he rose and stood almost straight up on his hind feet, and I, clasping his lean neck desperately, slid back into the saddle, and held on. He came down, and immediately hoisted his heels into the air, delivering a vicious kick at the sky, and stood on his fore feet. And then down he came once more, and began the original exercise of shooting me straight up again.

The third time I went up I heard a stranger say: "Oh, *don't* he buck, though!"

While I was up, somebody struck the horse a sounding thwack with a leathern strap, and when I arrived again the Genuine Mexican Plug was not there. A Californian youth chased him up and caught him, and asked if he might have a ride. I granted him that luxury. He mounted the Genuine, got lifted into the air once, but sent his spurs home as he descended, and the horse darted away like a telegram. . . .

I sat down on a stone with a sigh, and by a natural impulse one of my hands sought my forehead, and the other the base of my stomach. I believe I never appreciated, till then, the poverty of the human machinery—for I still needed a hand or two to place elsewhere. Pen cannot describe how I was jolted up. Imagination cannot conceive how disjointed I was—how internally, externally, and universally I was unsettled, mixed up, and ruptured. There was a sympathetic crowd around me, though.

One elderly-looking comforter said:

"Stranger, you've been taken in. Everybody in this camp knows that horse. Any child, any Injun, could have told you that he'd buck; he is the very worst devil to buck on the continent of America. You hear *me*. I'm Curry. *Old* Curry. Old *Abe* Curry. And moreover, he is a simon-pure, out-and-out, genuine d—d Mexican plug, and an uncommon mean one at that, too. Why, you turnip, if you had laid low and kept dark, there's chances to buy an *American* horse for mighty little more than you paid for that bloody old foreign relic."

I gave no sign; but I made up my mind that if the auctioneer's brother's funeral took place while I was in the territory I would postpone all other recreations and attend it.

After a gallop of sixteen miles the Californian youth and the Genuine Mexican Plug came tearing into town again, shedding foam-flakes like the spume-spray that drives before a typhoon, and, with one final skip over a wheelbarrow and a Chinaman, cast anchor in front of the "ranch."

Such panting and blowing! Such spreading and contracting of the red equine nostrils, and glaring of the wild equine eye! But was the imperial beast subjugated? Indeed, he was not. His lordship the Speaker of the House thought he was, and mounted him to go down to the Capitol; but the first dash the creature made was over a pile of telegraph-poles half as high as a church; and his time to the Capitol—one mile and three-quarters—remains unbeaten to this day. . . .

In the evening the Speaker came home afoot for exercise, and got the Genuine towed back behind a quartz-wagon. The next day I loaned the animal to the Clerk of the House to go down to the Dana silver mine, six miles, and *he* walked back for exercise, and got the horse towed. Everybody I loaned him to always walked back; they never could get enough exercise any other way. Still, I continued to loan him to anybody who was willing to borrow him, my idea being to get him crippled, and throw him on the borrower's hands, or killed, and make the borrower pay for him. But somehow nothing ever happened to him. He took chances that no other horse ever took and survived, but he always came out safe. It was his daily habit to try experiments that had always before been considered impossible, but he always got through. Sometimes he miscalculated a little, and did not get his rider through intact, but *he* always got through himself. Of course I had tried to sell him; but that was a stretch of simplicity which met with little sympathy. The auctioneer stormed up and down the streets on him for four days, dispersing the populace, interrupting business, and destroying children, and never got a bid—at least never any but the eighteen-dollar one he hired a notoriously substanceless bummer to make. The people only smiled pleasantly. . . . Then the auctioneer brought in his bill, and I withdrew the horse from the market. We tried to trade him off at private vendue next, offering him at a sacrifice for second-hand tombstones, old iron, temperance tracts—any kind of property. But holders were stiff, and we retired from the market again. I never tried to ride the horse any more. Walking was good enough exercise for a man like me, that had nothing the matter with him except ruptures, internal injuries, and such things. Finally I tried to *give* him away. But it was a failure. . . . As a last resort I offered him to the Governor for the use of the "Brigade." * His face lit up eagerly at first, but toned down again, and he said the thing would be too palpable.

Just then the livery-stable man brought in his bill for six weeks' keeping—stall-room for the horse, fifteen dollars; hay for the horse, two hundred and fifty! The Genuine Mexican Plug had eaten a ton of the article . . .

I will remark here, in all seriousness, that the regular price of hay during that year and a part of the next was really two hundred and fifty dollars a ton. . . . That same day I gave the Genuine Mexican Plug to a passing Arkansas emigrant whom fortune delivered into my hand.

* See p. 31—ED.

From *Following the Equator*—in India: The inn cow poked about the compound and emphasized the secluded and country air of the place, and there was a dog of no particular breed, who was . . . always stretched out baking in the sun and adding to the deep tranquillity and reposefulness of the place, . . . White-draperied servants were coming and going all the time, but they seemed only spirits, for their feet were bare and made no sound. Down the lane apiece lived an elephant in the shade of a noble tree, and rocked and rocked, and reached about with his trunk, begging of his brown mistress or fumbling the children playing at his feet. And there were camels about, but they go on velvet feet, and were proper to the silence and serenity of the surroundings.

HAWAIIAN HOLIDAY

He was being *paid,* Mark Twin wrote home triumphantly, when a Western newspaper sent him to Hawaii, and paid as much as if he'd stayed home—twenty dollars for each "travel letter." Some thirty years later he was traveling only for the money he desperately needed to save him from bankruptcy. On that "lecturing" trip around the world, his dear "enchanted islands" were to have been the first stop, but there was cholera there and he couldn't disembark. A tired man, suffering from a carbuncle, he gazed longingly from the ship: "If I might I would go ashore and never leave."

But here he is on his first visit and young enough to ride horseback ten hours a day, race across the burning floor of a dozing volcano, and be glad at everything he saw, from "smoke-dried children . . . clothed in nothing but sunshine" to "dusky native women sweeping by . . . on fleet horses and astride, with gaudy riding-sashes, streaming like banners behind them." The missionaries had reformed the women, he also wrote, by giving them "a profound respect for chastity—in other people."

It was after his return from the islands—a sea voyage of twenty-five days—that Mark Twin fell into the black mood during which, he said in later years, he put a gun to his head but lacked the courage to pull the trigger. Whatever his reasons, they were not connected with money or fame, for his Hawaiian letters had paid well, and his career as a national literary figure was just beginning. The best clue is this

entry in his notebook, made in 1866 just after his return from Hawaii:
"Aug. 13. San Francisco. Home again. No *not* home again—in
prison again and all the wide sense of freedom gone. The city seems so
cramped and so dreary with toil and care and business anxiety. God
help me, I wish I were at sea again."

He was to be at sea again very soon—on a cruise to Europe and the
Holy Lands, which he described in *The Innocents Abroad.* But he
didn't know that then, and he felt cornered. The very breath of life to
Mark Twain—and almost as necessary—was the act of wandering
over the world and reporting to all and sundry on its condition.

The Hawaiian Islands were the first foreign land Mark Twain ever
saw; along with India and England, they remained the foreign soil he
loved best.

The story is from *Roughing It.*

AT SEA

The scene is the schooner *Boomerang,* bound for the island of Hawaii from Honolulu. The *Boomerang* was "about as long as two street-
cars and about as wide as one."

The hold forward of the bulkhead had but little freight in it, and
from morning till night a portly old rooster, with a voice like Balaam's ass, and the same disposition to use it, strutted up and
down in that part of the vessel and crowed. He usually took dinner at six o'clock, and then, after an hour devoted to meditation,
he mounted a barrel and crowed a good part of the night. He got
hoarser and hoarser all the time, but he scorned to allow any
personal consideration to interfere with his duty, and kept up his
labors in defiance of threatened diphtheria.

Sleeping was out of the question when he was on watch. He
was a source of genuine aggravation and annoyance. It was
worse than useless to shout at him or apply offensive epithets to
him—he only took these things for applause, and strained himself to make more noise. Occasionally, during the day, I threw
potatoes at him through an aperture in the bulkhead, but he
only dodged and went on crowing.

The first night, as I lay in my coffin, idly watching the dim
lamp swinging to the rolling of the ship, and snuffing the nau-
seous odors of bilge-water, I felt something gallop over me. I

turned out promptly. However, I turned in again when I found it was only a rat. Presently something galloped over me once more. I knew it was not a rat this time, and I thought it might be a centipede, because the captain had killed one on deck in the afternoon. I turned out. The first glance at the pillow showed me a repulsive sentinel perched upon each end of it—cockroaches as large as peach leaves—fellows with long, quivering antennae and fiery, malignant eyes. They were grating their teeth like tobacco-worms, and appeared to be dissatisfied about something. I had often heard that these reptiles were in the habit of eating off sleeping sailors' toe-nails down to the quick, and I would not get in the bunk any more. I lay down on the floor. But a rat came and bothered me, and shortly afterward a procession of cockroaches arrived and camped in my hair. In a few moments the rooster was crowing with uncommon spirit, and a party of fleas were throwing double somersaults about my person in the wildest disorder, and taking a bite every time they struck. I was beginning to feel really annoyed. I got up and put my clothes on and went on deck.

It was compensation for my sufferings to come unexpectedly upon so beautiful a scene as met my eye—to step suddenly out of the sepulchral gloom of the cabin and stand under the strong light of the moon—in the center, as it were, of a glittering sea of liquid silver—to see the broad sails straining in the gale, the ship keeled over on her side, the angry foam hissing past her lee bulwarks, and sparkling sheets of spray dashing high over her bows and raining upon her decks; to brace myself and hang fast to the first object that presented itself, with hat jammed down and coat-tails whipping in the breeze, and feel that exhilaration that thrills in one's hair and quivers down his backbone when he knows that every inch of canvas is drawing and the vessel cleaving through the waves at her utmost speed. There was no darkness, no dimness, no obscurity there. All was brightness, every object was vividly defined. Every prostrate Kanaka; every coil of rope; every calabash of poi; every puppy; every seam in the flooring; every bolthead; every object, however minute, showed sharp and distinct in its every outline; and the shadow of the broad mainsail lay black as a pall upon the deck, leaving Billings' white upturned face glorified and his body in a total eclipse.

From *Roughing It*: I thought some of the things I said were rather fine. But he merely looked around at me, at distant intervals, something as I have seen a benignant old cat look around to see which kitten was meddling with her tail.

HORSEMANSHIP

Mark Twain rode so much horseback in Hawaii that he ended up incapacitated with saddle boils. But fortunately he came there fresh from the West and practice with Genuine Mexican Plugs.

The landlord of the American said the party had been gone nearly an hour, but that he could give me my choice of several horses that could overtake them. I said, never mind—I preferred a safe horse to a fast one—I would like to have an excessively gentle horse—a horse with no spirit whatever—a lame one, if he had such a thing. Inside of five minutes I was mounted, and perfectly satisfied with my outfit. I had no time to label him "This is a horse," and so if the public took him for a sheep I cannot help it. I was satisfied, and that was the main thing. I could see that he had as many fine points as any man's horse, and so I hung my hat on one of them, behind the saddle, and swabbed the perspiration from my face and started. I named him after this island, "Oahu" (pronounced O-waw-hee). The first gate he came to he started in; I had neither whip nor spur, and so I simply argued the case with him. He resisted argument, but ultimately yielded to insult and abuse. He backed out of that gate and steered for another one on the other side of the street. I triumphed by my former process. Within the next six hundred yards he crossed the street fourteen times and attempted thirteen gates, and in the meantime the tropical sun was beating down and threatening to cave the top of my head in, and I was literally dripping with perspiration. He abandoned the gate business after that and went along peaceably enough, but absorbed in meditation. I noticed this latter circumstance, and it soon began to fill me with apprehension. I said to myself, this creature is planning some new outrage, some fresh deviltry or other—no horse ever thought over a subject so profoundly as this one is doing just for nothing. The more this thing preyed upon my mind the more uneasy I became, until the suspense became almost unbearable, and I dismounted to see if there was anything wild in his eye—for I had heard that the eye of this noblest of our domestic animals is very expressive. I cannot describe what a load of anxiety was lifted from my mind when I found that he was only asleep. I woke him up and started him into a faster walk, and then the villainy of his nature came out again. He tried to climb over a stone wall five or six feet high. I saw that I must apply force to this horse, and that I might as well begin first as last. I plucked a stout switch from a tamarind tree, and the moment he saw it, he surrendered. He broke into a convulsive sort of a canter, which had three short steps in it and one long one, and reminded me alternately of the clattering shake of the great earthquake, and the sweeping plunge of the *Ajax** in a storm.

And now there can be no fitter occasion than the present to pronounce a left-handed blessing upon the man who invented the American saddle. There is no seat to speak of about it—one might as well sit in a shovel—and the stirrups are nothing but an ornamental nuisance. If I were to write down here all the abuse I expended on those stirrups, it would make a large book, even without pictures. Sometimes I got one foot so far through, that the stirrup partook of the nature of an anklet; sometimes both feet were through, and I was handcuffed by the legs; and sometimes my feet got clear out and left the stirrups wildly dangling about my shins. Even when I was in proper position and carefully balanced upon the balls of my feet, there was no comfort in it, on account of my nervous dread that they were going to slip one way or the other in a moment. But the subject is too exasperating to write about.

From *Roughing It*—in Hawaii: . . . we saw some horses that had been born and reared on top of the mountains, above the range of running water, and consequently they had never drunk that fluid in their lives, but had been always accustomed to quenching their thirst by eating dew-laden or shower-wetted leaves. And now it was destructively funny to see them sniff suspiciously at a pail of water, and then . . . try to take a *bite* out of the fluid, as if it were a solid. . . . When they became convinced at last that the water was friendly and harmless, they thrust in their noses . . . and proceeded to *chew* it complacently.

* The steamer from San Francisco to Honolulu—ED.

ADAM AND EVE AND KANGAROORUM ADAMIENSIS

Eve was alive when Mark Twain wrote "Extracts from Adam's Diary"; He began "Eve's Diary" the year he lost her. In life he called her Livy and he had been married to her for thirty-four years. "A delicate little beauty," his friend Howells once described her, "the very flower and perfume of *ladylikeness,* who simply adores him—but this leaves no word to describe his love for her." [1]

Both Adam's and Eve's diaries have been cut here, partly for reasons of space but mainly because some parts are better than others. This is much more true of Eve's diary than of Adam's. Eve is a little long-winded, or so I think, when she is made to speculate on why she loves Adam. She runs through most of the virtues and finds he doesn't have them. And those he does have aren't what matter. But her conclusion, especially from so young an Eve, is profound enough to be worth quoting: "I think I love him merely because he is *mine* and is *masculine.* There is no other reason. . . ."

Eve is not the wicked temptress in Mark Twain's version. On the contrary, it is Adam who is guilty of treachery for tattling to God that Eve offered him the apple. And Mark Twain did believe that the male was the treacherous sex. He makes Eve say: "He told on me, but I do not blame him; it is a peculiarity of sex, I think, and he did not make his sex. Of course I would not have told on him, I would have perished first; but that is a peculiarity of sex, too, and I do not take credit for it, for I did not make my sex."

Both in his life and work Mark Twain was prejudiced in favor of women. For example, Eve is clearly the artist; Mark Twain meant the act of naming things as an artist's activity, and she loves beauty as Adam does not. Eve is the hard worker, Adam the lazy one. By any standards Mark Twain was a woman's man. He once wrote in his *Notebook,* "We easily perceive that the peoples furtherest from civilization are the ones where equality between man and woman are the furthest apart—and we consider this one of the signs of savagery. But we are so stupid that we can't see that we thus plainly admit that no civilization can be perfect until exact equality between man and woman is included."

But equal did not mean alike to Mark Twain, as these diaries so plainly show.

"Extracts from Adam's Diary" was one of the very few pieces that Mark Twain had trouble selling. He finally disposed of it, in 1893, to *The Niagara Book,* an elaborate souvenir of Niagara Falls, which also contained contributions from W. D. Howells and assorted professors. There it was named "The First Authentic Mention of Niagara Falls." *Harper's Magazine* promptly republished it and published "Eve's Diary" in 1905.

Eve and creation are a day old when she begins her diary.

EVE'S DIARY

TRANSLATED FROM THE ORIGINAL

. . . Everything looks better today than it did yesterday. In the rush of finishing up yesterday, the mountains were left in a ragged condition, and some of the plains were so cluttered with rubbish and remnants that the aspects were quite distressing. . . . There are too many stars in some places and not enough in others, but that can be remedied presently, no doubt. The moon got loose last night, and slid down and fell out of the scheme—a very great loss; it breaks my heart to think of it. There isn't another thing among the ornaments and decorations that is comparable to it for beauty and finish. It should have been fastened better. If we can only get it back again—

But of course there is no telling where it went to. And besides, whoever gets it will hide it; I know it because I would do it myself. I believe I can be honest in all other matters, but I already begin to realize that the core and center of my nature is love of the beautiful, a passion for the beautiful, and that it would not be safe to trust me with a moon that belonged to another person. . . .

Stars are good, too. I wish I could get some to put in my hair. But I suppose I never can. You would be surprised to find how far-off they are, for they do not look it. When they first showed, last night, I tried to knock some down with a pole, but it didn't reach, which astonished me; then I tried clods till I was all tired out, but I never got one. It was because I am left-handed and cannot throw good. . . .

I followed the other Experiment around, yesterday afternoon, at a distance, to see what it might be for, if I could. But I was not able to make out. I think it is a man. I had never seen a man, but it looked like one, and I feel sure that that is what it is. I realize that I feel more curiosity about it than about any of the other reptiles. If it is a reptile, and I suppose it is; for it has frowsy hair and blue eyes, and looks like a reptile. It has no hips; it tapers like a carrot; when it stands, it spreads itself apart like a derrick; so I think it is a reptile, though it may be architecture.

I was afraid of it at first, and started to run every time it turned around, for I thought it was going to chase me; but by and by I found it was only trying to get away, so after that I was not timid any more, but tracked it along, several hours, about twenty yards behind, which made it nervous and unhappy. At last it was a good deal worried, and climbed a tree. I waited a good while, then gave it up and went home.

Today the same thing over. I've got it up the tree again.

Sunday—It is up there yet. Resting, apparently. But that is a subterfuge: Sunday isn't the day of rest; Saturday is appointed for that. It looks to me like a creature that is more interested in resting than in anything else. It would tire me to rest so much. It tires me just to sit around and watch the tree. I do wonder what it is for; I never see it do anything. . . .

It has low tastes, and is not kind. When I went there yesterday evening in the gloaming it had crept down and was trying to catch the little speckled fishes that play in the pool, and I had to clod it to make it go up the tree again and let them alone. I wonder if *that* is what it is for? Hasn't it any heart? . . . One of the clods took it back of the ear, and it used language. It gave me a thrill, for it was the first time I had ever heard speech, except my own. . . .

When I found it could talk I felt a new interest in it, for I love to talk; I talk, all day, and in my sleep, too, and I am very interesting, but if I had another to talk to I could be twice as interesting, and would never stop, if desired. . . .

Next week Sunday—All the week I tagged around after him

and tried to get acquainted. I had to do the talking, because he was shy, but I didn't mind it. He seemed pleased to have me around, and I used the sociable "we" a good deal, because it seemed to flatter him to be included.

Wednesday—We are getting along very well indeed, now, and getting better and better acquainted. He does not try to avoid me any more, which is a good sign, and shows that he likes to have me with him. That pleases me, and I study to be useful to him in every way I can, so as to increase his regard. During the last day or two I have taken all the work of naming things off his hands, and this has been a great relief to him, for he has not gift in that line, and is evidently very grateful. He can't think of a rational name to save him, but I do not let him see that I am aware of his defect. Whenever a new creature comes along I name it before he has time to expose himself by an awkward silence. In this way I have saved him many embarrassments. I have no defect like his. The minute I set eyes on an animal I know what it is. I don't have to reflect a moment; the right name comes out instantly, just as if it were an inspiration, as no doubt it is, for I am sure it wasn't in me half a minute before. I seem to know just by the shape of the creature and the way it acts what animal it is.

When the dodo came along he thought it was a wildcat—I saw it in his eye. But I saved him. And I was careful not to do it in a way that could hurt his pride. I just spoke up in a quite natural way of pleased surprise, and not as if I was dreaming of conveying information, and said, "Well, I do declare, if there isn't the dodo!" . . .

I tried to get him some of those apples, but I cannot learn to throw straight. I failed, but I think the good intention pleased him. They are forbidden, and he says I shall come to harm; but so I come to harm through pleasing him, why shall I care for that harm?

From "Eve's Diary": I *had* to have company—I was made for it, I think—so I made friends with the animals. . . . there's always a swarm of them around—sometimes as much as four or five acres—you can't count them; and when you stand on a rock in the midst and look out over the furry expanse it is so mottled and splashed and gay with color and frisking sheen and sun-flash, and so rippled with stripes, that you might think it was a lake, only you know it isn't; and there's storms of sociable birds, and hurricanes of whirring winds; and when the sun strikes all that feathery commotion, you have a blazing up of all the colors you can think of, enough to put your eyes out.

EXTRACTS FROM ADAM'S DIARY

There is no "Adam's Diary"—only these extracts. In order to distinguish between Mark Twain's own marks of ellipsis and mine, I have marked my cuts with asterisks.

Monday—This new creature with the long hair is a good deal in the way. It is always hanging around and following me about. I don't like this; I am not used to company. I wish it would stay with the other animals. . . . Cloudy today, wind in the east; think we shall have rain. . . . *We?* Where did I get that word?—I remember now—the new creature uses it.

Tuesday—Been examining the great waterfall. It is the finest thing on the estate, I think. The new creature calls it Niagara Falls—why, I am sure I do not know. Says it *looks* like Niagara Falls. That is not a reason, it is mere waywardness and imbecility. I get no chance to name anything myself. The new creature names everything that comes along, before I can get in a protest. And always that same pretext is offered—it *looks* like the thing. There is the dodo, for instance. Says the moment one looks at it one sees at a glance that it "looks like a dodo." It will have to keep that name, no doubt. It wearies me to fret about it, and it does no good, anyway. Dodo! It looks no more like a dodo than I do.

Wednesday—Built me a shelter against the rain, but could not have it to myself in peace. The new creature intruded. When I tried to put it out, it shed water out of the holes it looks with, and wiped it away with the back of its paws, and made a noise such as some of the other animals make when they are in distress. I wish it would not talk; it is always talking. That sounds like a cheap fling at the poor creature, a slur; but I do not mean it so. I have never heard the human voice before, and any new and strange sound intruding itself here upon the solemn hush of these dreaming solitudes offends my ear and seems a false note. . . .

Friday—The naming goes recklessly on, in spite of anything I can do. I had a very good name for the estate, and it was musical and pretty—GARDEN OF EDEN. Privately, I continue to call it that, but not any longer publicly. The new creature says it is all woods and rocks and scenery, and therefore has no resemblance to a garden. Says it *looks* like a park, and does not look like anything *but* a park. Consequently, without consulting me, it has been new-named—NIAGARA FALLS PARK. This is sufficiently high-handed, it seems to me. And already there is a sign up:

KEEP OFF
THE GRASS

My life is not as happy as it was.

Saturday—The new creature eats too much fruit. We are going to run short, most likely. "We" again—that is *its* word; mine, too, now, from hearing it so much. Good deal of fog this morning. I do not go out in the fog myself. The new creature does. It goes out in all weathers, and stumps right in with its muddy feet.* And talks. It used to be so pleasant and quiet here.

Sunday—Pulled through. This day is getting to be more and more trying. It was selected and set apart last November as a day of rest. I had already six of them per week before. This morning found the new creature trying to clod apples out of that forbidden tree.

Monday—The new creature says its name is Eve. That is all right, I have no objections. Says it is to call it by, when I want it to come. I said it was superfluous, then. The word evidently raised me in its respect; and indeed it is a large, good word and will bear repetition.† It says it is not an It, it is a She. This is probably doubtful; yet it is all one to me; what she is were nothing to me if she would but go by herself and not talk.

Tuesday—She has littered the whole estate with execrable names and offensive signs:

* Cf. "Eve's Diary": "He does not care for me, he does not care for flowers, he does not care for the painted sky at eventide—is there anything he does care for, except building shacks to coop himself up in from the good clean rain, and thumping the melons, and sampling the grapes . . . to see how those properties are coming along?"—ED.

† Cf. "Eve's Diary": "Although he talks so little, he has quite a considerable vocabulary. This morning he used a surprisingly good word. He evidently recognized, himself, that it was a good one, for he worked it in twice afterward, casually"—ED.

This Way to the Whirlpool
This Way to Goat Island
Cave of the Winds This Way

* * * *Friday*—She has taken to beseeching me to stop going over the Falls. What harm does it do? Says it makes her shudder. I wonder why; I have always done it—always liked the plunge, and coolness. I supposed it was what the Falls were for. They have no other use that I can see, and they must have been made for something. She says they were only made for scenery—like the rhinoceros and the mastodon.

I went over the Falls in a barrel—not satisfactory to her. Went over in a tub—still not satisfactory. Swam the Whirlpool and the Rapids in a fig-leaf suit. It got much damaged. Hence, tedious complaints about my extravagance. I am too much hampered here. What I need is change of scene.

Saturday—I escaped last Tuesday night, and traveled two days, and built me another shelter in a secluded place, and obliterated my tracks as well as I could, but she hunted me out by means of a beast which she has tamed and calls a wolf, and came making that pitiful noise again, and shedding that water out of the places she looks with. I was obliged to return with her, but will presently emigrate again when occasion offers. She engages herself in many foolish things; among others, to study out why the animals called lions and tigers live on grass and flowers,* when, as she says, the sort of teeth they wear would indicate that they were intended to eat each other. This is foolish, because to do that would be to kill each other, and that would introduce what, as I understand it, is called "death"; and death, as I have been told, has not yet entered the Park. Which is a pity, on some accounts.

Sunday—Pulled through.

Monday—I believe I see what the week is for: it is to give time to rest up from the weariness of Sunday. It seems a good idea. . . . She has been climbing that tree again. Clodded her out of it. She said nobody was looking. Seems to consider that a sufficient justification for chancing any dangerous thing. Told her that. The word justification moved her admiration—and envy, too, I thought. It is a good word.

---

* Cf. "Eve's Diary": "I found some tigers and nestled in among them and was most adorably comfortable, and their breath was sweet and pleasant, because they live on strawberries"—ED.

Tuesday—She told me she was made out of a rib taken from my body. This is at least doubtful, if not more than that. I have not missed any rib. . . . She is in much trouble about the buzzard; says grass does not agree with it; is afraid she can't raise it; thinks it was intended to live on decayed flesh. The buzzard must get along the best it can with what it is provided. We cannot overturn the whole scheme to accommodate the buzzard.

Saturday—She fell in the pond yesterday when she was looking at herself in it, which she is always doing. She nearly strangled, and said it was most uncomfortable. This made her sorry for the creatures which live in there, which she calls fish, for she continues to fasten names onto things that don't need them and don't come when they are called by them, which is a matter of no consequence to her, she is such a numskull, anyway; so she got a lot of them out and brought them in last night and put them in my bed to keep warm, but I have noticed them now and then all day and I don't see that they are any happier there then they were before, only quieter. When night comes I shall throw them outdoors. I will not sleep with them again, for I find them clammy and unpleasant to lie among when a person hasn't anything on.

Sunday—Pulled through.

Tuesday—She has taken up with a snake now. The other animals are glad, for she was always experimenting with them and bothering them; and I am glad because the snake talks, and this enables me to get a rest.

Friday—She says the snake advises her to try the fruit of that tree, and says the result will be a great and fine and noble education. I told her there would be another result, too—it would introduce death into the world. That was a mistake—it had been better to keep the remark to myself; it only gave her an idea—she could save the sick buzzard, and furnish fresh meat to the despondent lions and tigers. I advised her to keep away from the tree. She said she wouldn't. I foresee trouble. Will emigrate.

Wednesday—I have had a variegated time. I escaped last night, and rode a horse all night as fast as he could go, hoping to get clear out of the Park and hide in some other country before the trouble should begin; but it was not to be. About an hour after sunup, as I was riding through a flowery plain where thousands of animals were grazing, slumbering, or playing with each other, according to their wont, all of a sudden they broke into a tempest of frightful noises, and in one moment the plain was a frantic commotion and every beast was destroying its neighbor. I knew what it meant—Eve had eaten that fruit, and death was come into the world. . . . The tigers ate my horse, paying no attention when I ordered them to desist, and they would have eaten me if I had stayed—which I didn't, but went away in much haste. . . . I found this place, outside the Park, and was fairly comfortable for a few days, but she has found me out.

In fact I was not sorry she came, for there are but meager pickings here, and she brought some of those apples. I was obliged to eat them, I was so hungry. It was against my principles, but I find that principles have no real force except when one is well fed. . . . She came curtained in boughs and bunches of leaves, and when I asked her what she meant by such nonsense, and snatched them away and threw them down, she tittered and blushed. I had never seen a person titter and blush before, and to me it seemed unbecoming and idiotic. She said I would soon know how it was myself. This was correct. Hungry as I was, I laid down the apple half-eaten—certainly the best one I ever saw, considering the lateness of the season—and arrayed myself in the discarded boughs and branches, and then spoke to her with some severity and ordered her to go and get some more and not make such a spectacle of herself. She did it, and after this we crept down to where the wild-beast battle had been, and collected some skins, and I made her patch together a couple of suits proper for public occasions. They are uncomfortable, it is true, but stylish, and that is the main point about clothes. . . . I find she is a good deal of a companion. I see I should be lonesome and depressed without her, now that I have lost my property. Another thing, she says it is ordered that we work for our living hereafter. She will be useful. I will superintend. * * *

Next Year—We have named it Cain. She caught it while I was up-country trapping on the North Shore of the Erie; caught it in the timber a couple of miles from our dug-out—or it might have been four, she isn't certain which. It resembles us in some ways, and may be a relation. That is what she thinks, but this is an error, in my judgment. The difference in size warrants the conclusion that it is a different and new kind of animal—a fish, perhaps, though when I put it in the water to see, it sank, and she plunged in and snatched it out before there was opportunity for the experiment to determine the matter. I still think it is a fish, but she is indifferent about what it is, and will not let me have it to try. I do not understand this. The coming of the creature seems to have changed her whole nature and made her unreasonable about experiments. She thinks more of it than she does of any of the other animals, but is not able to explain why. Her mind is disordered—everything shows it. Sometimes she carries the fish in her arms half the night when it complains and wants to get to the water. At such times the water comes out of the places in her face that she looks out of, and she pats the fish on the back and makes soft sounds with her mouth to soothe it, and betrays sorrow and solicitude in a hundred ways. I have never seen her do like this with any other fish, and it troubles me greatly. She used to carry the young tigers around so, and play with them, before we lost our property, but it was only play; she never took on about them like this when their dinner disagreed with them.

Sunday—She doesn't work, Sundays, but lies around all tired out, and likes to have the fish wallow over her; and she makes fool noises to amuse it, and pretends to chew its paws, and that makes it laugh. I have not seen a fish before that could laugh. This makes me doubt. * * *

Wednesday—It isn't a fish. I cannot quite make out what it is. It makes curious devilish noises when not satisfied, and says "goo-goo" when it is. It is not one of us, for it doesn't walk; it is not a bird, for it doesn't fly; it is not a frog, for it doesn't hop; it is not a snake, for it doesn't crawl; I feel sure it is not a fish, though I cannot get a chance to find out whether it can swim or not. It merely lies around, and mostly on its back, with its feet up. I have not seen any other animal do that before. I said I believed it was an enigma; but she only admired the word without understanding it. In my judgment it is either an enigma or some kind of a bug. If it dies, I will take it apart and see what its arrangements are. I never had a thing perplex me so.

Three Months Later—The perplexity augments instead of diminishing. I sleep but little. It has ceased from lying around, and goes about on its four legs now. Yet it differs from the other four-legged animals, in that its front legs are unusually short, consequently this causes the main part of its person to stick up uncomfortably high in the air, and this is not attractive. It is built much as we are, but its method of traveling shows that it is not of our breed. The short front legs and long hind ones indicate that it is of the kangaroo family, but it is a marked variation of the species, since the true kangaroo hops, whereas this one never does. Still it is a curious and interesting variety, and has not been catalogued before. As I discovered it, I have felt justified in securing the credit of the discovery by attaching my name to it, and hence have called it *Kangaroorum Adamiensis.* . . . It must have been a young one when it came, for it has grown exceedingly since. It must be five times as big, now, as it was then, and when discontented it is able to make from twenty-two to thirty-eight times the noise it made at first. Coercion does not modify this, but has the contrary effect. For this reason I discontinued the system. She reconciles it by persuasion, and by giving it things which she had previously told me she wouldn't give it. As already observed, I was not at home when it first came, and she told me she found it in the woods. It seems odd that it should be the only one, yet it must be so, for I have worn myself out these many weeks trying to find another one to add to my collection, and for this one to play with; for surely then it would be quieter and we could tame it more easily. But I find none, nor any vestige of any; and strangest of all, no tracks. It has to live on the ground, it cannot help itself; therefore, how does it get about without leaving a track? I have set a dozen traps, but they do no good. I catch all small animals except that one; animals that merely go into the trap out of curiosity, I think, to see what the milk is there for. They never drink it.

Three Months Later—The kangaroo still continues to grow, which is very strange and perplexing. I never knew one to be so long getting its growth. It has fur on its head now; not like kangaroo fur, but exactly like our hair except that it is much finer and softer, and instead of being black is red. I am like to lose my mind over the capricious and harassing developments of this unclassifiable zoological freak. If I could catch another one—but that is hopeless; it is a new variety, and the only sample; this is plain. But I caught a true kangaroo and brought it in, thinking that this one, being lonesome, would rather have that for company than have no kin at all, or any animal it could feel a nearness to or get sympathy from in its forlorn condition here among strangers who do not know its ways or habits, or what to do to make it feel that it is among friends; but it was a mistake—it went into such fits at the sight of the kangaroo that I was convinced it had never seen one before. I pity the poor noisy little animal, but there is nothing I can do to make it happy. If I could tame it—but that is out of the question; the more I try the worse I seem to make it. It grieves me to the heart to see it in its little storms of sorrow and passion. I wanted to let it go, but she wouldn't hear of it. That seemed cruel and not like her. * * *

Five Months Later—It is not a kangaroo. No, for it supports itself by holding to her finger, and thus goes a few steps on its hind legs, and then falls down. It is probably some kind of a bear; and yet it has no tail—as yet—and no fur, except on its head. It still keeps on growing—that is a curious circumstance, for bears get their growth earlier than this. Bears are dangerous —since our catastrophe—and I shall not be satisfied to have this one prowling about the place much longer without a muzzle on. I have offered to get her a kangaroo if she would let this one go, but it did no good—she is determined to run us into all sorts of foolish risks, I think. She was not like this before she lost her mind.

A Fortnight Later—I examined its mouth. There is no danger yet: it has only one tooth. It has no tail yet. It makes more noise now than it ever did before—and mainly at night. I have moved out. But I shall go over, mornings, to breakfast, and see if it has more teeth. If it gets a mouthful of teeth it will be time for it to go, tail or no tail, for a bear does not need a tail in order to be dangerous.

Four Months Later—I have been off hunting and fishing a month, up in the region that she calls Buffalo; I don't know why, unless it is because there are not any buffaloes there. Meantime the bear has learned to paddle around all by itself on its hind legs, and says "poppa" and "momma." It is certainly a new species. This resemblance to words may be purely accidental, of course, and may have no purpose or meaning; but even in that case it is still extraordinary, and is a thing which no other bear can do. This imitation of speech, taken together with general absence of fur and entire absence of tail, sufficiently indicates that this is a new kind of bear. The further study of it will be exceedingly interesting. Meantime I will go off on a far expedition among the forests of the north and make an exhaustive search. There must certainly be another one somewhere, and this one will be less dangerous when it has company of its own species. I will go straightway; but I will muzzle this one first.

Three Months Later—It has been a weary, weary hunt, yet I have had no success. In the meantime, without stirring from the home estate, she has caught another one! I never saw such luck. I might have hunted these woods a hundred years, I never would have run across that thing.

Next Day—I have been comparing the new one with the old one, and it is perfectly plain that they are the same breed. I was going to stuff one of them for my collection, but she is prejudiced against it for some reason or other; so I have relinquished the idea, though I think it is a mistake. It would be an irreparable loss to science if they should get away. The old one is tamer than it was and can laugh and talk like the parrot, having learned this, no doubt, from being with the parrot so much, and having the imitative faculty in a highly developed degree. I shall be astonished if it turns out to be a new kind of parrot; and yet I ought not to be astonished, for it has already been everything else it could think of since those first days when it was a fish. The new one is as ugly now as the old one was at first; has the same sulphur-and-raw-meat complexion and the same singular head without any fur on it. She calls it Abel.

Ten Years Later— * * * I see that I was mistaken about Eve in the beginning; it is better to live outside the Garden with her than inside it without her. At first I thought she talked too much; but now I should be sorry to have that voice fall silent and pass out of my life. * * *

AT EVE'S GRAVE

ADAM: Wheresoever she was, *there* was Eden.

From Mark Twain's *Notebook*: Love seems the swiftest, but it is the slowest of all growths. No man or woman really knows what perfect love is until they have been married a quarter of a century.

AUTHORITIES

He who replies to words of Doubt
Doth put the Light of Knowledge out.

—WILLIAM BLAKE, "Auguries of Innocence"

When the physiologist Jacques Loeb predicted that life would be created by chemical agencies, scientists chuckled; Mark Twain bet on Loeb. He also remembered, with some heat, when the telephone and telegraph were considered "toys . . . of no practical value" and Pasteur was damned by "frenzied and ferocious consensuses of medical and chemical experts." [1]

But naturalists roused Mark Twain's mirth oftener than his blood pressure, for the term then included various wide-eyed literary gentlemen. One of these was John Burroughs, who appears in "The President and the Nature Fakir." The situation in "The Naturalist and the Ornithorhyncus" is more complicated; for there Mark Twain is not only ridiculing would-be scientific authorities, but is off on one of his favorite subjects: people who misuse impressive-sounding words. There is a whole regiment of these characters in Mark Twain's work, some handled fondly, some contemptuously. Mr. Ballou, of "Camping Out" is one who endeared himself to Mark Twain; the naturalist, with his flood of misinformation, is one who did not.

It might seem that such characters were imitations of Sheridan's Mrs. Malaprop, who also misued words. But this is a superficial view. When Mrs. Malaprop talked about an "allegory" on the banks of the Nile, her eighteenth-century audience knew perfectly well that she meant an alligator. But nobody, including themselves, knew what Mark Twain's characters meant once they turned themselves loose. Who, for example, shall say what the naturalist meant when he observed that "the only difference between a dingo and a dodo was that neither of them barked."

All of Mark Twain's characters inherited Mrs. Malaprop's self-assurance. The difference is that they are far more abandoned, word-drunk creatures, and when they aren't pretentious they can be as charming as his cultured horse, Soldier Boy, who didn't care what he said, or he heard either, so long as it had "a learned and cerebrospinal incandescent sound." [2] Then there is his self-educated collie, treated with deep sympathy because she listened to people; she would save their finest words for a "dogmatic gathering" where she would "surprise and distress them all, from pocket-pup to mastiff." Her great triumph was with "unintellectual," which she could define, Mark Twain claimed, as many ways as there were gatherings. She was not, he admitted, an educated dog, but she had presence of mind.[3]

But the geneaology of Mark Twain's naturalist is far more complicated than his collie's. The naturalist is descended, on his father's side, from a family of jargon-speaking pedants, and, on his mother's, from a renowned hog-wash artist. "Hog-wash" was Mark Twain's term for especially deplorable writing, which he, perversely, enjoyed.* It was always his contention that anything perfect of its kind is fascinating, whether it be the ugliest woman in the world or the most beautiful, the worst writing or the best. "None of us like mediocrity," he wrote in *A Tramp Abroad*, "but we all reverence perfection. This girl's music was perfection in its way; it was the worst music that had ever been achieved on our planet by a mere human being."

Finally, Mark Twain's naturalist is an illegitimate descendant of Darwin. So, for that matter, was Mark Twain—although in "Edison and the Animals" he is legitimate. Darwin might not have liked some of the editorializing, but it was Darwin's own discovery that "there is no fundamental difference between man and the higher mammals in their mental faculties." [4] Perhaps it was Mark Twain's merciless way of pounding home that point—a point so hard on human vanity—that made his version of Darwin so unpopular. Anyway, it still is.

"Edison and the Animals" comes from *What is Man?*, published anonymously in 1906—after the death of his wife, who hated it. A little later Mark Twain published the gist of it under his own name. Although our grandfathers took it calmly, our fathers did not, for they

---

* For a sample of it, see pp. 110–115.

had fallen passionately in love with human nature—"the spirit of man" as it was lovingly and reverently called—and if there was one human activity that pleased them more than another, it was "creativity." This was not precisely the right audience even for a legitimate Darwinian, who maintained that if man "created" or reasoned, so did the rat, the elephant, and the sea gull, and by the same process—and who declined to make an exception of Shakespeare.

Van Wyck Brooks's explanation of all this was sour grapes. Since Mark Twain could not create himself, said Brooks, it comforted him to imagine that nobody else could.[5] Less eminent critics have continued unhappy. According to Tony Tanner, writing in 1961, Mark Twain in *What Is Man?* was "almost vengeful" in his efforts to "humiliate" man by comparing him to "ignoble" animals.[6]

Actually no animal except man was ever ignoble to Mark Twain, and "Edison and the Animals" was its author's tamest interpretation of Darwin. When he was feeling his oats, he turned the great theories upside down and danced upon them, as in "The Lowest Animal" (pp. 152–161). Yet even that is Darwinian. Mark Twain might have managed without any of his literary contemporaries, but without Darwin he would have had to invent evolution himself.

It was all for the best, undoubtedly, that the great biologist never knew what a simple humorist did to his theories. For years Darwin peacefully read himself to sleep with *Tom Sawyer* and *Huckleberry Finn.* And Mark Twain meant it when he said he was proud that that mind should rest itself on him.[7] What he lacked in respect for other authorities, he more than made up for when it came to Darwin.

THE NATURALIST AND THE ORNITHORHYNCUS

This selection has been successfully used as a parlor game and, less successfully, as a test for English students' "comprehension"—an unhappy choice, since some is incomprehensible. It delighted Mark Twain when such deliberately senseless bits of his work were admired, or at least accepted—sliding, as he said, "through every reader's sensibilities like oil." The game, apparently, is to reveal which minds they slide through most easily, and which are more critical.

The Sweet Singer of Michigan was Julia Moore, a long-forgotten amateur poet, whose *Sentimental Song Book* Mark Twain so cherished that, at sixty, he carried it around the world. Of similar literature he once wrote that there was something so "innocent, so guileless, so complacent, so unearthly serene and self-satisfied about this peerless hog-wash, that the man must be made of stone who can read it without a dulcet ecstasy creeping along his backbone." [1] According to him, Shakespeare himself could not counterfeit the genuine article; certainly Mark Twain couldn't. His "Invocation" isn't even close. This was Mrs. Moore's style:

> Come all good people far and near
> Oh, come and see what you can hear,
> It's of a young man true and brave,
> That is now sleeping in his grave.
>
> Now, William Upson was his name—
> If it's not that, it's all the same—[2]

Notes for "The Naturalist and the Ornithorhyncus" were made on shipboard, approaching Australia in 1896. It is from *Following the Equator.*

. . . The most cultivated person in the ship was a young Englishman whose home was in New Zealand. He was a naturalist. His learning in his specialty was deep and thorough, his interest in his subject amounted to a passon, he had an easy gift of speech; and so, when he talked about animals it was a pleasure to listen to him. And profitable, too, though he was sometimes difficult to understand because now and then he used scientific technicalities which were above the reach of some of us. They were pretty sure to be above my reach, but as he was quite willing to explain them I always made it a point to get him to do it. I had a fair knowledge of his subject—layman's knowledge—to begin with, but it was his teachings which crystallized it into scientific form and clarity—in a word, gave it value.

His special interest was the fauna of Australasia, and his knowledge of the matter was as exhaustive as it was accurate. I already knew a good deal about the rabbits in Australasia and their marvelous fecundity, but in my talks with him I found that my estimate of the great hindrance and obstruction inflicted by the rabbit pest upon traffic and travel was far short of the facts.

He told me that the first pair of rabbits imported into Australasia bred so wonderfully that within six months rabbits were so thick in the land that people had to dig trenches through them to get from town to town.

He told me a great deal about worms, and the kangaroo, and other coleoptera, and said he knew the history and ways of all such pachydermata. He said the kangaroo had pockets, and carried its young in them when it couldn't get apples. And he said that the emu was as big as an ostrich, and looked like one, and had an amorphous appetite and would eat bricks. Also, that the dingo was not a dingo at all, but just a wild dog; and that the only difference between a dingo and a dodo was that neither of them barked; otherwise they were just the same.

He said that the only game bird in Australasia was the wombat, and the only songbird the larrikin, and that both were protected by government. . . . He explained that the "Sundowner" was not a bird, it was a man; sundowner was merely the Australian equivalent of our word, tramp. He is a loafer, a hard drinker, and a sponge. He tramps across the country in the sheep-shearing season, pretending to look for work; but he always times himself to arrive at a sheep-run just at sundown, when the day's labor ends; all he wants is whisky and supper and bed and breakfast; he gets them and then disappears. The naturalist spoke of the bell bird, the creature that at short intervals all day rings out its mellow and exquisite peal from the deeps of the forest. It is the favorite and best friend of the weary and thirsty sundowner; for he knows that wherever the bell bird is, there is water; and he goes somewhere else. The naturalist said that the oddest bird in Australasia was the Laughing Jackass, and the biggest the now extinct Great Moa.

The Moa stood thirteen feet high, and could step over an ordinary man's head or kick his hat off, and his head, too, for that matter. He said it was wingless, but a swift runner. The natives used to ride it. It could make forty miles an hour, and keep it up for four hundred miles and come out reasonably fresh. It was still in existence when the railway was introduced into New Zealand; still in existence, and carrying the mails. The railroad began with the same schedule it has now: two expresses a week —time, twenty miles an hour. The company exterminated the Moa to get the mails.

Speaking of the indigenous coneys and Bactrian camels, the naturalist said that the coniferous and bacteriological output of Australasia was remarkable for its many and curious departures from the accepted laws governing these species of tubercles, but that in his opinion Nature's fondness for dabbling in the erratic was most notably exhibited in that curious combination of bird, fish, amphibian, burrower, crawler, quadruped, and Christian called the Ornithorhyncus—grotesquest of animals, king of the animalculae of the world for versatility of character and make-up. Said he:

"You can call it anything you want to, and be right. It is a fish, for it lives in the river half the time; it is a land animal, for it resides on the land half the time; it is an amphibian, since it likes both . . . it is a hybernian, for when times are dull and nothing much going on it buries itself under the mud at the bottom of a puddle and hybernates there a couple of weeks at a time; it is a kind of duck, for it has a duck-bill and four webbed paddles; it is a fish and quadruped together, for in the water it swims with the paddles and on shore it paws itself across country with them; it is a kind of seal, for it has a seal's fur; it is carnivorous, herbivorous, insectivorous, and vermifuginous, for it eats fish and grass and butterflies, and in the season digs worms out of the mud and devours them; it is clearly a bird, for it lays eggs and hatches them; it is clearly a mammal, for it nurses its young; and it is manifestly a kind of Christian, for it keeps the Sabbath when there is anybody around, and when there isn't, doesn't. It has all the tastes there are except refined ones. . . .

"It is a survival—a survival of the fittest. Mr. Darwin invented the theory that goes by that name, but the Ornithorhyncus was the first to put it to actual experiment and prove that it could be done. Hence it should have as much of the credit as Mr. Darwin. It was never in the Ark; you will find no mention of it there; it nobly stayed out and worked the theory. Of all creatures in the world it was the only one properly equipped for the test. The Ark was thirteen months afloat, and all the globe submerged; no land visible above the flood, no vegetation, no food for a mammal to eat, nor water for a mammal to drink; for all mammal food was destroyed, and when the pure floods from heaven and the salt oceans of the earth mingled their waters and rose above the mountain tops, the result was a drink which no bird or beast of ordinary construction could use and live. But this combination was nuts for the Ornithorhyncus, if I may use a term like that without offense. Its river home had always been salted by the flood tides of the sea. On the face of the Noachian deluge innumerable forest trees were floating. Upon these the Ornithorhyncus voyaged in peace; voyaged from clime to clime, from hemisphere to hemisphere, in contentment and comfort, in virile interest in the constant change of scene, in humble thankfulness for its privileges, in ever-increasing enthusiasm in the development of the great theory upon whose validity it had staked its life, its fortunes, and its sacred honor, if I may use such expressions without impropriety in connection with an episode of this nature.

"It lived the tranquil and luxurious life of a creature of independent means. . . . When it wished to walk, it scrambled along the tree trunk; it mused in the shade of the leaves by day, it slept in their shelter by night; when it wanted the refreshment of a swim, it had it; it ate leaves when it wanted a vegetable diet, it dug under the bark for worms and grubs; when it wanted fish it caught them, when it wanted eggs it laid them. . . . And finally, when it was thirsty it smacked its chops in gratitude over a blend that would have slain a crococile.

"When at last, after thirteen months of travel and research in all the Zones, it went aground on a mountain summit, it strode ashore, saying in its heart, 'Let them that come after me invent theories and dream dreams about the Survival of the Fittest if they like, but I am the first that has *done* it!'

"This wonderful creature dates back, like the kangaroo and many other Australian hydrocephalous invertebrates, to an age long anterior to the advent of man upon the earth; they date back, indeed, to a time when a causeway, hundreds of miles wide and thousands of miles long, joined Australia to Africa, and the animals of the two countries were alike, and all belonged to that remote geological epoch known to science as the Old Red Grindstone Post-Pleosaurian. Later the causeway sank under the sea; subterranean convulsions lifted the African continent a thousand feet higher than it was before, but Australia kept her old level. In Africa's new climate the animals necessarily began to develop and shade off into new forms and families and species, but the animals of Australia as necessarily remained stationary, and have so remained until this day. In the course of some millions of years the African Ornithorhyncus developed and developed and developed, and sloughed off detail after detail of its make-up until at last the creature became wholly disintegrated and scattered. Whenever you see a bird or a beast or a seal or an otter in Africa you know that he is merely a sorry surviving fragment of that sublime original of whom I have been speaking—that creature which was everything in general and nothing in particular—the opulently endowed *e pluribus unum* of the animal world.

"Such is the history of the most hoary, the most ancient, the most venerable creature that exists in the earth today—*Ornithorhyncus Platypus Extraordinariensis*—whom God preserve!"

When he was strongly moved he could rise and soar like that with ease. And not only in the prose form, but in the poetical as well. He had written many pieces of poetry in his time, and these manuscripts he lent around among the passengers, and was willing to let them be copied. It seemed to me that the least technical one in the series, and the one which reached the loftiest note, perhaps, was his

INVOCATION

Come forth from thy oozy couch,
  O Ornithorhyncus dear!
And greet with a cordial claw
  The stranger that longs to hear

From thy own lips the tale
  Of thy origin all unknown:
Thy misplaced bone where flesh should be
  And flesh where should be bone;

And fishy fin where should be paw,
  And beaver-trowel tail,
And snout of beat equip'd with teeth
  Where gills ought *to* prevail.

Come, Kangaroo, the good and true!
  Foreshortened as to legs,
And body tapered like a churn,
  And sack marsupial, i' fegs,

> And tell us why you linger here,
> Thou relic of a vanished time,
> When all your friends as fossils sleep,
> Immortalized in lime!

Perhaps no poet is a conscious plagiarist; but there seems to be warrant for suspecting that there is no poet who is not at one time or another an unconscious one. The above verses are indeed beautiful, and, in a way, touching; but there is a haunting something about them which unavoidably suggests the Sweet Singer of Michigan. It can hardly be doubted that the author had read the works of that poet and been impressed by them.

From a letter to Rudyard Kipling, before going to India: I shall arrive next January, and you must be ready. I shall come riding my Ayah, with his tusks adorned with silver bells and ribbons, and escorted by a troop of native Howdahs, richly clad and mounted upon a herd of wild bungalows, and you must be on hand with a few bottles of ghee, for I shall be thirsty.

GLOSSARY

animalculae	minute or microscopic animals
Bactrian camel	two-humped camel, as distinguished from the one-humped Arabian kind dromedary
bell bird	Australian bird with a note like a bell; takes no special interest in water
coleoptera	order of insect which includes beetles
coneys	rabbits
coniferous	cone-bearing
dingo	Australian wild dog beloved by Mark Twain because it had no bark
dodo	extinct "flightless" bird that once lived on the island of Mauritius
emu	three-toed "flightless" Australian bird, related to the ostrich, but smaller

Great Moa	once a "flightless" ostrichlike bird at least ten feet high; believed extinct in New Zealand before the fourteenth century
hybernian	Unknown—Hibernians are Irish.
hydrocephalous invertebrates	hydrocephalus is water-on-the-brain; invertebrates are animals without backbones.
larrikin	native to Australia, from a species, according to Mark Twain, "variously called loafer, rough, tough, bummer, or blatherskite, according to his geographical distribution. The larrikin differs by a shade from those others, in that he is more . . . hearty, more friendly."
Laughing Jackass	harsh voiced crow-sized Australian bird
Old Red Grindstone Post-Pleosaurian	era unknown—Old Red Sandstone, however, is fossil-rich rock well known to geologists and to Mark Twain. With a slight alteration in spelling, Post-Pleosaurian means "after-the-dinosaurs."
Ornithorhyncus	a platypus
Pachydermata	a group of hoofed animals having thick skins, like the elephant or rhinoceros
Sundowner	correctly described by the naturalist
tubercles	rounded excrescences on the surface of the body, the characteristic lesion of tuberculosis
vermifuginous	able to expel worms or other animal parasites from the intestines
wombat	bearlike burrowing animal native to Australia

MOSQUITO STORY

In his middle years, Mark Twain went back down the Mississippi where he had once been a pilot, to enjoy himself and gather more material for his *Life on the Mississippi*. This time he was a passenger. Near Lake Providence, Louisiana, he got talking to a Mr. H. and "Mr. H. furnished some minor details of fact . . . which I would have hesitated to believe, if I had not known him to be a steamboat mate." Mr. H. was from Arkansas.

This story is from *Life on the Mississippi.*

. . . Among other things, he said that Arkansas had been in-jured and kept back by generations of exaggerations concerning the mosquitoes there. One may smile, said he, and turn the mat-ter off as being a small thing; but when you come to look at the effects produced, in the way of discouragement of immigration and diminished values of property, it was quite the opposite of a small thing, or thing in any wise to be coughed down or sneered at. These mosquitoes had been persistently represented as being formidable and lawless; whereas "the truth is, they are feeble, insignificant in size, diffident to a fault, sensitive"—and so on, and so on; you would have supposed he was talking about his family. But if he was soft on the Arkansas mosquitoes, he was hard enough on the mosquitoes of Lake Providence to make up for it—"those Lake Providence colossi," as he finely called them. He . . . referred in a sort of casual way—and yet significant way—to "the fact that the life policy in its simplest form is un-known in Lake Providence—they take out a mosquito policy be-sides." He told many remarkable things about those lawless in-sects. Among others, said he had seen them try to *vote*. Noticing that this statement seemed to be a good deal of a strain on us, he modified it a little; said he might have been mistaken as to that particular, but knew he had seen them around the polls "can-vassing."

There was another passenger—friend of H.'s—who backed up the harsh evidence against those mosquitoes, and detailed some stirring adventures which he had had with them. The stories were pretty sizable, merely pretty sizable; yet Mr. H. was contin-ually interrupting with a cold, inexorable "Wait—knock off twenty-five per cent of that; now go on"; or, "Wait—you are getting that too strong; cut it down, cut it down—you get a leetle too much costumery onto your statements: always dress a fact in tights, never in an ulster"; or, "Pardon, once more; if you are going to load anything more onto that statement, you want to get a couple of lighters and tow the rest, because it's drawing all the water there is in the river already; stick to facts—just stick to the cold facts; what these gentlemen want for a book is the fro-zen truth—ain't that so, gentlemen?" He explained privately that it was necessary to watch this man all the time, and keep him within bounds; it would not do to neglect this precaution, as he, Mr. H., "knew to his sorrow." Said he, "I will not deceive you; he told me such a monstrous lie once that it swelled my left ear up, and spread it so that I was actually not able to see out around it; it remained so for months, and people came miles to see me fan myself with it."

From *Following the Equator*—In Australia: A resident told me that those were not mountains; he said they were rabbit-piles. And explained that long exposure and the overripe condition of the rabbits was what made them look so blue. This man may have been right, but much reading of books of travel has made me distrustful of gratis information furnished by unofficial residents of a country. The facts which such people give to travelers are usually erroneous, and often intemperately so. The rabbit plague has indeed been very bad in Australia, and it could account for one mountain, but not for a mountain range, it seems to me.

EDISON AND THE ANIMALS

This selection comes from *What Is Man?* first privately published in 1906. As I have indicated, critical disapproval of that bit of philosophy has been relentless since the days of Van Wyck Brooks. A recurring critical theme has been that since Mark Twain argues in *What Is Man?* that man is only a machine, he wrote it to exonerate himself for all his misdoings. This is the view of Justin Kaplan, who in the 1960's applied modern psychiatric theories to Mark Twain,[1] just as Brooks, in 1920, applied the psychiatric theories of his own day.

YOUNG MAN. It is odious. Those drunken theories of yours, advanced a while ago—concerning the rat and all that—strip Man bare of all his dignities, grandeurs, sublimities.

Old Man. He hasn't any to strip—they are shams, stolen clothes. He claims credits which belong solely to his Maker.

Y. M. But you have no right to put him on a level with a rat.

O. M. I don't—morally. That would not be fair to the rat. The rat is well above him, there.

Y. M. Are you joking?

O. M. No, I am not.

Y. M. Then what do you mean?

O. M. That comes under the head of the Moral Sense. It is a large question. Let us finish with what we are about now, before we take it up.

Y. M. Very well. You have seemed to concede that you place Man and the rat on *a* level. What is it? The intellectual?

O. M. In form—not in degree.

Y. M. Explain.

O. M. I think that the rat's mind and the man's mind are the same machine, but of unequal capacities—like yours and Edison's; like the African pygmy's and Homer's; like the Bushman's and Bismarck's.

Y. M. How are you going to make that out, when the lower animals have no mental quality but instinct, while man possesses reason?

O. M. What is instinct?

Y. M. It is merely unthinking and mechanical exercise of inherited habit.

O. M. What originated the habit?

Y. M. The first animal started it, its descendants have inherited it.

O. M. How did the first one come to start it?

Y. M. I don't know; but it didn't *think* it out.

O. M. How do you know it didn't?

Y. M. Well—I have a right to suppose it didn't, anyway.

O. M. I don't believe you have. What is thought?

Y. M. I know what you call it: the mechanical and automatic putting together of impressions received from outside, and drawing an inference from them.

O. M. Very good. Now my idea of the meaningless term "instinct" is, that it is merely *petrified thought*; solidified and made inanimate by habit; thought which was once alive and awake, but is become unconscious—walks in its sleep, so to speak.

Y. M. Illustrate it.

O. M. Take a herd of cows feeding in a pasture. Their heads are all turned in one direction. They do that instinctively; they gain nothing by it, they have no reason for it, they don't know why they do it. It is an inherited habit which was originally thought—that is to say, observation of an exterior fact, and a valuable inference drawn from that observation and confirmed by experience. The original wild ox noticed that with the wind in his favor he could smell his enemy in time to escape; then he inferred that it was worth while to keep his nose to the wind. That is the process which man calls reasoning. Man's thought-machine works just like the other animals', but it is a better one and more Edisonian. Man, in the ox's place, would go further, reason wider: he would face part of the herd the other way and protect both front and rear.

Y. M. Did you say the term "instinct" is meaningless?

O. M. I think it is a bastard word. I think it confuses us; for as a rule it applies itself to habits and impulses which had a far-off origin in thought, and now and then breaks the rule and applies itself to habits which can hardly claim a thought origin.

Y. M. Give an instance.

O. M. Well, in putting on trousers a man always inserts the same old leg first—never the other one. There is no advantage in that, and no sense in it. All men do it, yet no man thought it out and adopted it of set purpose, I imagine. But it is a habit which is transmitted, no doubt, and will continue to be transmitted.

Y. M. Can you prove that the habit exists?

O. M. You can prove it, if you doubt. If you will take a man to a clothing store and watch him try on a dozen pairs of trousers, you will see.

Y. M. The cow illustration is not—

O. M. Sufficient to show that a dumb animal's mental machine is just the same as a man's and its reasoning processes the same? I will illustrate further. If you should hand Mr. Edison a box which you caused to fly open by some concealed device, he would infer a spring, and would hunt for it and find it. Now an uncle of mine had an old horse who used to get into the closed lot where the corncrib was and dishonestly take the corn. I got the punishment myself, as it was supposed that I had heedlessly failed to insert the wooden pin which kept the gate closed. These persistent punishments fatigued me; they also caused me to infer the existence of a culprit somewhere; so I hid myself and watched the gate. Presently the horse came and pulled the pin out with his teeth and went in. Nobody taught him that; he had observed—then thought it out for himself. His process did not differ from Edison's; he put this and that together and drew an inference—and the peg, too; but I made him sweat for it.

Y. M. It has something of the seeming of thought about it. Still it is not very elaborate. Enlarge.

O. M. Suppose that Edison has been enjoying someone's hospitalities. He comes again by and by, and the house is vacant. He infers that his host has moved. A while afterward, in another town, he sees the man enter a house; he infers that that is the new home, and follows to inquire. Here, now, is the experience of a gull, as related by a naturalist. The scene is a Scotch fishing village where the gulls were kindly treated. This particular gull visited a cottage; was fed; came next day and was fed again; came into the house next time and ate with the family; kept on doing this almost daily thereafter. But once the gull was away on a journey for a few days, and when it returned the house was vacant. Its friends had removed to a village three miles distant. Several months later it saw the head of the family on the street there, followed him home, entered the house without excuse or apology, and became a daily guest again. Gulls do not rank high mentally, but this one had memory and the reasoning faculty, you see, and applied them Edisonially.

Y. M. Yet it was not an Edison and couldn't be developed into one.

O. M. Perhaps not. Could you?

Y. M. That is neither here nor there. Go on.

O. M. If Edison were in trouble and a stranger helped him out of it and next day he got into the same difficulty again, he would infer the wise thing to do in case he knew the stranger's address. Here is a case of a bird and a stranger as related by a naturalist. An Englishman saw a bird flying around about his dog's head, down in the grounds, and uttering cries of distress. He went there to see about it. The dog had a young bird in his mouth—unhurt. The gentleman rescued it and put it on a bush and brought the dog away. Early the next morning the mother bird came for the gentleman, who was sitting on his veranda, and by its maneuvers persuaded him to follow it to a distant part of the grounds—flying a little way in front of him and waiting for him to catch up, and so on; and keeping to the winding path, too, instead of flying the near way across lots. The distance covered was four hundred yards. The same dog was the culprit; he had the young bird again, and once more he had to give it up. Now the mother bird had reasoned it all out: since the stranger had helped her once, she inferred that he would do it again; she knew where to find him, and she went upon her errand with confidence. Her mental processes were what Edison's would have been. She put this and that together—and that is all that thought *is*—and out of them built her logical arrangement of inferences. Edison couldn't have done it any better himself.

Y. M. Do you believe that many of the dumb animals can think?

O. M. Yes—the elephant, the monkey, the horse, the dog, the parrot, the macaw, the mockingbird, and many others. The elephant whose mate fell into a pit, and who dumped dirt and rubbish into the pit till the bottom was raised high enough to enable the captive to step out, was equipped with the reasoning quality. I conceive that all animals that can learn things through teaching and drilling have to know how to observe, and put this and that together and draw an inference—the process of thinking. Could you teach an idiot the manual of arms, and to advance, retreat, and go through complex field maneuvers at the word of command?

Y. M. Not if he were a thorough idiot.

O. M. Well, canary birds can learn all that; dogs and elephants learn all sorts of wonderful things. They must surely be able to notice, and to put things together, and say to themselves, "I get the idea, now: when I do so and so, as per order, I am praised and fed; when I do differently I am punished." Fleas can be taught nearly anything that a Congressman can.

Y. M. Granting, then, that dumb animals are able to think upon a low plane, is there any that can think upon a high one? Is there one that is well up toward Man?

O. M. Yes. As a thinker and planner the ant is the equal of any savage race of men; as a self-educated specialist in several arts she is the superior of any savage race of men; and in one or two high mental qualities she is above the reach of any man, savage or civilized!

Y. M. Oh, come! you are abolishing the intellectual frontier which separates man and beast.

O. M. I beg your pardon. One cannot abolish what does not exist.

From *Following the Equator*: One morning the master of the house was in his bath, and the window was open. Near it stood a pot of yellow paint and a brush. Some monkeys appeared in the window; to scare them away, the gentleman threw his sponge at them. They did not scare at all; they jumped into the room and threw yellow paint all over him from the brush, and drove him out; then they painted the walls and the floor and the tank and the windows and the furniture yellow, and were in the dressing room painting that when help arrived and routed them.

THE PRESIDENT AND THE NATURE FAKIR

Once upon a time, in the quiet pages of the *Atlantic Monthly,* a nature writer named John Burroughs disagreed with a nature writer named the Reverend William Long. In time a third writer, named Theodore Roosevelt, intervened.

"You will be pleased to know," he wrote Burroughs in 1907, "that I finally proved unable to contain myself and . . . sailed into Long and Jack London and one or two others of the more preposterous writers of 'unnatural' history. I know that as President I ought not to do this, but I was having an awful time toward the end of the session and I felt I simply had to permit myself some diversion."

Shortly thereafter *Roosevelt on the Nature Fakirs* appeared, the opening gun of a war joyfully reported from coast to coast. Roosevelt, the well-known author of *Hunting Trips of a Ranchman* and similar works, made an aggressive and colorful general; Burroughs, equally famous for such titles as *Wake Robin* and *The Breath of Life,* an amiable second lieutenant.

"Don't you think," Roosevelt once wrote him, "that you perhaps scarcely allow sufficiently for the extraordinary change made in the habits of wild animals by experiences with man?"

"I shall never cease to marvel," Burroughs replied, "at the variety of your interests and the extent of your knowledge. You seem to be able to discipline and correct any one of us in his chosen field."

And, in the other corner, peppery, low-brow Long poured forth lively "public letters." "I find," he said, "after carefully reading two of his big books, that every time Mr. Roosevelt gets near the heart of a wild thing he invariably puts a bullet through it. From his own records I have reckoned a full thousand hearts which he has thus known intimately." [1]

Roosevelt's prowess as a huntsman is discussed by Mark Twain in "The President and the Cow (pp. 136–140). And when he mentions Roosevelt's "thundering from our Olympus about football and baseball and mollycoddles and all sorts of little nursery matters," Mark Twain is referring to the President's lifelong preoccupation with manly virtues and manly sports, which another humorist of the time also found ridiculous. Finley Peter Dunn, better known to newspaper readers of the day as the Irish bartender Mr. Dooley, thus describes the beginning of a day in which ". . . th' head iv th' nation thransacts th' nation's business as follows: four A.M., a plunge into th' salt, salt sea an' a swim iv twenty miles; five A.M., horse-back ride, th' prisidint insthructin' his two sons, aged two and four rayspictively, to jump th' first Methodist church without knockin' off th' shingles; six A.M., wrestles with a thrained grizzly bear; sivin A.M. breakfast; eight A.M., Indyan clubs; nine A.M., boxes with Sharkey; tin A.M., bates th' tinnis champeen. . . . Whin our rayporther was dhriven off th' premises . . . th' head iv th' nation was tachin' Lord Dum de Dum an' Sicrety Hay how to do a handspring. . . ." [2]

The "illegal Order 78" that Mark Twain discusses was the once notorious Executive Order by which Roosevelt, in an election year, enlarged the Civil War "pension list," a list corrupt enough just as it stood. It had begun as honest bonus legislation, but various congresses had made their own vote-hungry additions and by the time Roosevelt finished it was a national joke. Only the national humorist was not amused.

This story comes from the sections of Mark Twain's *Autobiography,* edited by Bernard DeVoto, published in 1940 under the title *Mark Twain in Eruption.*

> President Roosevelt has been having a scrap with the Rev. Dr. Long, who is a naturalist equipped with a pleasant and entertaining pen. Mr. Long is not a heavyweight like John Burroughs and has never intimated, as John has seemed to intimate, that he knows more about an animal than the animal knows about itself. Mr. Long's books are very popular, particularly among young people. He tells many amusing and interesting things

about the wild creatures of the forest, and he does not speak from hearsay but from observation. He tells what *he* has seen the animal do, not what it is reported to have done. If he misinterprets the actions of the animals and infers from them intellectual qualities of a higher order than they perhaps possess, is that a crime? I think not—although the President of the United States thinks it is. I think it is far from being a crime. Ninety-six per cent of our newspapers and ninety-eight per cent of our eighty million citizens believe that the President is possessed of high intellectual qualities. Is that a crime? I do not think so. I think it is merely stupidity, and stupidity is not a crime. The other day the President allowed the affairs of the universe to stand unmolested during thirty minutes, while he got himself interviewed for the *Outlook* and launched a devastating assault upon poor obscure little Mr. Long, and made a noise over him the like of which has not been heard on the planet since the hostile fleets opened upon each other with two thousand shells a minute in the Japan Sea.[3]

What had Mr. Long been doing? He had merely been telling how he had found a deer whose breast had just been fatally torn by a wolf, and how he had also seen a wild bird mend its broken leg by smart devices invented by itself and successfully consummated without anybody else's help. No doubt these were extraordinary incidents, but what of that? Does their unusualness make them incredible? Indeed it does not. Wild creatures often do extraordinary things. Look at Mr. Roosevelt's own performances. . . . Didn't he promulgate the illegal Order 78? . . . Hasn't he tacitly claimed some dozens of times that he is the only person in America who knows how to speak the truth—quite ignoring me and other professionals? Hasn't he kept up such a continual thundering from our Olympus about football and baseball and mollycoddles and all sorts of little nursery matters that we have come to stand in fear that the first time an exigency of real importance shall arise, our thunders will not be able to attract the world's notice or exert any valuable influence upon ourselves. And so on and so on—the list of unpresidential things, things hitherto deemed impossible, wholly impossible, measurelessly impossible for a president of the United States to do, is much too long for invoicing here.

When a president can do these extraordinary things, why

can't he allow a poor little unoffending bird to work a marvelous surgical operation without finding fault with it? That surgical operation is impossible at first glance, but it is not any more impossible than is Order 78. It is not easy to believe that either of them happened; but we all know that Order 78 happened, therefore we are justified in believing in the bird's surgery. Order 78 should make it easy for us to believe in anything that can be charged against a bird. . . .

Perhaps it is a marvelous thing for a bird to mend its broken leg; but is it half as marvelous, as extraordinary, as incredible, as that the autocrat over a nation of eighty millions should come down from his summit in the clouds to destroy a wee little naturalist who was engaged in the harmless business of amusing a nursery? Is it as extraordinary as the spectacle of a president of the United States attacking a private citizen without offering anything describable as evidence that he is qualified for the office of critic—and then refusing to listen to the man's defense, and following this uncourteous attack by backing out of the dispute upon the plea that it would not be consonant with the dignity of his great office to further notice such a person?

The President is badly worsted in the scrap, and I think he is wise in backing out of it. There was no respectable way out, and I think it was plainly best for him to accept and confess defeat in silence.[4] And he would be safe in any course he might pursue, whatever that course might be, for the newspapers would praise it and admire it and the nation would applaud. It is long since the head of any nation has been so blindly and unreasoningly worshiped as is President Roosevelt by this nation today. If he should die now, he would be mourned as no ruler has been mourned save Nero. . . .

I think it is not wise for an emperor, or a king, or a president, to come down into the boxing ring, so to speak, and lower the dignity of his office by meddling in the small affairs of private citizens. I think it is not even discreet in a private citizen to come out in public and make a large noise, and by criticism and faultfinding try to cough down and injure another citizen whose trade he knows nothing valuable about. It seems to me that natural history is a pretty poor thing to squabble about anyway, because it is not an exact science. What we know about it is built out of the careful or careless observations of students of animal nature, and no man can be accurate enough in his observations to safely pose as the last and unassailable authority in the matter—not even Aristotle, not even Pliny, not even Sir John Mandeville, not even Jonah, not even Theodore Roosevelt. All these professionals ought to stand ready to accept each other's facts, closing one eye furtively now and then, perhaps, but keeping strictly quiet and saying nothing. The professional who disputes another professional's facts damages the business and imperils his own statistics, there being no statistics connected with the business that are absolute and unassailable. The only wise and safe course is for all the naturalists to stand by each other and accept and endorse every discovery, or seeming discovery, that any one of them makes. Mr. Roosevelt is immeasurably indiscreet. He accepts as an established fact that the ravens fed Elijah; it is then bad policy in him to question the surgical ability of Mr. Long's bird. I accept the raven's work, and admire it. I know the raven; I know him well; I know he has no disposition to share his food, inferior and overdue as it is, with prophets or presidents or anyone else—yet I feel that it would not be right nor judicious in me to question the validity of the hospitalities of those ravens while trying to market natural-history marvels of my own which are of a similar magnitude.

I know of a turkey hen that tried during several weeks to hatch out a porcelain egg, then the gobbler took the job and sat on that egg two entire summers and at last hatched it. He hatched out of it a doll's tea set of fourteen pieces, and all perfect except that the teapot had no spout, on account of the material running out. I know this to be true, of my own personal knowledge, and I do as Mr. Roosevelt and Mr. Burroughs and Jonah and Aristotle, and all the other naturalists do—that is to say, I merely make assertions and back them up with just my say-so, offering no other evidence of any kind. I personally know that that unusual thing happened; I knew the turkey; I furnished the egg and I have got the crockery.

Mark Twain's note in his copy of Alexander Winchell's *Sketches of Creation*: And all these eons and eons of trivial fussing in order that we might have [Teddy] Roosevelt! The dignity of God is established.

THE SCOT AND THE FLYING FISH

This nonsense is from Mark Twain's *Notebook*. I don't know whether it's true or not. It happened, if it happened, in March 1896 while Mark Twain was on his way from India to England.

Our Captain is a handsome Hercules; young, resolute, manly, and has a huge great splendid head, a satisfaction to look at. He has this odd peculiarity: he cannot tell the truth in a plausible way. He is the very opposite of the austere Scot who sits midway on the table: he cannot tell a lie in an *un*plausible way. When the Captain finishes a statement, the passengers glance at each other privately, as who would say—"Do you believe that?" When the Scot finishes one, the look says—"How strange and interesting." The whole secret is in the matter and method of the two men. The Captain is a little shy and diffident, and he states the simplest fact as if he were a little afraid of it, while the Scot delivers himself of the most atrocious lie with such an air of stern veracity that one is forced to believe it although he knows it isn't so. For instance: the Captain told how he carried home sixty-two children under seven, one voyage, nearly all of them bad, ungoverned creatures, because they had been allowed all their little lives to abuse and insult the native servants; and how a boy of seven was shoving a boy of three overboard one day when the Captain caught the victim by the leg and saved him—then slapped the persecutor, and straightway got a couple of stinging slaps himself from the persecutor's mother. The private comment among the ladies at the table was "Do you really believe she slapped him?"

Presently the Scot told how he caught a shark down on the frozen shores of the Antarctic Continent, and the natives took the shark away from him and cut it open, and began to take out cigars and hair-brushes and hymn books and corkscrews and revolvers and other things belonging to a missionary who had been missed . . . and when he demanded a share of the find the natives laughed in his face and would give him no part of it ex-

cept a sodden wad of crumpled paper. But this paper turned out
to be a lottery ticket, and with it the Scot afterward collected a
prize of 500,000 francs in Paris. Everybody agreed that this was
"remarkable and interesting," but nobody tried to throw any
doubt upon it.

The Captain told how a maniac chased him round and round
the main mast one day with an ax, until he was nearly exhausted, and at last the racket brought the mate up from below
who threw a steamer chair in the way, the maniac stumbled over
it and fell, then the mate jumped on his back and got the ax
away from him, and the Captain's life was saved. There was
nothing unreasonable or unlikely about this, yet the Captain
told it in such an unplausible way that it was plain nobody believed him.

Presently the Scot told about a pet flying-fish he once owned,
that lived in a little fountain in his conservatory and supported
itself by catching birds and frogs in the neighboring field. He
was believed.

From Mark Twain's *Notebook*—approaching Australia: We have
the snake liar and the fish liar always with us. Now . . . we are getting
toward the atmosphere breathed by the boomerang liar. The first officer
has seen a man escape behind the trees but his pursuer sent his boomerang high over and beyond the tree; then it turned, descended, and
killed the man. The Australian passenger has seen it done to *two* behind
two trees, with one throw. Maturin Ballon *heard* of a case where the
boomerang killed a bird and brought it back to the thrower.

THE JOY OF KILLING

Each outcry of the hunted Hare
A fibre from the Brain does tear.

—WILLIAM BLAKE, "Auguries of Innocence"

Until the twentieth century the joys of killing were not recognized, except by Mark Twain. Public executioners or slaughterhouse employees were supposedly working only for the money. Big-game hunters were allegedly after the thrill of danger in the open air and nothing more—including, of course, the world's most famous hunter, Theodore Roosevelt, whose exploits Mark Twain discusses in this section.

Roosevelt began as a frail lad who idealized the masculine virtues. He became a cheerful boyish man, our most two-fisted President, and the only one to practice jujitsu on foreign diplomats. Later he became the only candidate to seek the Presidency on the grounds that he was strong as a bull moose and "battling for the Lord."

Although Roosevelt freely expressed his distaste for "slothful ease and ignoble peace," [1] he was inhibited by the moral standards of his time. Killing men or animals might be manly or character-building or even fun, but nobody glorified killing for its own sake. It was also assumed that killers who acted in cold blood either had practical motives or were insane; pleasure was admitted, as a partial motive only, in the killing of animals.

Mark Twain, on the other hand, knew that people killed people as well as animals for fun, because he once investigated the Thugs, a sect in India dedicated to hunting and strangling human prey, not for profit but for pleasure. In Mark Twain's account, the Thugs are understandable human beings. They are not ridiculed; Mark Twain ridiculed only hypocrisy. They are not preached over. The thrill of inflicting death, he said, or of watching it inflicted, is universal.

He hoped, however, that the thrill would gradually die out. Already, he bragged in *Following the Equator,* "We have reached a little altitude where we may look down upon the Indian Thugs with a complacent shudder; and we may even hope for a day, many centuries hence, when our posterity will look down upon us in the same way." His favorite proof of progress was that public executions were no longer public entertainments; he even believed that this fact would eventually weaken human public lust, which fed, so he claimed, on the sight and smell of blood. But that day was not yet: "We have no tourists of either sex or any religion who are able to resist the delights of the bull ring."

It remained for the twentieth century to celebrate those delights in its literature. The American fad for bullfighting is not yet extinct—memoirs of matadors still sell—but it has declined since Ernest Hemingway started it all in *Death in the Afternoon,* a technical handbook and ode to bullfighting. Teddy Roosevelt and Hemingway would have understood each other; they could have swapped tales of war, of simple virile men, and of African lion hunts, for both men traveled to Africa to kill big game. Thus in two centuries—by coincidence, let us hope—the world's most articulate hunter was an American. But the sort of swaggering and aggressive masculinity that characterized both Teddy Roosevelt and Hemingway is not typically American; in fact, it is the Spanish-speaking countries that have a word for it that carries strong connotations of admiration: *machismo.* Our nearest equivalents are used in mild derision; men like Roosevelt and Hemingway, we are apt to say, are "hairy-chested."

At any rate, hunting has always been a super-masculine—almost exclusively masculine—sport. Mark Twain was addicted to no sport except billiards, but he loathed only the blood sports. Moreover he was shameless about this soft, or feminine, side of his nature, as may be noted in his "In Defense of Cockfighting" when he admits the spectacle was "too pitiful" for him and he had to leave before it was over.

Mark Twain was not born hating the hunt. Various bits of his *Autobiography* testify to how much he enjoyed it as a boy, in the country town of Hannibal, Missouri:

> I remember the 'coon and 'possum hunts, nights, with the Negroes, and the long marches through the black gloom of the woods, and the excitement which fired everybody when the dis-

tant bay of an experienced dog announced that the game was treed; then the wild scramblings and stumblings through briers and bushes and over roots to get to the spot . . . I remember it all well, and the delight that everyone got out of it, except the 'coon.

But that was when he was a boy, and it is his contention in "The President and the Cow" that hunter-President Roosevelt was a boy. American philosopher William James agreed with him. "He is still mentally in the *Sturm und Drang* period of early adolescence," James wrote in 1900 of the man who was to be President the next year.[2]

This is Mark Twain's account of how he was cured of the hunting fever:

> Conscious teaching is good and necessary, and in a hundred instances it effects its purpose, while in a hundred others it fails and the purpose, if accomplished at all, is accomplished by some other agent or influence. . . . When I was a boy my mother pleaded for the fishes and the birds and tried to persuade me to spare them, but I went on taking their lives unmoved, until at last I shot a bird that sat in a high tree, with its head tilted back, and pouring out a grateful song from an innocent heart. It toppled from its perch and came floating down limp and forlorn and fell at my feet, its song quenched and its unoffending life extinguished. . . . I felt all that an assassin feels, of grief and remorse when his deed comes home to him. . . .[3]

BULLFIGHT

This comes from "A Horse's Tale," a story that failed, but is redeemed by a few pages. Thorndike and Antonio are army scouts on the frontier. At this point Spanish-born Antonio is going back to Spain. American-born Thorndike is speaking.

> "I wish I was going, Antonio. There's two things I'd give a lot to see. One's a railroad. . . . The other's a bullfight."
> "I've seen lots of them; I wish I could see another."

"I don't know anything about it, except in a mixed-up, foggy way, Antonio, but I know enough to know it's grand sport."

"The grandest in the world! There's no other sport that begins with it. I'll tell you what I've seen, then you can judge. It was my first, and it's as vivid to me now as it was when I saw it. It was a Sunday afternoon, and beautiful weather, and my uncle, the priest, took me as a reward for being a good boy and because of my own accord and without anybody asking me I had bankrupted my savings-box and given the money to a mission that was civilizing the Chinese and sweetening their lives and softening their hearts with the gentle teachings of our religion, and I wish you could have seen what we saw that day, Thorndike.

"The amphitheater was packed, from the bull ring to the highest row—twelve thousand people in one circling mass, one slanting, solid mass—royalties, nobles, clergy, ladies, gentlemen, state officials, generals, admirals, soldiers, sailors, lawyers, thieves, merchants, brokers, cooks, housemaids, scullery-maids, doubtful women, dudes, gamblers, beggars, loafers, tramps, American ladies, gentlemen, preachers, English . . . German . . . French . . . all the world represented: Spaniards to admire and praise, foreigners to enjoy and go home and find fault—there they were, one solid, sloping, circling sweep of rippling and flashing color under the downpour of the summer sun—just a garden, a gaudy, gorgeous flower garden! Children munching oranges, six thousand fans fluttering and glimmering . . . lovely girl-faces smiling recognition and salutation to other lovely girl-faces, gray old ladies and gentlemen dealing in the like exchanges with each other—ah, such a picture of cheery contentment and glad anticipation! not a mean spirit, nor a sordid soul, nor a sad heart there—ah, Thorndike, I wish I could see it again.

"Suddenly, the martial note of a bugle cleaves the hum and murmur—clear the ring!

"They clear it. The great gate is flung open, and the procession marches in, splendidly costumed and glittering: the marshals of the day, then the picadores on horseback, then the matadores on foot, each surrounded by his quadrille of *chulos*. They march to the box of the city fathers, and formally salute. The key is thrown, the bull gate is unlocked. Another bugle blast—the gate flies open, the bull plunges in, furious, trembling, blinking in the blinding light, and stands there, a magnificent creature, center of those multitudinous and admiring eyes . . . He sees his enemy: horsemen sitting motionless, with long spears in rest, upon blindfolded broken-down nags, lean and starved, fit only for sport and sacrifice, then the carrion heap.

"The bull makes a rush, with murder in his eye, but a picador meets him with a spear thrust in the shoulder. He flinches with the pain, and the picador skips out of danger. A burst of applause for the picador, hisses for the bull. Some shout "Cow!" at the bull, and call him offensive names. But he is not listening to them, he is there for business; he is not minding the cloak-bearers that come fluttering around to confuse him; he chases this way, he chases that way, and hither and yon, scattering the nimble banderillos in every direction like a spray, and receiving their maddening darts in his neck as they dodge and fly—oh, but it's a lively spectacle, and brings down the house! Ah, you should hear the thundering roar that goes up when the game is at its wildest and brilliant things are done!

"Oh, that first bull, that day, was great! From the moment the spirit of war rose to flood tide in him and he got down to his work, he began to do wonders. He tore his way through his persecutors, flinging one of them clear over the parapet; he bowled a horse and his rider down, and plunged straight for the next, got home with his horns, wounding both horse and man; on again, here and there and this way and that; and one after another he tore the bowels out of two horses so that they gushed to the ground, and ripped a third one so badly that although they rushed him to cover and shoved his bowels back and stuffed the rents with tow and rode him against the bull again, he couldn't make the trip; he tried to gallop, under the spur, but soon reeled and tottered and fell, all in a heap. For a while, that bull ring was the most thrilling and glorious and inspiring sight that ever was seen. The bull absolutely cleared it, and stood there alone! monarch of the place. The people went mad for pride in him, and joy and delight, and you couldn't hear yourself think, for the roar and boom and crash of applause."

"Antonio, it carries me clear out of myself just to hear you tell it . . . If I live, I'll see a bullfight yet before I die. Did they kill him?"

"Oh yes; that is what the bull is for. They tired him out, and got him at last. He kept rushing the matador, who always

slipped smartly and gracefully aside in time, waiting for a sure
chance; and at last it came; the bull made a deadly plunge for
him—was avoided neatly, and as he sped by, the long sword
glided silently into him, between left shoulder and spine—in and
in, to the hilt. He crumpled down, dying."

"Ah, Antonio, it *is* the noblest sport that ever was. I would
give a year of my life to see it. Is the bull always killed?"

"Yes. Sometimes a bull is timid, finding himself in so strange a
place, and he stands trembling, or tries to retreat. Then everybody despises him for his cowardice and wants him punished
and made ridiculous; so they hough him from behind, and it is
the funniest thing in the world to see him hobbling around on
his severed legs; the whole vast house goes into hurricanes of
laughter over it; I have laughed till the tears ran down my
cheeks to see it. When he has furnished all the sport he can, he is
not any longer useful, and is killed."

"Well, it is perfectly grand, Antonio, perfectly beautiful.
Burning a nigger don't begin."

From Mark Twain's *Notebook* : To create man was a fine and original
idea; but to add the sheep was tautology.

THE PRESIDENT AND THE COW

Understandably, this little hunting sketch was unpublishable while
Theodore Roosevelt was still President of the United States. It was
dictated three years before Mark Twain's death and left to be published someday. It appeared in 1940, in *Mark Twain in Eruption*, the
parts of Mark Twain's *Autobiography* edited by Bernard DeVoto.

It was a mild joke to say that Roosevelt wanted war with Japan.
When he sent the navy there, in 1907, all he wanted was to show off
the fleet and, perhaps, frighten the Japanese. But he wanted war with
Spain (1898), and with England (1895) and with Germany (1912). And
in 1897: "I should welcome almost any war, for I think this country
needs one." [1]

The "skirmish" at San Juan Hill was, of course, the most famous
battle of the Spanish American War. It was waged between the Span-

iards and a private regiment—mainly cowboys, Indians, policemen, and Ivy League athletes—recruited and paid by Colonel Theodore Roosevelt and called the Rough Riders.

Two colossal historical incidents took place yesterday, incidents which must go echoing down the corridors of time for ages, incidents which can never be forgotten while histories shall continue to be written. Yesterday, for the first time, business was opened to commerce by the Marconi Company and wireless messages sent entirely across the Atlantic, straight from shore to shore; and on that same day the President of the United States for the fourteenth time came within three miles of flushing a bear. As usual he was far away, nobody knew where, when the bear burst upon the multitude of dogs and hunters and equerries and chamberlains in waiting, and sutlers and cooks and scullions, and Rough Riders and infantry and artillery, and had his customary swim to the other side of a pond and disappeared in the woods. While half the multitude watched the place where he vanished, the other half galloped off, with horns blowing, to scour the State of Louisiana in search of the great hunter. Why don't they stop hunting the bear altogether and hunt the President? He is the only one of the pair that can't be found when he is wanted.

By and by the President was found and laid upon the track and he and the dogs followed it several miles through the woods, then gave it up, because Rev. Dr. Long, the "nature fakir," came along and explained that it was a cow track.* This is a sorrowful ending to a mighty enterprise. His Excellency leaves for Washington today, to interest himself further in his scheme of provoking a war with Japan with his battleships. Many wise people contend that his idea, on the contrary, is to compel peace with Japan but I think he wants a war. He was in a skirmish once at San Juan Hill, and he got so much moonshine glory out of it that he has never been able to stop talking about it since. I remember that at a small luncheon party of men at Brander Matthews' house once, he dragged San Juan Hill in three or four times, in spite of all attempts of the judicious to abolish the subject and introduce an interesting one in its place. I think the

* See "The President and the Nature Fakir," pp. 123–127—ED.

President is clearly insane in several ways, and insanest upon war and its supreme glories. . . .

Alas, the President has got that cow after all! If it was a cow. Some say it was a bear—a real bear. These were eyewitnesses, but they were all White House domestics; they are all under wages to the great hunter, and when a witness is in that condition it makes his testimony doubtful. The fact that the President himself thinks it was a bear does not diminish the doubt but enlarges it. . . .

I am sure he honestly thinks it was a bear, but the circumstantial evidence that it was a cow is overwhelming. It acted just as a cow would act; in every detail from the beginning to the end it acted precisely as a cow would act when in trouble; it even left a cow track behind, which is what a cow would do when in distress, or indeed at any other time if it knew a President of the United States was after it—hoping to move his pity, you see; thinking maybe he would spare her life on account of her sex, her helpless situation, and her notorious harmlessness. In her flight she acted just as a cow would have done when in a frenzy of fright, with a President of the United States and a squadron of bellowing dogs chasing after her; when her strength was exhausted, and she could drag herself no further, she did as any other despairing cow would have done—she stopped in an open spot, fifty feet wide, and humbly faced the President of the United States with the tears running down her cheeks, and said to him with the mute eloquence of surrender: "Have pity, sir, and spare me. I am alone, you are many; I have no weapon but my helplessness, you are a walking arsenal; I am in awful peril, you are as safe as you would be in a Sunday school; have pity, sir—there is no heroism in killing an exhausted cow."

Here are the scareheads that introduce the wonderful dime-novel performance:

ROOSEVELT TELLS OF HUNTING TRIP

Ate All the Game, Except a Wildcat, and That Had a Narrow Escape.

Swam Despite Alligators.

Charged Into the Canebrake After Bear and Hugged the Guides After the Kill.

There it is—he hugged the guides after the kill. It is the President all over; he is still only fourteen years old after living half a century; he takes a boy's delight in showing off; he is always hugging something or somebody—when there is a crowd around to see the hugging and envy the hugged. A grown person would have milked the cow and let her go; but no, nothing would do this lad but he must kill her and be a hero. The account says: "The bear slain by the President was killed Thursday, and the killing was witnessed by one of the McKenzies and by Alex Ennolds."

These names will go down in history forever, in the company of an exploit which will take a good deal of the shine out of the twelve labors of Hercules. Testimony of the witnesses: "They say that the President's bearing was extremely sportsmanlike."

Very likely. Everybody knows what mere sportsmanlike bearing is, unqualified by an adverb, but none of us knows quite what it is when it is extremely sportsmanlike, because we have never encountered that inflamed form of the thing before. The probabilities are that the sportsmanlike bearing was not any more extremely sportsmanlike than was that of Hercules; it is quite likely that the adverb is merely emotional and has the hope of a raise of wages back of it. The chase of the frightened creature lasted three hours and reads like a hectic chapter in a dime novel—and this time it is a chapter of pathetically humble heroics.

In the outcome the credit is all with the cow, none of it is with the President. When the poor hunted thing could go no further it turned, in fine and picturesque defiance, and gallantly faced its enemies and its assassin. From a safe distance Hercules sent a bullet to the sources of its life; then, dying, it made fight—so there *was* a hero present after all. Another bullet closed the tragedy, and Hercules was so carried away with admiration of himself that he hugged his domestics and bought a compliment from one of them for twenty dollars. But this resumé of mine is pale; let us send it down to history with the colors all in it:

> The bear slain by the President was killed Thursday, and the killing was witnessed by one of the McKenzies and by Alex Ennolds. They say that the President's bearing was extremely sportsmanlike. The animal had been chased by the dogs for three hours, the Presi-

dent following all the time. When at last they came within hearing distance the President dismounted, threw off his coat, and dashed into the canebrake, going to within twenty paces of the beast. The dogs were coming up rapidly, with the President's favorite, Rowdy, in the lead.

The bear had stopped to bid defiance to the canines when the President sent a fatal bullet from his rifle through the animal's vitals. With the little life left in it the bear turned on the dogs. The President then lodged a second bullet between the bear's shoulders, breaking the creature's neck. Other members of the party soon came up, and the President was so rejoiced over his success that he embraced each of his companions. Ennolds said: "Mr. President, you are no tenderfoot."

Mr. Roosevelt responded by giving Ennold a $20 note.

There was little hunting yesterday, because the dogs encountered a drove of wild hogs, more ferocious than bears. One of the best dogs was killed by a boar.

There were daily swims in the lake by members of the party, including the President.

"The water was fine," he said, "and I did not have the fear of alligators that some seem to have."

. . . Mr. Ennolds lost a chance; if he had been judiciously on watch he could have done the alligator compliment himself, and got another twenty for it.

From *The Adventures of Tom Sawyer*: The minister made a grand and moving picture of the assembling together of the world's hosts at the millennium when the lion and the lamb should lie down together and a little child should lead them. But the pathos, the lesson, the moral of that great spectacle were lost upon the boy; he only thought of the conspicuousness of the principal character before the onlooking nations; his face lit with the thought, and he said to himself he wished he could be that child, if it was a tame lion.

MASTER OF THE BUCKHOUNDS

This chat took place in Australia and was published in *Following the Equator*. It contains at least one lie: Mark Twain was not "diffident about horses." He had ridden them through Hawaii, Palestine, and large chunks of Nevada and California.

This story reads best if it be remembered that Mark Twain talked with a pronounced drawl.

Mr. G. called. I had not seen him since Nauheim, Germany—several years ago . . . We talked of the people we had known there, or had casually met; and G. said:

"Do you remember my introducing you to an earl—the Earl of C.?"

"Yes. . . ."

"I remember it too, because of a thing which happened then which I was not looking for . . . when I introduced you, you said, 'I am glad to meet your lordship—again.' The 'again' was the surprise. He is a little hard of hearing, and didn't catch that word, and I thought you hadn't intended that he should . . . He and I talked it over, but could not guess it out. . . . because he knew you had never met him before. . . ."

"Yes, I had."

"Is that so? Where?"

"At a fox-hunt, in England."

"How curious that is. Why, he hadn't the least recollection of it. Had you any conversation with him?"

"Some—yes."

"Well, it left not the least impression upon him. What did you talk about?"

"About the fox. I think that was all."

"Why, *that* would interest him; that ought to have left an impression. What did *he* talk about?"

"The fox."

"It's very curious. I don't understand it. Did what he said leave an impression upon you?"

"Yes. It showed me that he was a quick judge of—however, I will tell you all about it, then you will understand. It was a quarter of a century ago—1873 or '74. I had an American friend in London named F., who was fond of hunting, and his friends the Blanks invited him and me to come out to a hunt and be their guests at their country place. In the morning the mounts were provided, but when I saw the horses I changed my mind and asked permission to walk. I had never seen an English hunter before, and it seemed to me that I could hunt a fox safer on the ground. I had always been diffident about horses, anyway, even those of the common altitudes, and I did not feel competent to hunt on a horse that went on stilts. So then Mrs. Blank came to my help and said I could go with her in the dog-cart and we would drive to a place she knew of, and there we should have a good glimpse of the hunt as it went by.

"When we got to that place I got out and went and leaned my elbows on a low stone wall which enclosed a turfy and beautiful great field with heavy wood on all its sides except ours. Mrs. Blank sat in the dog-cart fifty yards away, which was as near as she could get with the vehicle. I was full of interest, for I had never seen a fox-hunt. I waited, dreaming and imagining, in the deep stillness and impressive tranquillity which reigned in that retired spot. Presently, from away off in the forest on the left, a mellow bugle-note came floating; then all of a sudden a multitude of dogs burst out of that forest and went tearing by and disappeared in the forest on the right; there was a pause, and then a cloud of horsemen in black caps and crimson coats plunged out of the left-hand forest and went flaming across the field like a prairie-fire, a stirring sight to see. There was one man ahead of the rest, and he came spurring straight at me. He was fiercely excited. It was fine to see him ride; he was a master horseman. He came like a storm till he was within seven feet of me, where I was leaning on the wall, then he stood his horse straight up in the air on his hind toe-nails, and shouted like a demon:

" 'Which way'd the fox go?'

"I didn't much like the tone, but I did not let on; for he was excited, you know. But I was calm; so I said softly, and without acrimony:

" '*Which* fox?'

"It seemed to anger him. I don't know why; and he thundered out:

" '*Which* fox? Why, *the* fox! Which way did the *fox* go?'

"I said, with great gentleness—even argumentatively:

" 'If you could be a little more definite—a little less vague— because I am a stranger, and there are many foxes, as you will know even better than I, and unless I know which one it is that you desire to identify, and—'

" 'You're certainly the damnedest idiot that has escaped in a thousand years!' and he snatched his great horse around as easily as I would snatch a cat, and was away like a hurricane. A very excitable man.

"I went back to Mrs. Blank, and *she* was excited, too—oh, all alive. She said:

" 'He *spoke* to you!—*didn't* he?'

" 'Yes, it is what happened.'

" 'I *knew* it! I couldn't hear what he said, but I *knew* he spoke to you! Do you know who it was? It was Lord C.—and he is Master of the Buckhounds! Tell me—what do you think of him?'

" 'Him? Well, for sizing up a stranger, he's got the most sudden and accurate judgment of any man I ever saw.'

"It pleased her. I thought it would."

From Mark Twain's *Autobiography*: It was a curious place. Two rooms of considerable size—parlors opening together . . . and the floors, the walls, the ceilings cluttered up and overlaid with lion skins, tiger skins, leopard skins, elephant skins; photographs of the general . . . gushing sprays of swords fastened in trophy form against the wall . . . more skins . . . skins of wild creatures always, I believe; beautiful skins. . . . You couldn't put out a hand anywhere without laying it upon a velvety, exquisite tiger skin or leopard skin . . . it was as if a menagerie had undressed in the place.

In Defense of Cockfighting

From the second volume of *Life on the Mississippi*:

We went to a cockpit in New Orleans on a Saturday afternoon. I had never seen a cockfight before. There were men and boys there of all ages and all colors, and of many languages and nationalities. But I noticed one quite conspicuous and surprising absence: the traditional brutal faces. There were no brutal faces. With no cockfighting going on, you could have played the gathering on a stranger for a prayer-meeting; and after it began, for a revival—provided you blindfolded your stranger—for the shouting was something prodigious.

A Negro and a white man were in the ring; everybody else
outside. The cocks were brought in in sacks; and when time was
called, they were taken out by the two bottle-holders, stroked,
caressed, poked toward each other, and finally liberated. The big
black cock plunged instantly at the little gray one and struck
him on the head with his spur. The gray responded with spirit.
Then the Babel of many-tongued shoutings broke out, and
ceased not thenceforth. When the cocks had been fighting some
little time, I was expecting them momently to drop dead, for
both were blind, red with blood, and so exhausted that they frequently fell down. Yet they would not give up, neither would
they die. The Negro and the white man would pick them up
every few seconds, wipe them off, blow cold water on them in a
fine spray, and take their heads in their mouths and hold them
there a moment—to warm back the perishing life perhaps; I do
not know. Then, being set down again, the dying creatures
would totter gropingly about, with dragging wings, find each
other, strike a guesswork blow or two, and fall exhausted once
more.

I did not see the end of the battle. I forced myself to endure it
as long as I could, but it was too pitiful a sight; so I made frank
confession to that effect, and we retired. We heard afterward
that the black cock died in the ring, and fighting to the last.

Evidently there is abundant fascination about this "sport" for
such as have had a degree of familiarity with it. I never saw people enjoy anything more than this gathering enjoyed this fight.
The case was the same with old gray-heads and with boys of ten.
They lost themselves in frenzies of delight. The "cocking-main"
is an inhuman sort of entertainment, there is no question about
that; still, it seems a much more respectable and far less cruel
sport than fox hunting—for the cocks like it; they experience, as
well as confer enjoyment; which is not the fox's case.

From *A Connecticut Yankee in King Arthur's Court*: . . . I . . .
dozed off to slumber, thinking about what a pity it was that men with
such superb strength—strength enabling them to stand up cased in
cruelly burdensome iron and drenched with perspiration, and hack and
batter and bang each other for six hours on a stretch—should not have
been born at a time when they could put it to some useful purpose.
Take a jackass, for instance; a jackass has that kind of strength, and

puts it to a useful purpose, and is valuable to this world because he *is* a jackass; but a nobleman is not valuable because he is a jackass.

Hunting the Deceitful Turkey

From Mark Twain's *Autobiography*, as published in the *North American Review*, 1906:

When I was a boy my uncle and his big boys hunted with the rifle, the youngest boy Fred and I with a shotgun—a small single-barreled shotgun which was properly suited to our size and strength; it was not much heavier than a broom. We carried it turn about, half an hour at a time. I was not able to hit anything with it, but I liked to try. Fred and I hunted feathered small game, the others hunted deer, squirrels, wild turkeys, and such things. My uncle and the big boys were good shots. They killed hawks and wild geese and such like on the wing; and they didn't wound or kill squirrels, they *stunned* them. When the dogs treed a squirrel, the squirrel would scamper aloft and run out on a limb and flatten himself along it, hoping to make himself invisible in that way—and not quite succeeding. You could see his wee little ears sticking up. You couldn't see his nose, but you knew where it was. Then the hunter, despising a "rest" for his rifle, stood up and took offhand aim at the limb and sent a bullet into it immediately under the squirrel's nose, and down tumbled the animal, unwounded but unconscious; the dogs gave him a shake and he was dead. Sometimes when the distance was great and the wind not accurately allowed for, the bullet would hit the squirrel's head; the dogs could do as they pleased with that one —the hunter's pride was hurt, and he wouldn't allow it to go into the gamebag.

In the first faint gray of the dawn the stately wild turkeys would be stalking around in great flocks, and ready to be sociable and answer invitations to come and converse with other excursionists of their kind. The hunter concealed himself and imitated the turkey-call by sucking the air through the legbone of a turkey which had previously answered a call like that and lived only just long enough to regret it. There is nothing that furnishes a perfect turkey-call except that bone. Another of Nature's treacheries, you see. She is full of them; half the time she doesn't know which she likes best—to betray her child or protect it. In the case of the turkey she is badly mixed: she gives it a bone to be used in getting it into trouble, and she also furnishes it with a trick for getting itself out of the trouble again. When a mamma turkey answers an invitation and finds she has made a mistake in accepting it, she does as the mamma partridge does—remembers a previous engagement and goes limping and scrambling away, pretending to be very lame; and at the same time she is saying to her not visible children, "Lie low, keep still, don't expose yourselves; I shall be back as soon as I have beguiled this shabby swindler out of the country."

When a person is ignorant and confiding, this immoral device can have tiresome results. I followed an ostensibly lame turkey over a considerable part of the United States one morning, because I believed in her and could not think she would deceive a mere boy, and one who was trusting her and considering her honest. I had the single-barreled shotgun, but my idea was to catch her alive. I often got within rushing distance of her, and then made my rush; but always, just as I made my final plunge and put my hand down where her back had been, it wasn't there; it was only two or three inches from there and I brushed the tail-feathers as I landed on my stomach—a very close call, but still not quite close enough; that is, not close enough for success, but just close enough to convince me that I could do it next time. She always waited for me, a little piece away, and let on to be resting and greatly fatigued; which was a lie, but I believed it, for I still thought her honest long after I ought to have begun to doubt her, suspecting that this was no way for a high-minded bird to be acting. I followed, and followed, and followed, making my periodical rushes, and getting up and brushing the dust off, and resuming the voyage with patient confidence; indeed, with a confidence which grew, for I could see by the change of climate and vegetation that we were getting up into the high latitudes, and as she always looked a little tireder and a little more discouraged after each rush, I judged that I was safe to win, in the end, the competition being purely a matter of staying power and the advantage lying with me from the start because she was lame.

Along in the afternoon I began to feel fatigued myself. Neither of us had had any rest since we first started on the excursion, which was upwards of ten hours before, though latterly we had paused awhile after rushes, I letting on to be thinking about something else; but neither of us sincere, and both of us waiting for the other to call game but in no real hurry about it, for indeed those little evanescent snatches of rest were very grateful to the feelings of us both; it would naturally be so, skirmishing along like that ever since dawn and not a bite in the meantime; at least for me, though sometimes as she lay on her side fanning herself with a wing and praying for strength to get out of this difficulty a grasshopper happened along whose time had come, and that was well for her, and fortunate, but I had nothing— nothing the whole day.

More than once, after I was very tired, I gave up taking her alive, and was going to shoot her, but I never did it, although it was my right, for I did not believe I could hit her; and besides, she always stopped and posed, when I raised the gun, and this made me suspicious that she knew about me and my marksmanship, and so I did not care to expose myself to remarks.

I did not get her, at all. When she got tired of the game at last, she rose from almost under my hand and flew aloft with the rush and whir of a shell and lit on the highest limb of a great tree and sat down and crossed her legs and smiled down at me, and seemed gratified to see me so astonished.

From *Mark Twain, Business Man* by Samuel C. Webster, Mark Twain's grand-nephew: When Sam was about three he was distressed because he had "no tail bebind." He said, "The dog has a tail bebind, the cat has a tail bebind, and I haven't any tail bebind at all at all." His uncle . . . made a tail of paper and pinned it on his little dress, and he went around very proud and happy.

SERMONS

The Catterpiller on the Leaf
Repeats to thee thy Mother's grief.

—WILLIAM BLAKE, "Auguries of Innocence"

Mark Twain heard his best sermons from a Scot named Macfarlane
and a slave named Jerry. One was a Marxist who'd never read Marx
and the other a Darwinian who'd never heard of Darwin.

Jerry was a "satirical and delightful young black man" who daily
preached from the top of his master's woodpile, "with me for sole audience." His prime sermon was as simple as Marx, though gayer:
"You tell me whar a man gits his corn pone, en I'll tell you what his
'pinions is." The boy who heard that quivered with delight, but it was
too simple for the man. "I think Jerry was right, in the main," he
wrote half a century later, "but . . . it was his idea that a man con-
forms to the majority view of his locality by calculation and intention.
This happens, but I think it is not the rule."

Far more important than "pocketbook" conformity, he said, was
the kind born of man's yearning to be approved by his own group—
"to hear the precious words, '*He's* on the right track!' Uttered, perhaps, by an ass but still an ass of high degree, an ass whose approval is
gold and diamonds to a smaller ass, and confers glory and honor and
happiness and membership in the herd. For these gauds many a man
will dump his lifelong principles into the street and his conscience
along with them. We have seen it happen. In some millions of instances." [1] He had his own instances, of course. It was a long road
that led Mark Twain—via Jerry, the Blaine-Cleveland campaign,
Macfarlane, and a revolution in Crete—to "The Lowest Animal."

The campaign was most important. It was what first convinced him
that the human race was damned by corn-pone opinions. And when
he wrote that these blossomed in "a political emergency" he knew
what he was talking about, for he'd lived his early married life in a
Hartford suburb, knee-deep in ministers, lawyers, insurance men,
writers, would-be writers, reformers, and would-be reformers. They
were his friends. One—the Reverend Joseph Twitchell—he loved.
Then came 1884.

Hartford had long been Republican; so, for that matter, had been
every anti-Confederate in the land, including Mark Twain. But by
1884 Reconstruction was dead, and the issue was simply between an
honest Democrat and a dishonest Republican—that and sex morals.
For Cleveland, the Democrat, had admitted that he had probably fa-
thered an illegitimate child. "To see grown men," Mark Twain wrote
Howells, "apparently in their right minds, seriously arguing against a
bachelor's fitness for President because he has had private intercourse
with a consenting widow!"

Our grandfathers, slanderously called stuffy, elected Grover Cleveland, love life and all. For Blaine had been caught with his hand in the
public pocket. Mark Twain's Hartford friends had been calling Blaine
a thief for years, in public and private. When they all, except Twitchell, frantically supported him—and when Twitchell was abused and
almost lost his pulpit for refusing to—Mark Twain wrote "Concerning
Man." It's in his *Autobiography* and is a savage early version of "The
Lowest Animal."

He wrote "The Lowest Animal" thirteen years later, when the
Christian Greeks of Crete, who wanted autonomy with Greece, re-
volted against their ruling class of Moslem Turks. The atrocities committed by the religious zealots on both sides inspired Mark Twain to
remember Macfarlane. He remembered him often, in many sermons
and much blasphemy, but "The Lowest Animal" is his purest Macfarlanism, as surely as "The Low-minded Ant", also in this section,
reflects the teachings of the slave Jerry on corn-pone opinions.

Clemens was twenty when he met Macfarlane. He'd been earning
his keep as a printer and a printer's apprentice since he was twelve.
He'd drudged on his brother's newspaper until, at eighteen, he decided it would never put a square meal on the family table. The row
began when he demanded from his brother enough wages to buy a
gun to provide meat, for he was a teetotaler only when it came to

hunting for pleasure. The demand was refused. He had long yearned
to see the World's Fair in New York. And so his home life ended. He
said he was going to see relatives in St. Louis (and he did), but he was
soon seeing the fair and earning top printer's pay. He was still a jour-
neyman printer when he met Macfarlane two years later in a Cincinnati boardinghouse. The other boarders were "oppressively uninter-
esting" and so his evenings were spent by the fireside with a
forty-year-old, self-educated working man, "listening in comfort to his
tireless talk."

The gist of it—this was before Darwin—was that animal life had
evolved from "a microscopic seed germ," the various species improving steadily until the advent of man, when the process reversed. For
man's heart, said Macfarlane, was "the only bad heart in the animal
kingdom" and man "the only animal capable of feeling malice, envy,
vindictiveness, revengefulness, hatred. . . ."

Macfarlane invented Macfarlanism; Mark Twain merely translated
it into literature. And the recurrent critical problem has been: why
should anyone say such dreadful things? The answer has been sought
by carefully examining the author's life. Something, so the premise
runs, must have upset and embittered him. Was it all that money he
lost in the '90's? Deaths in the family? Old age? But Mark Twain was
writing Macfarlanism in the 80's, with the family fine and the world in
his lap. The most famous theory has been that of Van Wyck Brooks—
that Mark Twain knew he was a literary failure, and the knowledge
soured him.[2] But there is no evidence that he regarded himself in that
light; once he even dared to hope that he would walk with Cervantes
in a better world.

Mark Twain learned further morality from the religious, on a
cruise. It was a round-the-world affair, which wound up in the Holy
Land; that was why so many clergymen took it. They did not always
practice what they preached and so inspired "The Ways of Righteousness." That selection comes from *The Innocents Abroad*, which was
written during the period that Mark Twain fell in love for the first
time—and the last. The affair began on shipboard, when he saw the
girl's portrait; she was the sister of fellow passenger Charles Langdon,
and very beautiful indeed. If "The Ways of Righteousness" seems un-
naturally restrained, it may be because he met her soon after landing.
For his Livy was devout, and during the courtship Mark Twain tried
earnestly to become a good Christian. He was still trying, for love's

sake, when he made the last revisions in *The Innocents Abroad* and toned down the anti-Christian sentiments. And the end of that story was that after they were married, Livy lost her religion too.

THE LOWEST ANIMAL

Twenty-year-old Samuel Clemens, in a Cincinnati boardinghouse, was so curious about Macfarlane that, he says, he fished for information every night for half a year until exactly ten o'clock. At that hour, Macfarlane always grilled a herring, which was "his nightcap and my signal to go."

Macfarlane dropped one fact: he was self-educated. Clemens induced a few more: since Macfarlane's hands were rough, since he left early and returned late, and since his clothes were cheap, he must work long hours, at "some mechanical calling." And Clemens was sure he'd find out what that was, for, as he said, "technicalities of a man's vocation, and figures and metaphors drawn from it" always slip out. But they did not in Macfarlane's case. He had a few dozen weighty books that he always read for a few hours after his nightly herring; he loved his Bible and dictionary best and he made good his boast that Clemens could not find an English word that he could not correctly define and spell. He was tall, thin, and Scottish; he had not a vestige of humor. All else—"whether he was bachelor, widower, or grass widower"—remains a mystery still. Personal questions did not offend him. "He merely turned the matter aside and flowed placidly on." The flow was his own theory of evolution, conceived before Darwin and immortalized, half a century later, by Mark Twain.

"The Lowest Animal" is Mark Twain's most brilliant exposition of Macfarlanism. It wasn't published until 1962, but there was a summary of Macfarlane's thinking in Mark Twain's biography, and as a result the earnest Scot was listed by Van Wyck Brooks as one of the many bad influences on Mark Twain. The theory was that young people could be seriously injured by such cynical ideas.[1]

The concept of the moral sense here is Mark Twain's, and the bare bones of Macfarlanism are, of course, considerably supplemented. The experiment of the caged animals was probably suggested by the possibilities in his own kitchen in his later years. "The materials for war were all there," he wrote in his unpublished "A Family Sketch." "There was a time when we had a colored cook—Presbyterian; George—Methodist; Rosa—Lutheran; Katy, American-Irish— Roman Catholic; Elise Koslowska of Polish descent—Greek Catholic; English Mary, some kind of non-conformist . . ." [2] (In the Clemens household, however, peace was maintained, according to Mark Twain, by the tactful supervision of George Griffin, the black butler.)

The French were Mark Twain's least favorite people, and his remarks in his selection are part of a savage literature on them. There were exceptions, of course: Joan of Arc, whom he adored; Napoleon, so infamously betrayed by the English; he also never forgot French help in the American revolution. But far more typical was a comment inspired by the Dreyfus case: "Oh, the French! The unspeakables! . . . I don't think they have improved a jot since they were turned out of hell!"

The newspaper clippings that Mark Twain intended to head this selection have been lost. It comes from the book *Letters from the Earth*, edited by Bernard DeVoto and published in 1962.

. . . I have been studying the traits and dispositions of the "lower animals" (so-called), and contrasting them with the traits and dispositions of man. I find the result humiliating to me. For it obliges me to renounce my allegiance to the Darwinian theory of the Ascent of Man from the Lower Animals; since it now seems plain to me that that theory ought to be vacated in favor of a new and truer one, this new and truer one to be named the *De*scent of Man from the Higher Animals.

In proceeding toward this unpleasant conclusion I have not guessed or speculated or conjectured, but have used what is commonly called the scientific method. That is to say, I have subjected every postulate that presented itself to the crucial test of actual experiment, and have adopted it or rejected it according to the result. . . . These experiments were made in the London Zoological Gardens, and covered many months of painstaking and fatiguing work.

Before particularizing any of the experiments, I wish to state one or two things which seem to more properly belong in this place than further along. This in the interest of clearness. The

massed experiments established to my satisfaction certain gener-
alizations, to wit:

1. That the human race is of one distinct species. It exhibits
slight variations—in color, stature, mental caliber, and so on—
due to climate, environment, and so forth; but it is a species by
itself, and not to be confounded with any other.

2. That the quadrupeds are a distinct family, also. This family
exhibits variations—in color, size, food preferences, and so on;
but it is a family by itself.

3. That the other families—the birds, the fishes, the insects,
the reptiles, etc.—are more or less distinct, also. They are in the
procession. They are links in the chain which stretches down
from the Higher Animals to man at the bottom.

Some of my experiments were quite curious. In the course of
my reading I had come across a case where, many years ago,
some hunters on our Great Plains organized a buffalo hunt for
the entertainment of an English earl—that, and to provide some
fresh meat for his larder. They had charming sport. They killed
seventy-two of those great animals; and ate part of one of them
and left the seventy-one to rot. In order to determine the difference between an anaconda and an earl—if any—I caused
seven young calves to be turned into the anaconda's cage. The
grateful reptile immediately crushed one of them and swallowed
it, then lay back satisfied. It showed no further interest in the
calves, and no disposition to harm them. I tried this experiment
with other anacondas; always with the same result. The fact
stood proven that the difference between an earl and an anaconda is that the earl is cruel and the anaconda isn't; and that
the earl wantonly destroys what he has no use for, but the anaconda doesn't. This seemed to suggest that the anaconda was
not descended from the earl. It also seemed to suggest that the
earl was descended from the anaconda, and had lost a good deal
in the transition.

I was aware that many men who have accumulated more millions of money than they can ever use have shown a rabid hunger for more, and have not scrupled to cheat the ignorant and
the helpless out of their poor servings in order to partially appease that appetite. I furnished a hundred different kinds of wild
and tame animals the opportunity to accumulate vast stores of
food, but none of them would do it. The squirrels and bees and

certain birds made accumulations, but stopped when they had gathered a winter's supply, and could not be persuaded to add to it either honestly or by chicane. In order to bolster up a tottering reputation the ant pretended to store up supplies, but I was not deceived. I know the ant. These experiments convinced me that there is this difference between man and the Higher Animals: he is avaricious and miserly, they are not.

In the course of my experiments I convinced myself that among the animals man is the only one that harbors insults and injuries, broods over them, waits till a chance offers, then takes revenge. The passion of revenge is unknown to the Higher Animals.

Roosters keep harems, but it is by consent of their concubines; therefore no wrong is done. Men keep harems, but it is by brute force, privileged by atrocious laws which the other sex were allowed no hand in making. In this matter man occupies a far lower place than the rooster.

Cats are loose in their morals, but not consciously so. Man, in his descent from the cat, has brought the cat's looseness with him but has left the unconsciousness behind—the saving grace which excuses the cat. The cat is innocent, man is not.

Indecency, vulgarity, obscenity—these are strictly confined to man; he invented them. Among the Higher Animals there is no trace of them. They hide nothing; they are not ashamed. Man, with his soiled mind, covers himself. He will not even enter a drawing room with his breast and back naked, so alive are he and his mates to indecent suggestion. Man is "The Animal that Laughs." But so does the monkey, as Mr. Darwin pointed out; and so does the Australian bird that is called the laughing jackass. No—Man is the Animal that Blushes. He is the only one that does it—or has occasion to.

At the head of this article we see how "three monks were burnt to death" a few days ago, and a prior "put to death with atrocious cruelty." Do we inquire into the details? No; or we should find out that the prior was subjected to unprintable mutilations. Man—when he is a North American Indian—gouges out his prisoner's eyes; when he is King John, with a nephew to render untroublesome, he uses a red-hot iron; when he is a religious zealot dealing with heretics in the Middle Ages, he skins his captive alive and scatters salt on his back; in the first Rich-

ard's time he shuts up a multitude of Jew families in a tower and
sets fire to it; in Columbus' time he captures a family of Spanish
Jews and—but *that* is not printable; in our day in England a
man is fined ten shillings for beating his mother nearly to death
with a chair, and another man is fined forty shillings for having
four pheasant eggs in his possession without being able to satis-
factorily explain how he got them. Of all the animals, man is the
only one that is cruel. He is the only one that inflicts pain for the
pleasure of doing it. It is a trait that is not known to the Higher
Animals. The cat plays with the frightened mouse; but she has
this excuse, that she does not know that the mouse is suffering.
The cat is moderate—unhumanly moderate: she only scares the
mouse, she does not hurt it; she doesn't dig out its eyes, or tear
off its skin, or drive splinters under its nails—man-fashion; when
she is done playing with it she makes a sudden meal of it and
puts it out of its trouble. Man is the Cruel Animal. He is alone in
that distinction.

The Higher Animals engage in individual fights, but never in
organized masses. Man is the only animal that deals in that
atrocity of atrocities, War. He is the only one that gathers his
brethren about him and goes forth in cold blood and with calm
pulse to exterminate his kind. He is the only animal that for sordid wages will march out, as the Hessians did in our Revolution,
and as the boyish Prince Napoleon did in the Zulu war, and help
to slaughter strangers of his own species who have done him no
harm and with whom he has no quarrel.

Man is the only animal that robs his helpless fellow of his
country—takes possession of it and drives him out of it or destroys him. Man has done this in all the ages. There is not an
acre of ground on the globe that is in possession of its rightful
owner, or that has not been taken away from owner after owner,
cycle after cycle, by force and bloodshed.

Man is the only Slave. And he is the only animal who en-
slaves. He has always been a slave in one form or another, and
has always held other slaves in bondage under him in one way
or another. In our day he is always some man's slave for wages,
and does that man's work; and this slave has other slaves under
him for minor wages, and they do *his* work. The Higher Animals
are the only ones who exclusively do their own work and provide their own living.

Man is the only Patriot. He sets himself apart in his own country, under his own flag, and sneers at the other nations, and keeps multitudinous uniformed assassins on hand at heavy expense to grab slices of other people's countries, and keep *them* from grabbing slices of *his*. And in the intervals between campaigns he washes the blood off his hands and works for "the universal brotherhood of man"—with his mouth.

Man is the Religious Animal. He is the only Religious Animal. He is the only animal that has the True Religion—several of them. He is the only animal that loves his neighbor as himself, and cuts his throat if his theology isn't straight. He has made a graveyard of the globe in trying his honest best to smooth his brother's path to happiness and heaven. He was at it in the time of the Caesars, he was at it in Mohammed's time, he was at it in the time of the Inquisition, he was at it in France a couple of centuries, he was at it in England in Mary's day, he has been at it ever since he first saw the light, he is at it today in Crete—as per the telegrams quoted above—he will be at it somewhere else tomorrow. The Higher Animals have no religion. And we are told that they are going to be left out, in the Hereafter. I wonder why? It seems questionable taste.

Man is the Reasoning Animal. Such is the claim. I think it is open to dispute. . . . His record is the fantastic record of a maniac. I consider that the strongest count against his intelligence is the fact that with that record back of him he blandly sets himself up as the head animal of the lot: whereas by his own standards he is the bottom one.

In truth, man is incurably foolish. Simple things which the other animals easily learn, he is incapable of learning. Among my experiments was this. In an hour I taught a cat and a dog to be friends. I put them in a cage. In another hour I taught them to be friends with a rabbit. In the course of two days I was able to add a fox, a goose, a squirrel, and some doves. Finally a monkey. They lived together in peace; even affectionately.

Next, in another cage I confined an Irish Catholic from Tipperary, and as soon as he seemed tame I added a Scotch Presbyterian from Aberdeen. Next a Turk from Constantinople; a Greek Christian from Crete; an Armenian; a Methodist from the wilds of Arkansas; a Buddhist from China; a Brahman from Benares. Finally, a Salvation Army Colonel from Wapping.

Then I stayed away two whole days. When I came back to note results, the cage of Higher Animals was all right, but in the other there was but a chaos of gory odds and ends of turbans and fezzes and plaids and bones and flesh—not a specimen left alive. These Reasoning Animals had disagreed on a theological detail and carried the matter to a Higher Court.

One is obliged to concede that in true loftiness of character, Man cannot claim to approach even the meanest of the Higher Animals. It is plain that he is . . . constitutionally afflicted with a Defect which must make such approach forever impossible, for it is manifest that this Defect is permanent in him, inde-structible, ineradicable.

I find this Defect to be *the Moral Sense*. He is the only animal that has it. It is the secret of his degradation. It is the quality *which enables him to do wrong*. It has no other office. It is incapa-ble of performing any other function. It could never have been intended to perform any other. Without it, man could do no wrong. He would rise at once to the level of the Higher Animals.

Since the Moral Sense has but the one office, the one capacity —to enable man to do wrong—it is plainly without value to him. It is as valueless to him as is disease. In fact, it manifestly *is* a disease. *Rabies* is bad, but it is not so bad as this disease. Rabies enables a man to do a thing which he could not do when in a healthy state: kill his neighbor with a poisonous bite. No one is the better man for having rabies. The Moral Sense enables a man to do wrong. It enables him to do wrong in a thousand ways. Rabies is an innocent disease, compared to the Moral Sense. No one, then, can be the better man for having the Moral Sense. What, now, do we find the Primal Curse to have been? Plainly what it was in the beginning: the infliction upon man of the Moral Sense; the ability to distinguish good from evil; and with it, necessarily, the ability to *do* evil; for there can be no evil act without the presence of consciousness of it in the doer of it.

And so I find that we have descended and degenerated, from some far ancestor—some microscopic atom wandering at its pleasure between the mighty horizons of a drop of water per-chance—insect by insect, animal by animal, reptile by reptile, down the long highway of smirchless innocence, till we have reached the bottom stage of development—namable as the Human Being. Below us—nothing. Nothing but the Frenchman.

There is only one possible stage below the Moral Sense; that is the Immoral Sense. The Frenchman has it. Man is but little lower than the angels. This definitely locates him. He is between the angels and the French.

Man seems to be a rickety poor sort of a thing, any way you take him; a kind of British Museum of infirmities and inferiorities. He is always undergoing repairs. A machine that was as unreliable as he is would have no market. On top of his specialty— the Moral Sense—are piled a multitude of minor infirmities; such a multitude, indeed, that one may broadly call them countless. The Higher Animals get their teeth without pain or inconvenience. Man gets his through months and months of cruel torture; and at a time of life when he is but ill able to bear it. As soon as he has got them they must all be pulled out again, for they were of no value in the first place, not worth the loss of a night's rest. The second set will answer for a while, by being reinforced occasionally with rubber or plugged up with gold; but he will never get a set which can really be depended on till a dentist makes him one. . . .

In a wild state—a natural state—the Higher Animals have a few diseases; diseases of little consequence; the main one is old age. But man starts in as a child and lives on diseases till the end, as a regular diet. He has mumps, measles, whooping cough, croup, tonsilitis, diphtheria, scarlet fever, almost as a matter of course. Afterward, as he goes along, his life continues to be threatened at every turn: by colds, coughs, asthma, bronchitis, itch, cholera, cancer, consumption, yellow fever, bilious fever, typhus fevers, hay fever, ague, chilblains, piles, inflammation of the entrails, indigestion, toothache, earache, deafness, dumbness, blindness, influenza, chicken pox, cowpox, smallpox, liver complaint, constipation, bloody flux, warts, pimples, boils, carbuncles, abscesses, bunions, corns, tumors, fistulas, pneumonia, softening of the brain, melancholia and fifteen other kinds of insanity; dysentery, jaundice, diseases of the heart, the bones, the skin, the scalp, the spleen, the kidneys, the nerves, the brain, the blood; scrofula, paralysis, leprosy, neuralgia, palsy, fits, headache, thirteen kinds of rheumatism, forty-six of gout, and a formidable supply of gross and unprintable disorders of one sort and another. Also—but why continue the list? . . . He is but a basket of pestilent corruption provided for the support and en-

tertainment of swarming armies of bacilli . . . The process of
waylaying him, persecuting him, rotting him, killing him, begins
with his first breath, and there is no mercy, no pity, no truce till
he draws his last one.

Look at the workmanship of him, in certain of its particulars.
What are his tonsils for? . . . They have but the one office, the
one industry: to provide tonsilitis and quinsy and such things for
the possessor of them. And what is the vermiform appendix for?
It has no value; it cannot perform any useful service. It is but an
ambuscaded enemy whose sole interest in life is to lie in wait for
stray grapeseeds and employ them to breed strangulated hernia.
And what are the male's mammals for? For business, they are
out of the question; as an ornament, they are a mistake. What is
his beard for? It performs no useful function; it is a nuisance
and a discomfort; all nations hate it; all nations persecute it with
the razor. And because it is a nuisance and a discomfort, Nature
never allows the supply of it to fall short, in any man's case, between puberty and the grave. You never see a man bald-headed
on his chin. But his hair! It is a graceful ornament, it is a comfort, it is the best of all protections against certain perilous ail-
ments, man prizes it above emeralds and rubies. And because of
these things Nature puts it on, half the time, so that it won't stay.
Man's sight, smell, hearing, sense of locality—how inferior they
are. The condor sees a corpse at five miles; man has no telescope
that can do it. The bloodhound follows a scent that is two days
old. The robin hears the earthworm burrowing his course under
the ground. The cat, deported in a closed basket, finds its way
home again through twenty miles of country which it has never
seen.

Certain functions lodged in the other sex perform in a lament-
ably inferior way as compared with the performance of the same
functions in the Higher Animals. In the human being, menstrua-
tion, gestation, and parturition are terms which stand for horrors. In the Higher Animals these things are hardly even incon-
veniences.

For style, look at the Bengal tiger—that ideal of grace, beauty,
physical perfection, majesty. And then look at Man—that poor
thing. He is the Animal of the Wig, the Trepanned Skull, the Ear
Trumpet, the Glass Eye, the Pasteboard Nose, the Porcelain
Teeth, the Silver Windpipe, the Wooden Leg—a creature that is

mended and patched all over, from top to bottom. If he can't get renewals of his bric-a-brac in the next world, what will he look like?

He has just one stupendous superiority. In his intellect he is supreme. The Higher Animals cannot touch him there. It is curious, it is noteworthy, that no heaven has ever been offered him wherein his one sole superiority was provided with a chance to enjoy itself. Even when he himself has imagined a heaven, he has never made provision in it for intellectual joys. It is a striking omission. It seems a tacit confession that heavens are provided for the Higher Animals alone. This is matter for thought; and for serious thought. . . .

From *Tom Sawyer Abroad*: It was strange and unnatural to see lion eat lion, and we thought maybe they warn't kin. But Jim said that didn't make no difference. He said a hog was fond of her own children, and so was a spider, and he reckoned maybe a lion was pretty near as unprincipled, though maybe not quite. He thought likely a lion wouldn't eat his own father, if he knowed which was him, but reckoned he would eat his brother-in-law if he was uncommon hungry. . . .

FLEAS IN PROPORTION

This story comes from *Tom Sawyer Abroad*, which is, I believe, Mark Twain's most neglected masterpiece. It's been so long ignored primarily because it's been criminally misrepresented as a children's story. Mark Twain himself may have thought of it that way, since he first published it, serially (1893–1894) in *St. Nicholas*, a magazine for young folks. Young folks may or may not enjoy it; certainly they could not begin to appreciate it.

The story line: Huck Finn, Tom Sawyer, and the slave Jim are stowaways in a balloon invented by a mad scientist. Shortly after the balloon takes off the scientist goes overboard and the three others float around the world, landing where it suited Mark Twain. In between adventures, Tom, the educated member of the trio, tries to educate Huck and Jim. Huck tells the story. (Technically a flea is not a bug; it's an insect.)

Jim said he reckoned a balloon was a good deal the fastest thing in the world, unless it might be some kinds of birds—a wild pigeon, maybe, or a railroad.

But Tom said he had read about railroads in England going nearly a hundred miles an hour for a little ways, and there never was a bird in the world that could do that—except one, and that was a flea.

"A flea? Why, Mars Tom, in de fust place he ain't a bird, strickly speakin'—"

"He ain't a bird, eh? Well, then, what is he?"

"I don't rightly know, Mars Tom, but I speck he's only jist a' animal. No, I reckon dat won't do, nuther, he ain't big enough for a' animal. He mus' be a bug. Yassir, dat's what he is, he's a bug."

"I bet he ain't, but let it go. What's your second place?"

"Well, in de second place, birds is creturs dat goes a long ways, but a flea don't."

"He don't, don't he? Come, now, what *is* a long distance, if you know?"

"Why, it's miles, and lots of 'em—anybody knows dat."

"Can't a man walk miles?"

"Yassir, he kin."

"As many as a railroad?"

"Yassir, if you give him time."

"Can't a flea?"

"Well—I s'pose so—ef you gives him heaps of time."

"Now you begin to see, don't you, that *distance* ain't the thing to judge by, at all; it's the time it takes to go the distance *in* that *counts,* ain't it?"

"Well, hit do look sorter so, but I wouldn't 'a' b'lieved it, Mars Tom."

"It's a matter of *proportion,* that's what it is; and when you come to gauge a thing's speed by its size, where's your bird and your man and your railroad 'longside of a flea? The fastest man can't run more than about ten miles in an hour—not much over ten thousand times his own length. But all the books says any common ordinary third-class flea can jump a hundred and fifty times his own length; yes, and he can make five jumps a second too—seven hundred and fifty times his own length, in one little second—for he don't fool away any time stopping and starting

—he does them both at the same time; you'll see, if you try to put your finger on him. Now that's a common, ordinary, third-class flea's gait; but you take an Eyetalian *first*-class, that's been the pet of the nobility all his life, and hasn't ever knowed what want or sickness or exposure was, and he can jump more than three hundred times his own length, and keep it up all day, five such jumps every second, which is fifteen hundred times his own length. Well, suppose a man could go fifteen hundred times his own length in a second—say, a mile and a half. It's ninety miles a minute; it's considerable more than five thousand miles an hour. Where's your man *now?*—yes, and your bird, and your railroad, and your balloon? Laws, they don't amount to shucks 'longside of a flea. A flea is just a comet b'iled down small."

Jim was a good deal astonished, and so was I. Jim said:

"Is dem figgers jist edjackly true, en no jokin' en no lies, Mars Tom?"

"Yes, they are; they're perfectly true."

"Well, den, honey, a body's got to respec' a flea. I ain't had no respec' for um befo', sca'sely, but dey ain't no gittin' round' it, dey do deserve it, dat's certain."

"Well, I bet they do. They've got ever so much more sense, and brains, and brightness, in proportion to their size, than any other cretur in the world. A person can learn them 'most anything; and they learn it quicker than any other cretur, too. They've been learnt to haul little carriages in harness, and go this way and that way and t'other way according to their orders; yes, and to march and drill like soldiers, doing it as exact, according to orders, as soldiers does it. They've been learnt to do all sorts of hard and troublesome things. S'pose you could cultivate a flea up to the size of a man, and keep his natural smartness a-growing and a-growing right along up, bigger and bigger, and keener and keener, in the same proportion—where'd the human race be, do you reckon? That flea would be President of the United States, and you couldn't any more prevent it than you can prevent lightning."

"My lan', Mars Tom, I never knowed dey was so much *to* de beas'. No, sir, I never had no idea of it, and dat's de fac'."

"There's more to him, by a long sight, than there is to any other cretur, man or beast, in proportion to size. He's the interestingest of them all. People have so much to say about an ant's

strength, and an elephant's, and a locomotive's. Shucks, they
don't begin with a flea. He can lift two or three hundred times
his own weight. And none of them can come anywhere near it.
And, moreover, he has got notions of his own, and is very particular, and you can't fool him; his instinct, or his judgment, or
whatever it is, is perfectly sound and clear, and don't ever make
a mistake. People think all humans are alike to a flea. It ain't so.
There's folks that he won't go near, hungry or not hungry, and
I'm one of them. I've never had one of them on me in my life."

"Mars Tom!"

"It's so; I ain't joking."

"Well, sah, I hain't ever heard de likes o' dat befo'."

Jim couldn't believe it, and I couldn't; so we had to drop
down to the sand and git a supply and see. Tom was right. They
went for me and Jim by the thousand, but not a one of them lit
on Tom. There warn't no explaining it. . . .

From *Pudd'nhead Wilson*: Consider well the proportions of things. It
is better to be a young June-bug than an old bird of paradise.

REPTILES

There was point and truth in this parable partly because Ulysses
Grant was a trusting and unwordly man. Mark Twain sent it to be
read to a Knights of Saint Patrick banquet that he couldn't attend.
This was in 1876, when Grant was completing his second term as
President. At that point his Secretary of War, William Belknap, had
been impeached for selling trade posts in the Indian territory, and his
private secretary, General Babcock, indicted, along with hundreds of
others, for conspiracy to defraud the government of the whiskey tax;
Grant himself intervened to save Babcock from conviction.

Nevertheless, nobody loved and revered Grant more than Mark
Twain, who came to know him, years later, when he published Grant's
Personal Memoirs. In the man he saw unpretentious nobility; he was
also the first to recognize that *Personal Memoirs* was a truly great
book—or, as Sir Dennis Brogan said many years later, "a masterpiece
of narrative power, of candor and of historical intelligence." [1]

HARTFORD, CONN., March 16, 1876

TO THE CHAIRMAN:

DEAR SIR—

I am very sorry that I cannot be with the Knights of St. Patrick to-morrow evening. In this centennial year we ought to find a peculiar pleasure in doing honor to the memory of a man whose good name has endured through fourteen centuries. We ought to find pleasure in it for the reason that at this time we naturally have a fellow-feeling for such a man. He wrought a great work in his day. He found Ireland a prosperous republic, and looked about him to see if he might find some useful thing to turn his hand to. He observed that the president of that republic was in the habit of sheltering his great officials from deserved punishment, so he lifted up his staff and smote him, and he died. He found that the Secretary of War had been so unbecomingly economical as to have laid up $12,000 a year out of a salary of $8,000, and he killed him. He found that the Secretary of the Interior always prayed over every separate and distinct barrel of salt beef that was intended for the unconverted savage, and then kept that beef himself, so he killed him also. He found that the Secretary of the Navy knew more about handling suspicious claims than he did about handling a ship, and he at once made an end of him. He found that a very foul private secretary had been engineered through a sham trial, so he destroyed him. He discovered that the congress which pretended to prodigious virtue was very anxious to investigate an ambassador who had dishonored the country abroad, but was equally anxious to prevent the appointment of any spotless man to a similar post; that this congress had no God but party; no system of morals but party policy; no vision but a bat's vision; and no reason or excuse for existing anyhow. Therefore he massacred that congress to the last man.

When he had finished his great work, he said, in his figurative way, "Lo, I have destroyed all the reptiles in Ireland."

St. Patrick had no politics; his sympathies lay with the right— that was politics enough. When he came across a reptile, he forgot to inquire whether he was a democrat or a republican, but simply exalted his staff and "let him have it." Honored be his name—I wish we had him here to trim us up for the centennial. But that cannot be. His staff, which was the symbol of real, not sham reform, is idle. However, we still have with us the symbol of Truth— George Washington's little hatchet—for I know where they've buried it.

Yours truly,

MARK TWAIN

From **Mark Twain's** *Notebook* : This B. I. Company had a dead py-
thon landed once. A year later this ship brought one to Calcutta zoo.
Our captain was instructed to see for himself that this one was alive before he accepted it. The man, a half-caste, said, yes, he was alive; and
opened the door of the box and gave the snake a punch with an old umbrella and asked him to show up. The snake snatched the umbrella and
made a rush, and showed up on deck—forty feet long and as big as a
barrel. Everybody went aloft, but the half-caste said: "There's no harm
in him, he just had a feed that will last him two years; come a couple of
you and take him by the tail and help me steer him into the box."
Which they did without trouble.

THE WAYS OF RIGHTEOUSNESS

Sixty-five Americans took the trip through Europe and the Holy
Land described in *The Innocents Abroad*, whence this story comes. But
only eight, including Mark Twain, made the terrible journey described in "Pilgrims and Horseflesh"; nowadays no sane Westerner,
not even an archaeologist, would brave summer in the Syrian desert.

As Mark Twain feared, they did catch "the fevers of the country";
he himself came down with cholera in Damascus—which was "pleas-
anter than traveling in Syria." However in this little tale he has altered
many facts. In life, he was not the one who was so deadly ill. The real-
life victim was Dan Slote, described by Mark Twain as his "splendid,
immoral, tobacco-smoking, wine-drinking, godless roommate," and
the pilgrims did leave him behind, not just threaten to, as this selection describes it. Clemens alone stayed behind with Dan and finally
brought him into Jerusalem alive.

These facts were given to Mark Twain's biographer, A. B. Paine, by
Clemens' fellow traveler, Deacon William Church, who in life, had
abandoned Dan, though you'd never guess it from this story. Church
added that Mark Twain was "the worst man I ever knew—and the
best."

Some of Mark Twain's best friends were ministers, and one of his
very best was Hartford's Reverend Joseph Twitchell. But whatever
Joe's faults, they were not those of the Plymouth Church Brethren of
The Innocents Abroad—called "the pilgrims" by the few sinners on a

"pleasure cruise" which was sponsored by the church and which Mark Twain was covering for a Western newspaper.

On this side trip, which was strictly for strong young men, the sinners outnumbered the pilgrims. But how quickly and thoroughly the sinners were cowed is plain in "Pilgrim at the Zoo," written at Marseilles early on the voyage. It is also plain in the letter Mark Twain wrote for the New York *Herald,* just two hours after the ship docked in New York.

"Anybody's and everybody's notion of a pleasure excursion," he said—he was then a restless bachelor of thirty-four—"is that the parties to it will of a necessity be young and giddy and somewhat boisterous." However: "Three-fourths of the *Quaker City*'s passengers were between forty and seventy years of age! . . . Is any man insane enough to imagine that this picnic of patriarchs sang, made love, danced, laughed, told anecdotes, dealt in ungodly levity?" On the contrary, the "venerable excursionists" studied their guidebooks and "shirked not the irksome journal, for alas! most of them were even writing books." For recreation they played dominoes and "blackguarded each other privately till prayer-time."

The Innocents Abroad inflicted a shock on the right-minded that a century has not completely dispelled. Volume I, about Europe, is still considered hopelessly philistine. This selection is from Volume II, on the Near East, which Mark Twain was unable to appreciate, according to critic Justin Kaplan, because of a "vision colored by the American present with its saloons and oyster restaurants, its addiction to whiskey and poker. . . ."[1] The luncheon party in it, according to Louis J. Budd, suggests that Mark Twain felt "more resentment than sorrow" at the sight of starving children.[2]

PILGRIMS AND HORSEFLESH

Properly, with the sorry relics we bestrode, it was a three days' journey to Damascus. It was necessary that we should do it in less than two. It was necessary because our three pilgrims would not travel on the Sabbath day. We were all perfectly willing to keep the Sabbath day, but there are times when to keep the *letter* of a sacred law, whose spirit is righteous, becomes a sin, and this was a case in point. We pleaded for the tired, ill-treated horses, and tried to show that their faithful service deserved kindness in return, and their hard lot compassion. But when did ever self-righteousness know the sentiment of pity? What were a few long hours added to the hardships of some overtaxed brutes when weighed against the peril of those human souls? It was not the most promising party to travel with and hope to gain a higher veneration for religion through the example of its devotees. We said the Saviour, who pitied dumb beasts and taught that the ox must be rescued from the mire even on the Sabbath day, would not have counseled a forced march like this. We said the "long trip" was exhausting and therefore dangerous in the blistering heats of summer, even when the ordinary days' stages were traversed, and if we persisted in this hard march, some of us might be stricken down with the fevers of the country in consequence of it. Nothing could move the pilgrims. They *must* press on. Men might die, horses might die, but they must enter upon holy soil next week, with no Sabbath-breaking stain upon them. Thus they were willing to commit a sin against the spirit of religious law, in order that they might preserve the letter of it. It was not worthwhile to tell them "the letter kills." I am talking now about personal friends; men whom I like; men who are good citizens; who are honorable, upright, conscientious: but whose idea of the Saviour's religion seems to me distorted. They lecture our shortcomings unsparingly, and every night they call us together and read to us chapters from the Testament that are full of gentleness, of charity, and of tender mercy; and then all the next day they stick to their saddles clear up to the summits of these rugged mountains, and clear down again. Apply the Testament's gentleness, and charity, and tender mercy to a toiling, worn, and weary horse? Nonsense—these are for God's human creatures, not His dumb ones. . . .

We have given the pilgrims a good many examples that might benefit them, but it is virtue thrown away. They have never heard a cross word out of our lips toward each other—but *they* have quarreled once or twice. We love to hear them at it, after they have been lecturing us. The very first thing they did, coming ashore at Beirut, was to quarrel in the boat. I have said I like them, and I do like them—but every time they read me a scorcher of a lecture I mean to talk back in print.

Not content with doubling the legitimate stages, they switched off the main road and went away out of the way to visit an absurd fountain called Figia, because Balaam's ass had drank there once. So we journeyed on, through the terrible hills and deserts and the roasting sun, and then far into the night, seeking the honored pool of Balaam's ass, the patron saint of all pilgrims like us. I find no entry but this in my notebook:

> Rode today, altogether, thirteen hours, through deserts, partly, and partly over barren, unsightly hills, and latterly through wild, rocky scenery, and camped at about eleven o'clock at night on the banks of a limpid stream, near a Syrian village. Do not know its name—do not wish to know it—want to go to bed. Two horses lame (mine and Jack's) and the others worn out. Jack and I walked three or four miles, over the hills, and led the horses. Fun—but of a mild type.

Twelve or thirteen hours in the saddle, even in a Christian land and a Christian climate, and on a good horse, is a tiresome journey; but in an oven like Syria, in a ragged spoon of a saddle that slips fore and aft, and "thort-ships," and every way, and on a horse that is tired and lame, and yet must be whipped and spurred with hardly a moment's cessation all day long, till the blood comes from his side, and your conscience hurts you every time you strike, if you are half a man—it is a journey to be remembered in bitterness of spirit and execrated with emphasis for a liberal division of a man's lifetime.

The next day was an outrage upon men and horses both. It was another thirteen-hour stretch (including an hour's "noon-ing"). It was over the barrenest chalk-hills and through the baldest cañons that even Syria can show. The heat quivered in the air everywhere. In the cañons we almost smothered in the baking atmosphere. On high ground, the reflection from the chalk-hills was blinding. It was cruel to urge the crippled horses, but it had to be done in order to make Damascus Saturday night. We saw ancient tombs and temples of fanciful architecture carved out of the solid rock high up in the face of precipices above our heads, but we had neither time nor strength to climb up there and examine them. The terse language of my notebook will answer for the rest of this day's experiences:

> Broke camp at 7 A.M., and made a ghastly trip through the Zeb Dana valley and the rough mountains—horses limping and that Arab screech-owl that does most of the singing and carries the water-skins, always a thousand miles ahead of course, and no water to drink—will he *never* die? Beautiful stream in a chasm, lined thick

with pomegranate, fig, olive, and quince orchards, and nooned an
hour at the celebrated Balaam's Ass Fountain of Figia, second in size
in Syria, and the coldest water out of Siberia—guidebooks do not say
Balaam's ass ever drank there—somebody been imposing on the pilgrims, maybe. Bathed in it—Jack and I. Only a second—ice water.
. . . Beautiful place—giant trees all around—*so* shady and cool, if
one could keep awake. . . . Over it is a very ancient ruin, with no
known history—supposed to have been for the worship of the deity
of the fountain or Balaam's ass or somebody. Wretched nest of
human vermin about the fountain—rags, dirt, sunken cheeks, pallor
of sickness, sores, projecting bones, dull, aching misery in their eyes
and ravenous hunger speaking from every eloquent fiber and muscle
from head to foot. How they sprang upon a bone, how they crunched
the bread we gave them! Such as these to swarm about one and
watch every bite he takes with greedy looks, and swallow uncon-
sciously every time he swallows, as if they half fancied the precious
morsel went down their own throats—hurry up the caravan!—I
never shall enjoy a meal in this distressful country. To think of eating
three times every day under *such* circumstances for three weeks yet—
it is worse punishment than riding all day in the sun. There are sixteen starving babies from one to six years old in the party, and their
legs are no larger than broom-handles. . . .

Lest any man think I mean to be ill-natured when I talk about
our pilgrims as I have been talking, I wish to say in all sincerity
that I do not. I would not listen to lectures from men I did not
like and could not respect; and none of these can say I ever took
their lectures unkindly, or was restive under the infliction, or
failed to try to profit by what they said to me. They are better
men than I am; I can say that honestly; they are good friends of
mine, too—and besides, if they did not wish to be stirred up occasionally in print, why in the mischief did they travel with me?
They knew me. They knew my liberal way—that I like to give
and take—when it is for me to give and other people to take.
When one of them threatened to leave me in Damascus when I
had the cholera, he had no real idea of doing it—I know his pas-
sionate nature and the good impulses that underlie it. And did I
not overhear Church, another pilgrim, say he did not care who
went or who stayed, *he* would stand by me till I walked out of
Damascus on my own feet or was carried out in a coffin, if it was
a year? And do I not include Church every time I abuse the pilgrims—and would I be likely to speak ill-naturedly of him? I
wish to stir them up and make them healthy; that is all.

From Mark Twain's unpublished papers: It is not his ambition to purify himself, but his unselfish diligence in trying to purify his neighbor, that enobles the polecat.

PILGRIM AT THE ZOO

In the great Zoological Gardens we found specimens of all the animals the world produces, I think, including a dromedary, a monkey ornamented with tufts of brilliant blue and carmine hair—a very gorgeous monkey he was—a hippopotamus from the Nile, and a sort of tall, long-legged bird with a beak like a powder-horn, and close-fitting wings like the tails of a dress-coat. This fellow stood up with his eyes shut and his shoulders stooped forward a little, and looked as if he had his hands under his coat-tails. Such tranquil stupidity, such supernatural gravity, such self-righteousness, and such ineffable self-complacency as were in the countenance and attitude of that gray-bodied, dark-winged, bald-headed, and preposterously uncomely bird! He was so ungainly, so pimply about the head, so scaly about the legs; yet so serene, so unspeakably satisfied! He was the most comical-looking creature that can be imagined. It was good to hear Dan and the doctor laugh—such natural and such enjoyable laughter had not been heard among our excursionists since our ship sailed away from America. This bird was a godsend to us, and I should be an ingrate if I forgot to make honorable mention of him in these pages. Ours was a pleasure excursion; therefore we stayed with that bird an hour, and made the most of him. We stirred him up occasionally, but he only unclosed an eye and slowly closed it again, abating no jot of his stately piety of demeanor or his tremendous seriousness. He only seemed to say, "Defile not Heaven's anointed with unsanctified hands." We did not know his name, and so we called him "The Pilgrim."

From a letter to W. D. Howells: We all belong to the nasty stinking little human race, and of course it is not nice for God's beloved vermin to scoff at each other; but how can I help it . . . ?

ARAB STEEDS

Arab steeds are doubtless all very well in their way, for the children of the desert who love to ride wild horses "bare-backed," and take their chances of a broken neck. But Christian people, who want a safe and respectable turnout, and don't like to risk their precious carcasses with unbroken nags, will prefer to patronize PORTER and COVEY'S fashion livery stable, no. 16 Sutton Street. . . .

—advertisement in the San
Francisco *Chronicle*, April 13, 1865

"Arab Steeds," from Chapters 14, 15, and 18 of *The Innocents Abroad*, is a companion piece to "Pilgrims and Horseflesh," another view of the terrible ride down Syria to Jerusalem, which began in the mountains of Lebanon. Along the way Mark Twain made the discovery that is in *Roughing It*—why Western man still feels the thrill of camping out: "We are descended from desert-lounging Arabs, and countless ages . . . have failed to root out of us the nomadic instinct."

Baalbek, that magnificent four-footed ruin, was named for Baalbek, once Heliopolis, City of the Sun, and still earlier a shrine to Baal. It moved Mark Twain as nothing "old" in Europe did, certainly not the "old masters," though the far older Praxiteles and Phidias he deeply admired. Critic Constance Rourke was mistaken when she said that Mark Twain "followed the cult of newness like a thousand comic prophets . . . before him." [1]

"That polite dragoman, Abraham" was called Ferguson because by then the American had given up on the "dreadful foreign names" of their guides, and were calling them all Ferguson. They also renamed some Syrian villages like Temnin-el-Foka, a name, said Mark Twain, "which the boys have simplified a good deal, for the sake of convenience in spelling. They call it Jacksonville." And even these mild little facts have been explained. The Americans adopted these linguistic short cuts, according to critic Douglas Grant, because "foreignness frightened" Mark Twain, and "he hid his fear in the harsh, the insensitive jest." [2]

We were to select our horses at 3 P.M., At that hour Abraham, the dragoman, marshaled them before us. With all solemnity I set it down here, that those horses were the hardest lot I ever did come across, and their accoutrements were in exquisite keeping with their style. One brute had an eye out; another had his tail sawed off close, like a rabbit, and was proud of it; another had a bony ridge running from his neck to his tail, like one of those ruined aqueducts one sees about Rome, and had a neck on him like a bowsprit; they all limped, and had sore backs, and likewise raw places and old scales scattered about their persons like brass nails in a hair trunk; their gaits were marvelous to contemplate, and replete with variety—under way the procession looked like a fleet in a storm. It was fearful. Blucher shook his head and said:

"That dragon is going to get himself into trouble fetching these old crates out of the hospital the way they are, unless he has got a permit."

I said nothing. The display was exactly according to the guidebook, and were we not traveling by the guidebook? I selected a certain horse because I thought I saw him shy, and I thought that a horse that had spirit enough to shy was not to be despised. . . .

Shortly after six, our pack-train arrived. I had not seen it before, and a good right I had to be astonished. We had nineteen serving-men and twenty-six pack-mules! It was a perfect caravan. It looked like one, too, as it wound among the rocks. I wondered what in the very mischief we wanted with such a vast turnout as that, for eight men. I wondered awhile, but soon I began to long for a tin plate, and some bacon and beans. I had camped out many and many a time before, and knew just what was coming. I went off, without waiting for serving-men, and unsaddled my horse, and washed such portions of his ribs and his spine as projected through his hide, and when I came back, behold five stately circus-tents were up—tents that were brilliant, within, with blue and gold and crimson, and all manner of splendid adornment! I was speechless. Then they brought eight little iron bedsteads, and set them up in the tents; they put a soft mattress and pillows and good blankets and two snow-white sheets on each bed. Next, they rigged a table about the center-pole, and on it placed pewter pitchers, basins, soap, and the whitest of towels —one set for each man; they pointed to pockets in the tent, and said we could put our small trifles in them for convenience, and if we needed pins or such things, they were sticking everywhere. Then came the finishing touch—they spread carpets on the floor! I simply said, "If you call this camping out, all right—but it isn't the style *I* am used to; my little baggage that I brought along is at a discount."

It grew dark, and they put candles on the tables—candles set in bright, new, brazen candlesticks. And soon the bell—a genuine, simon-pure bell—rang, and we were invited to "the saloon." I had thought before that we had a tent or so too many, but now here was one, at least, provided for; it was to be used for nothing but an eating-saloon. Like the others, it was high enough for a family of giraffes to live in, and was very handsome and clean and bright-colored within. It was a gem of a place. A table for eight, and eight canvas chairs . . . knives and forks, soup plates, dinner plates—everything, in the handsomest kind of style. It was wonderful! And they call *this* camping out. Those stately fellows in baggy trousers and turbaned fezzes brought in a dinner which consisted of roast mutton, roast chicken, roast goose, potatoes, bread, tea, pudding, apples, and delicious grapes; the viands were better cooked than any we had eaten for weeks . . . and yet that polite dragoman, Abraham, came bowing in and apologizing for the whole affair, on account of the unavoidable confusion of getting under way for a very long trip, and promising to do a great deal better in future!

. . . I have a horse now by the name of "Jericho." . . . I wanted a horse that could shy, and this one fills the bill. I had an idea that shying indicated spirit. If I was correct, I have got the most spirited horse on earth. He shies at everything he comes across, with the utmost impartiality. He appears to have a mortal dread of telegraph-poles, especially; and it is fortunate that these are on both sides of the road, because as it is now, I never fall off twice in succession on the same side. . . .

He is not particularly fast, but I think he will get me through the Holy Land. He has only one fault. His tail has been chopped off or else he has sat down on it too hard, some time or other, and he has to fight the flies with his heels. This is all very well, but when he tries to kick a fly off the top of his head with his hind foot, it is too much variety. . . .

I think the owner of this prize had a wrong opinion about him.

He had an idea that he was one of those fiery, untamed steeds, but he is not of that character. I know the Arab had this idea, because when he brought the horse out for inspection in Beirut, he kept jerking at the bridle and shouting in Arabic, "Whoa! will you? Do you want to run away, you ferocious beast, and break your neck?" when all the time the horse was not doing anything in the world, and only looked like he wanted to lean up against something and think. Whenever he is not shying at things, or reaching after a fly, he wants to do that yet. How it would surprise his owner to know this. . . .

Jericho and I have parted company. The new horse is not much to boast of, I think. One of his hind legs bends the wrong way, and the other one is as straight and stiff as a tent-pole. Most of his teeth are gone, and he is as blind as a bat. His nose has been broken at some time or other, and is arched like a culvert now. His under-lip hangs down like a camel's, and his ears are chopped off close to his head. I had some trouble at first to find a name for him, but I finally concluded to call him Baalbek, because he is such a magnificent ruin. I cannot keep from talking about my horses, because I have a very long and tedious journey before me, and they naturally occupy my thoughts about as much as matters of apparently much greater importance.

We satisfied our pilgrims by making those hard rides from Baalbek to Damascus, but Dan's horse and Jack's were so crippled we had to leave them behind and get fresh animals for them. The dragoman says Jack's horse died. I swapped horses with Mohammed, the kingly-looking Egyptian who is our Ferguson's lieutenant. By Ferguson I mean our dragoman Abraham, of course. I did not take this horse on account of his personal appearance, but because I have not seen his back. I do not wish to see it. I have seen the backs of all the other horses, and found most of them covered with dreadful saddle-boils which I know have not been washed or doctored for years. The idea of riding all day long over such ghastly inquisitions of torture is sickening. My horse must be like the others, but I have at least the consolation of not knowing it to be so.

I hope that in future I may be spared any more sentimental praises of the Arab's idolatry of his horse. In boyhood I longed to be an Arab of the desert and have a beautiful mare, and call

her Selim or Benjamin or Mohammed, and feed her with my
own hands, and let her come into the tent, and teach her to caress me and look fondly upon me with her great tender eyes;
and I wished that a stranger might come at such a time and offer
me a hundred thousand dollars for her, so that I could do like
the other Arabs—hesitate, yearn for the money, but, overcome
by my love for my mare, at last say, "Part with thee, my beautiful one! Never with my life! Away, tempter, I scorn thy gold!"
and then bound into the saddle and speed over the desert like
the wind!

But I recall those aspirations. If these Arabs be like the other
Arabs, their love for their beautiful mares is a fraud. These of
my acquaintance have no love for their horses, no sentiment of
pity for them, and no knowledge of how to treat them or care for
them. The Syrian saddle-blanket is a quilted mattress two or
three inches thick. It is never removed from the horse, day or
night. It gets full of dirt and hair, and becomes soaked with
sweat. It is bound to breed sores. These pirates never think of
washing a horse's back. They do not shelter the horses in the
tents, either; they must stay out and take the weather as it
comes. Look at poor cropped and dilapidated Baalbek, and
weep for the sentiment that has been wasted upon the Selims of
romance.

From *The Innocents Abroad* : I cannot think of anything now more
certain to make one shudder, than to have a soft-footed camel sneak up
behind him and touch him on the ear with its cold, flabby under-lip. A
camel did this for one of the boys, who was drooping over his saddle in
a brown study. He glanced up and saw the majestic apparition hovering
above him and made frantic efforts to get out of the way, but the camel
reached out and bit him on the shoulder before he accomplished it. This
was the only pleasant incident of the journey.

NATURE'S WISDOM

In the first part of this selection, from *Roughing It*, Mark Twain is in
California. The waters of Lake Mono were alkaline. "Nearly pure

lye," it lay in the midst of a "lifeless, treeless, hideous desert." Mark Twain and some friends camped out there on their way to a fabulous cement mine loaded with gold. They never found the mine.

The rest, from *Following the Equator*, was written twenty-five years later. In the second part, Mark Twain is in Hobart, Tasmania—an island off Australia. In the third part, he is in Dunedin, New Zealand, visiting a Doctor Hockin whose house was a "museum of Maori art" and other curiosities.

BOARDINGHOUSE

There are no fish in Mono Lake—no frogs, no snakes, no polliwogs—nothing, in fact, that goes to make life desirable. Millions of wild ducks and sea gulls swim about the surface, but no living thing exists *under* the surface, except a white feathery sort of worm, one-half an inch long, which looks like a bit of white thread frayed out at the sides. If you dip up a gallon of water, you will get about fifteen thousand of these. They give to the water a sort of grayish-white appearance. Then there is a fly, which looks something like our housefly. These settle on the beach to eat the worms that wash ashore—and any time, you can see there a belt of flies an inch deep and six feet wide, and this belt extends clear around the lake—a belt of flies one hundred miles long. If you throw a stone among them, they swarm up so thick that they look dense, like a cloud. You can hold them underwater as long as you please—they do not mind it— they are only proud of it. When you let them go, they pop up to the surface as dry as a patent-office report, and walk of as unconcernedly as if they had been educated especially with a view to affording instructive entertainment to man in that particular way. Providence leaves nothing to go by chance. All things have their uses and their part and proper place in Nature's economy: the ducks eat the flies—the flies eat the worms—the Indians eat all three—the wildcats eat the Indians—the white folks eat the wildcats—and thus all things are lovely.

Mono Lake is a hundred miles in a straight line from the ocean—and between it and the ocean are one or two ranges of mountains—yet thousands of sea gulls go there every season to lay their eggs and rear their young. One would as soon expect to find sea gulls in Kansas. And in this connection let us observe another instance of Nature's wisdom. The islands in the lake being merely huge masses of lava, coated over with ashes and pumice stone, and utterly innocent of vegetation or anything that would burn; and sea gulls' eggs being entirely useless to anybody unless they be cooked, Nature has provided an unfailing spring of boiling water on the largest island, and you can put your eggs in there, and in four minutes you can boil them as hard as any statement I have made during the past fifteen years. Within ten feet of the boiling spring is a spring of pure cold water, sweet and wholesome. So, in that island you get your board and washing free of charge—and if Nature had gone further and furnished a nice American hotel clerk who was crusty and disobliging, and didn't know anything about the timetables, or the railroad routes—or—anything—and was proud of it—I would not wish for a more desirable boardinghouse.

From Mark Twain's _Notebook_: The porpoise is the clown of the sea —evidently does his wild antics for pure fun; there is no sordid profit in it.

PARROT

We had a glimpse of the museum, by courtesy of the American gentleman who is curator of it. It has samples of half a dozen different kinds of marsupials* . . . And there was a fish with lungs. When the water dries up, it can live in the mud. Most curious of all was a parrot that kills sheep. On one great sheep-run this bird killed a thousand sheep in a whole year. He doesn't want the whole sheep, but only the kidney fat. This restricted taste makes him an expensive bird to support. To get the fat he drives his beak in and rips it out; the wound is mortal. This parrot furnishes a notable example of evolution brought about by changed conditions. When the sheep culture was introduced, it

---

* A marsupial is a plantigrade vertebrate whose specialty is its pocket. In some countries it is extinct, in the others it is rare. The first American marsupials were Stephen Girard, Mr. Astor, and the opposum; the principal marsupials of the Southern Hemisphere are Mr. Rhodes and the kangaroo. I, myself, am the latest marsupial. Also, I might boast that I have the largest pocket of them all. But there is nothing in that. [Girard was a French-American banker who made a fortune during the American Revolution; John Jacob Astor did well in furs; Cecil Rhodes in diamonds—ED.]

presently brought famine to the parrot by exterminating a kind of grub which had always thitherto been the parrot's diet. The miseries of hunger made the bird willing to eat raw flesh, since it could get no other food, and it began to pick remnants of meat from sheep skins hung out on the fences to dry. It soon came to prefer sheep meat to any other food, and by and by it came to prefer the kidney fat to any other detail of the sheep. The parrot's bill was not well shaped for digging out the fat, but Nature fixed that matter; she altered the bill's shape, and now the parrot can dig out kidney fat better than the Chief Justice of the Supreme Court, or anybody else, for that matter . . .

From "Little Bessie Would Assist Providence": "[Mr. Hollister] says the wasps catch spiders and cram them down into their nests in the ground—*alive,* mama!—and there they live and suffer days and days and days and the hungry little wasps chewing their legs and gnawing into their bellies all the time, to make them good and religious and praise God for his infinite mercies. *I* think Mr. Hollister is just lovely, and ever so kind; for when I asked him if *he* would treat a spider like that he said he hoped to be damned if he would; and then he— *Dear* mama, have you fainted!"

CATERPILLARS AND STARFISH

Dr. Hockin gave us a ghastly curiosity—a lignified caterpillar with a plant growing out of the back of its neck—a plant with a slender stem four inches high. It happened not by accident, by be design—Nature's design. This caterpillar was in the act of loyally carrying out a law inflicted upon him by Nature—a law purposely inflicted upon him to get him into trouble—a law which was a trap; in pursuance of this law he made the proper preparations for turning himself into a night-moth; that is to say, he dug a little trench, a little grave, and then stretched himself out in it on his stomach and partially buried himself—then Nature was ready for him. She blew the spores of a peculiar fungus through the air—with a purpose. Some of them fell into a crease in the back of the caterpillar's neck, and began to sprout and grow—for there was soil there—he had not washed his neck. The roots forced themselves down into the worm's person, and rearward along through its body, sucking up the creature's juices for sap; the worm slowly died, and turned to wood. And here he was now, a wooden caterpillar, with every detail of his former physique delicately and exactly preserved and perpetuated, and with that stem standing up out of him for his monument—monument commemorative of his own loyalty and of Nature's unfair return for it.

Nature is always acting like that. Mrs. X. said (of course) that the caterpillar was not conscious and didn't suffer. She should have known better. No caterpillar can deceive Nature. If this one couldn't suffer, Nature would have known it and would have hunted up another caterpillar. Not that she would have let this one go, merely because it was defective. No. She would have waited and let him turn into a night-moth; and then fried him in the candle.

Nature cakes a fish's eyes over with parasites, so that it shan't be able to avoid its enemies or find its food. She sends parasites into a starfish's system, which clog up its prongs and swell them and make them so uncomfortable that the poor creature delivers itself from the prong to ease its misery; and presently it has to part with another prong for the sake of comfort, and finally with a third. If it regrows the prongs, the parasite returns and the same thing is repeated. And finally, when the ability to reproduce prongs is lost through age, that poor old starfish can't get around any more, and so it dies of starvation.

From Mark Twain's *Notebook*: Idiots argue that nature is kind and fair to us, if we . . . obey her laws. . . . Good God! Cholera comes out of Asia and cuts me down when I have taken every pains to have myself and house in good sanitary condition. Oh, in that case, my *neighbors* violated Nature's law—and Nature makes *me* responsible. . . . Very well, the caterpillar doesn't know what the laws are—how then are these people going to excuse Nature for afflicting that helpless and ignorant creature?

Bashful Boy

JIM WOLF AND THE CATS

When Sam Clemens was fourteen, and his pretty sister Pamela twenty-two, their widowed mother advertized for boarders. The only customer was Jim Wolf, come to Hannibal to learn the printing trade. No bashful boy ever received more embarrassing publicity than Jim. His last appearance was as a case of indecent exposure, with his nightshirt "up around his neck" and it came along with a careful list of all the other inadequately clad characters, and all the references to nakedness, in the works of Sam Clemens. According to this theory, propounded by critic Alexander Jones, Mark Twain was a sexual exhibitionist.[1]

"Jim Wolf and the Cats" is the most famous of Mark Twain's Jim Wolf stories; it comes from the sections of his *Autobiography* edited by A. B. Paine.

It was back in those far-distant days—1848 or '49—that Jim Wolf came to us. He was from a hamlet thirty or forty miles back in the country, and he brought all his native sweetnesses and gentlenesses and simplicities with him. He was approaching seventeen, a grave and slender lad, trustful, honest, honorable, a creature to love and cling to. And he was incredibly bashful. He was with us a good while, but he could never conquer that peculiarity; he could not be at ease in the presence of any woman, not even in my good and gentle mother's; and as to speaking to any girl, it was wholly impossible. . . .

It is to this kind that untoward things happen. My sister gave a "candy-pull" on a winter's night. I was too young to be of the company, and Jim was too diffident. I was sent up to bed early, and Jim followed of his own motion. His room was in the new part of the house and his window looked out on the roof of the L annex. That roof was six inches deep in snow, and the snow had an ice crust upon it which was as slick as glass. Out of the comb of the roof projected a short chimney, a common resort for sentimental cats on moonlight nights—and this was a moonlight night. Down at the eaves, below the chimney, a canopy of dead vines spread away to some posts, making a cozy shelter, and after an hour or two the rollicking crowd of young ladies and gentlemen grouped themselves in its shade, with their saucers of liquid and piping-hot candy disposed about them on the frozen ground to cool. There was joyous chaffing and joking and laughter—peal upon peal of it.

About this time a couple of old, disreputable tomcats got up on the chimney and started a heated argument about something; also about this time I gave up trying to get to sleep and went visiting to Jim's room. He was awake and fuming about the cats and their intolerable yowling. I asked him, mockingly, why he didn't climb out and drive them away. He was nettled, and said overboldly that for two cents he *would*.

It was a rash remark and was probably repented of before it was fairly out of his mouth. But it was too late—he was committed. I knew him; and I knew he would rather break his neck than back down, if I egged him on judiciously.

"Oh, of course you would! Who's doubting it?"

It galled him, and he burst out, with sharp irritation, "Maybe *you* doubt it!"

"I? Oh no! I shouldn't think of such a thing. You are always doing wonderful things, with your mouth."

He was in a passion now. He snatched on his yarn socks and began to raise the window, saying in a voice quivering with anger:

"*You* think I dasn't—you do! Think what you blame please. *I* don't care what you think. I'll show you!"

The window made him rage; it wouldn't stay up.

I said, "Never mind, I'll hold it."

Indeed, I would have done anything to help. I was only a boy and was already in a radiant heaven of anticipation. He climbed carefully out, clung to the window sill until his feet were safely placed, then began to pick his perilous way on all fours along the glassy comb, a foot and a hand on each side of it. I believe I enjoy it now as much as I did then; yet it is nearly fifty years ago. The frosty breeze flapped his short shirt about his lean legs; the crystal roof shone like polished marble in the intense glory of the moon; the unconscious cats sat erect upon the chimney, alertly watching each other, lashing their tails and pouring out their hollow grievances; and slowly and cautiously Jim crept on, flapping as he went, the gay and frolicsome young creatures under the vine canopy unaware, and outraging these solemnities with their misplaced laughter. Every time Jim slipped I had a hope; but always on he crept and disappointed it. At last he was within reaching distance. He paused, raised himself carefully up, measured his distance deliberately, then made a frantic grab at the nearest cat—and missed it. Of course he lost his balance. His heels flew up, he struck on his back, and like a rocket he darted down the roof feet first, crashed through the dead vines, and landed in a sitting position in fourteen saucers of red-hot candy, in the midst of all that party—and dressed as *he* was—this lad who could not look a girl in the face with his clothes on. There was a wild scramble and a storm of shrieks, and Jim fled up the stairs, dripping broken crockery all the way.

From *Tom Sawyer Abroad*—from a balloon: The moon made it just like daylight, only a heap softer; and once we see a lion standing all alone by himself, just all alone on the earth, it seemed like, and his shadder laid on the sand by him like a puddle of ink. That's the kind of moonlight to have.

STORY OF A STORY

"Jim Wolf and the Cats" was the first humorous story Mark Twain ever told. He was fourteen and his audience was Jimmie McDaniel, the most envied boy in town because his father owned a candy store. Jimmie's public position was that candy bored him because he saw so much of it, but "circumstantial evidence," Mark Twain remembered more than half a century later, told another story, for Jimmie had the worst teeth in town.

Sam Clemens told Jimmie about Jim Wolf and the cats the morning after it all happened, and, "I thought he would laugh his remaining teeth out. I had never been so proud and happy before, and I have seldom been so proud and happy since."

But that is only the first of the stories, in Mark Twain's *Autobiography*, about his success with "Jim Wolf and the Cats." What follows was dictated when he was sixty-three. He is remembering when he was thirty-two and "had failed in all my other undertakings and had stumbled into literature."

The original of this story, from the sections of Mark Twain's *Autobiography* edited by A. B. Paine, seemed to me a little garrulous and I have made various unimportant deletions.

. . . I was offered a large sum to write something for the *Sunday Mercury*, and I answered with the tale of "Jim Wolf and the Cats." I also collected the money for it—twenty-five dollars. It seemed over-pay, but I did not say anything about that, for I was not so scrupulous then as I am now.

A year or two later "Jim Wolf and the Cats" appeared in a Tennessee paper in a new dress—as to spelling it; it was masquerading in a Southern dialect. . . .

A couple of years went by; then the original story cropped up again and went floating around in the original spelling, and with my name to it. Soon, first one paper and then another fell upon me vigorously for "stealing" "Jim Wolf and the Cats" from the Tennessee man. I got a merciless basting, but I did not mind it. It's all in the game. Besides, I had learned, a good while before that, that it is not wise to keep the fires going under a slander unless you can get some large advantage out of keeping it alive. Few slanders can stand the wear of silence.

But I was not done with "Jim and the Cats" yet. In 1873 I was lecturing in London . . . I had . . . no official household except George Dolby, lecture agent, and Charles Warren Stoddard, the Californian poet . . . Ostensibly Stoddard was my private secretary; in reality . . . I hired him in order to have his company. . . . He was . . . charming, gentle, generous, unsuspicious . . . and I think he was the purest male I have known, in mind and speech. George Dolby was something of a contrast . . . large and ruddy, full of life and strength and spirits . . . bursting with jollity. It was a choice and satisfactory menagerie, this pensive poet and this gladsome gorilla.

Dolby had been agent for . . . Charles Dickens, and all sorts of "attractions" . . . He had known the human being in many aspects, and he didn't much believe in him. But the poet did. The waifs and estrays found a friend in Stoddard; Dolby tried to persuade him that he was dispensing his charities unworthily, but he was never able to succeed. One night a young American

got access to Stoddard . . . He said . . . his remittances had
failed to arrive from home . . . he was out of employment and
friendless; his girl wife and his new baby were actually suffering
for food. For the love of Heaven could he lend him a sovereign
until his remittance should resume? Stoddard . . . gave him a
sovereign on my account. Dolby scoffed, but Stoddard stood his
ground. Each told me his story . . . and I backed Stoddard's
judgment. Dolby said we were women in disguise, and not a
sane kind of woman, either. The next week the young man came
again. His wife was ill with the pleurisy, the baby had the botts
or something—I am not sure of the name of the disease; the
doctor and the drugs had eaten up the money . . . If Stoddard,
"in the kindness of his heart . . ." etc., etc. Stoddard . . .
spared him a sovereign for me. Dolby . . . said to the customer:

"Now, young man, you are going to the hotel with us and
state your case to the other member of the family. If you don't
make him believe in you, I shan't honor this poet's drafts in your
interest any longer, for I don't believe in you myself."

The young man was quite willing. . . . I believed in him at
once and was solicitous to heal the wounds inflicted by Dolby's
too frank incredulity; therefore I did everything I could think of
to cheer him up and entertain him and make him . . . comfortable. I spun many yarns; among others . . . "Jim Wolf and the
Cats." Learning that he had done something in a small way in literature, I offered to try to find a market for him in that line. His
face lighted . . . and he said that if I could only sell a small
manuscript to Tom Hood's *Annual* for him . . . he would hold
me in grateful remembrance. . . .

Next week the baby died. Meantime I had spoken to Tom
Hood . . . The young man had sent his manuscript to him, and
the very day the child died the money for the Ms. came—three
guineas. The young man came with a poor little strip of crape
around his arm and thanked me. . . . He wept . . . Also Dolby
wept. At least he wiped his eyes and wrung out his handkerchief,
and sobbed stertorously and made other exaggerated shows of
grief. Stoddard and I . . . tried to make the young man understand that he meant no harm . . . The young man said sadly
that he was not minding it . . . that he was only thinking of the
funeral and the heavy expenses which—

We cut that short and told him . . . to . . . leave it all to us; send the bills to Mr. Dolby and—

"Yes," said Dolby, with a mock tremor in his voice, "send them to me and I will pay them. What, are you going? You must not go alone in your worn and broken condition. Mr. Stoddard and I will go with you. Come, Stoddard. We will comfort the bereaved mamma and get a lock of the baby's hair."

It was shocking. We were ashamed of him . . . But he was not disturbed. He said:

"Oh, I know this kind; the woods are full of them. I'll make this offer: if he will show me his family I will give him twenty pounds. Come!"

The young man . . . said good-night and took his hat. But Dolby said he would go with him and stay by him until he found the family. Stoddard went along to soothe the young man and modify Dolby. They drove . . . all over Southwork, but did not find the family. At last the young man confessed that there wasn't any.

The thing he sold to Tom Hood's *Annual* for three guineas was "Jim Wolf and the Cats." And he did not put my name to it.

So that small tale was sold three times. I am selling it again now. It is one of the best properties I have come across.

From Mark Twain's *Autobiography*: An autobiography is the most treacherous thing there is. It lets out every secret the author is trying to keep; it lets the truth shine unobstructed through every harmless deception he tries to play. . . . I am speaking from autobiographical personal experience. . . .

JIM WOLF AND THE WASPS

"Harris" was Joel Chandler Harris, the literary father of Bre'r Rabbit and Uncle Remus, and in the matter of writing Negro dialect, he was "the only master the country has produced"—or so said Mark Twain, commonly considered a master himself. Harris was too shy to read his own work aloud, even to console some unhappy children who had discovered he was white.

This same Joel Chandler Harris was "the bashfulest grown person I have ever met." And that reminded Mark Twain—. The story comes from the sections of his *Autobiography* edited by Bernard DeVoto under the title *Mark Twain in Eruption.*

It may be that Jim Wolf was as bashful as Harris. It hardly seems possible, yet as I look back fifty-six years and consider Jim Wolf, I am almost persuaded that he was. He was our long slim apprentice in my brother's printing office in Hannibal. . . . He was seventeen and yet he was as much as four times as bashful as I was, though I was only fourteen. He boarded and slept in the house but he was always tongue-tied in the presence of my sister, and when even my gentle mother spoke to him he could not answer save in frightened monosyllables. He would not enter a room where a girl was; nothing could persuade him to do such a thing.

Once when he was in our small parlor alone, two majestic old maids entered and seated themselves in such a way that Jim could not escape without passing by them. He would as soon have thought of passing by one of Harris' plesiosaurians, ninety feet long. I came in presently, was charmed with the situation, and sat down in a corner to watch Jim suffer and to enjoy it. My mother followed, a minute later, and sat down with the visitors and began to talk. Jim sat upright in his chair and during a quarter of an hour he did not change his position by a shade—neither General Grant nor a bronze image could have maintained that immovable pose more successfully. I mean as to body and limbs; with the face there was a difference. By fleeting revealments of the face I saw that something was happening—something out of the common. There would be a sudden twitch of the muscles of the face, an instant distortion which in the next instant had passed and left no trace. These twitches gradually grew in frequency but no muscle outside of the face lost any of its rigidity, or betrayed any interest in what was happening to Jim. I mean if something *was* happening to him, and I knew perfectly well that that was the case. At last a pair of tears began to swim slowly down his cheeks amongst the twitchings, but Jim sat still and let them run; then I saw his right hand steal along his thigh until halfway to his knee, then take a vigorous grip upon the cloth.

That was a wasp that he was grabbing. A colony of them were climbing up his legs and prospecting around, and every time he winced they stabbed him to the hilt—so for a quarter of an hour one group of excursionists after another climbed up Jim's legs and resented even the slightest wince or squirm that he indulged himself with in his misery. When the entertainment had become nearly unbearable, he conceived the idea of gripping them between his fingers and putting them out of commission. He succeeded with many of them but at great cost, for as he couldn't see the wasp he was as likely to take hold of the wrong end of him as he was the right; then the dying wasp gave him a punch to remember the incident by.

If those ladies had stayed all day and if all the wasps in Missouri had come and climbed up Jim's legs, nobody there would ever have known it but Jim and the wasps and me. There he would have sat until the ladies left. When they were gone we went upstairs and he took his clothes off, and his legs were a picture to look at. They looked as if they were mailed all over with shirt buttons, each with a single red hole in the center. The pain was intolerable—no, would have been intolerable, but the pain of the presence of those ladies had been so much harder to bear that the pain of the wasps' stings was quite pleasant and enjoyable by comparison.

Jim never could enjoy wasps. I remember once—

From *A Connecticut Yankee in King Arthur's Court*: Pretty soon, various kinds of bugs and ants and worms and things began to flock in out of the wet and crawl down inside my armor to get warm; and while some of them behaved well enough, and snuggled up amongst my clothes and got quiet, the majority were of a restless, uncomfortable sort, and never stayed still, but went on prowling and hunting for they did not know what; especially the ants, which went tickling along in wearisome procession from one end of me to the other by the hour, and are the kind of creatures which I never wish to sleep with again. It would be my advice to persons situated in this way, to not roll or thrash around, because this excites the interest of all the different sorts of animals and makes every last one of them want to turn out and see what is going on, and this makes things worse than they were before, and of course makes you objurgate harder, too, if you can. Still, if one did not roll and thrash around he would die . . . there is no real choice.

JIM WOLF AND MORE WASPS

From *Mark Twain in Eruption*:

During three-fourths of my life I have held the practical joker in limitless contempt and detestation; I have despised him as I have despised no other criminal, and when I am delivering my opinion about him the reflection that I have been a practical joker myself seems to increase my bitterness rather than to modify it.

One afternoon I found the upper part of the window in Jim's bedroom thickly cushioned with wasps. Jim always slept on the side of his bed that was against the window. I had what seemed to me a happy inspiration: I turned back the bedclothes and, at cost of one or two stings, brushed the wasps down and collected a few hundred of them on the sheet on that side of the bed, then turned the covers over them and made prisoners of them. I made a deep crease down the center of the bed to protect the front side from invasion by them, and then at night I offered to sleep with Jim. He was willing.

I made it a point to be in bed first to see if my side of it was still a safe place to rest in. It was. None of the wasps had passed the frontier. As soon as Jim was ready for bed I blew out the candle and let him climb in in the dark. He was talking as usual but I couldn't answer, because by anticipation I was suffocating with laughter, and although I gagged myself with a hatful of the sheet I was on the point of exploding all the time. Jim stretched himself out comfortably, still pleasantly chatting; then his talk began to break and become disjointed; separations intervened between his words and each separation was emphasized by a more or less sudden and violent twitch of his body, and I knew that the immigrants were getting in their work. I knew I ought to evince some sympathy, and ask what was the matter, but I couldn't do it because I should laugh if I tried. Presently he stopped talking altogether—that is on the subject which he had been pursuing, and he said, "There is something in this bed."

I knew it but held my peace.

He said, "There's thousands of them."

Then he said he was going to find out what it was. He reached down and began to explore. The wasps resented this intrusion and began to stab him all over and everywhere. Then he said he had captured one of them and asked me to strike a light. I did it, and when he climbed out of bed his shirt was black with half-crushed wasps dangling by one hind leg, and in his two hands he held a dozen prisoners that were stinging and stabbing him with energy, but his grit was good and he held them fast. By the light of the candle he identified them, and said, "Wasps!"

It was his last remark for the night. He added nothing to it. In silence he uncovered his side of the bed and, dozen by dozen, he removed the wasps to the floor and beat them to a pulp with the bootjack, with earnest and vindictive satisfaction, while I shook the bed with mute laughter—laughter which was not all a pleasure to me, for I had the sense that his silence was ominous. The work of extermination being finally completed, he blew out the light and returned to bed and seemed to compose himself to sleep—in fact he did lie stiller than anybody else could have done in the circumstances.

I remained awake as long as I could and did what I could to keep my laughter from shaking the bed and provoking suspicion, but even my fears could not keep me awake forever and I finally fell asleep and presently woke again—under persuasion of circumstances. Jim was kneeling on my breast and pounding me in the face with both fists. It hurt—but he was knocking all the restraints of my laughter loose; I could not contain it any longer and I laughed until all my body was exhausted, and my face, as I believed, battered to a pulp.

Jim never afterward referred to that episode and I had better judgment than to do it myself, for he was a third longer than I was, although not any wider.

I played many practical jokes upon him but they were all cruel and all barren of wit. Any brainless swindler could have invented them. When a person of mature age perpetrates a practical joke it is fair evidence, I think, that he is weak in the head and hasn't enough heart to signify.

From Mark Twain's *Autobiography*: Along the outside of the front fence ran the country road, dusty in the summertime, and a good place for snakes . . . when they were "house snakes," or "garters," we carried them home and put them in Aunt Patsy's work basket for a surprise; for she was prejudiced against snakes, and always when she took the basket in her lap and they began to climb out of it it disordered her mind.

ROYAL CATS

A Connecticut Yankee in King Arthur's Court is the story of an American mechanic who comes to life in sixth-century England, where he persuades the king that he is a magician and is allowed to do as he pleases. He improves the condition of the people, to whom he is affectionately known as The Boss, but his advanced political ideas lead to his own destruction.

When the book was published (1889) The Boss's ideas so infuriated the English that they boycotted all Mark Twain's work. For various reasons, modern critics have been equally alarmed and angry. Beginning in the 1960's the hero of the book has been described, by some critics, as a sadistic dictator operating with Mark Twain's approval. Sometimes such points have been made by words taken out of context. An example is the strange use made of three sentences—those which I have italicized—from the following three passages:

From Mark Twain's Chapter 40: Consider the three years sped. Now look around on England. A happy and prosperous country, and strangely altered. Schools everywhere, and several colleges; a number of pretty good newspapers. Even authorship was taking a start; Sir Dinadan the Humorist was first in the field, with a volume of gray-headed jokes which I had been familiar with during thirteen centuries. If he had left out that old rancid one about the lecturer I wouldn't have said anything; but I couldn't stand that one. *I suppressed the book and hanged the author.*

From Mark Twain's Chapter 40: [King] Arthur was good for thirty years yet, he being about my own age—that is to say, forty—and I believed that in that time I could easily have the active part of the population of that day ready and eager for an event which should be the first of its kind in the history of the world—a rounded and complete governmental revolution without bloodshed. The result to be a republic. Well, I may as well confess, though I do feel ashamed when I think of it: *I was beginning to have a base hankering to be its first president myself.*

From Mark Twain's Chapter 10: *Unlimited power IS the ideal thing when it is in safe hands.* The despotism of heaven is the one absolutely perfect government. An earthly despotism would be the absolutely perfect earthly government, if the conditions were the same, namely, the despot the perfectest individual of the human race, and his lease of life perpetual. But as a perishable perfect man must die, and leave his despotism in the hands of an imperfect successor, the earthly despotism is not merely a bad form of government, it is the worst form that is possible.

And on this basis, Allen Guttmann offers this summary of The Boss: "The time comes when The Boss is indistinguishable from history's wittier despots, for he replaces feudal institutions with a 'Bossism' complete with a censorship that involves suppressing joke-books and hanging authors. Eventually, The Boss admits his 'base hankering' to be president of an English republic, but long before this admission he had espoused the theory of benevolent dictatorship. 'Unlimited power *is* the ideal thing when it is in safe hands.' " [1]

Clarence was originally a court page—"an airy slim boy in shrimp-colored tights that made him look like a forked carrot." But by now he is The Boss's right-hand man, and only occasionally lapses into his old frivolous ways.

Clarence was with me as concerned the revolution, but in a modified way. His idea was a republic, without privileged orders, but with a hereditary royal family at the head of it instead of an elective chief magistrate. He believed that no nation that had ever known the joy of worshiping a royal family could ever be robbed of it and not fade away and die of melancholy. I urged that kings were dangerous. He said, then have cats. He was sure that a royal family of cats would answer every purpose. They would be as useful as any other royal family, they would know as much, they would have the same virtues and the same treacheries, the same disposition to get up shindies with other royal cats, they would be laughably vain and absurd and never know it, they would be wholly inexpensive; finally, they would have as sound a divine right as any other royal house, and "Tom VII, or Tom XI, or Tom XIV by the grace of God King," would sound as well as it would when applied to the ordinary royal tomcat with tights on. "And as a rule," said he, in his neat modern English, "the character of these cats would be considerably above the character of the average king, and this would be an immense moral advantage to the nation, for the reason that a nation always models its morals after its monarch's. The worship of royalty being founded in unreason, these graceful and harmless cats would easily become as sacred as any other royalties, and indeed more so, because it would presently be noticed that they hanged nobody, beheaded nobody, imprisoned nobody, inflicted no cruelties or injustices of any sort, and so must be worthy of a deeper love and reverence than the customary human king, and would certainly get it. The eyes of the whole harried world would soon be fixed upon this humane and gentle system, and royal butchers would presently begin to disappear; their subjects would fill the vacancies with catlings from our own royal house; we should become a factory; we should supply the thrones of the world; within forty years all Europe would be governed by cats, and we should furnish the cats. The reign of universal peace would begin then, to end no more forever. . . . *Me-e-e-yow-ow-ow-ow—fzt!—wow!*"

Hang him, I supposed he was in earnest, and was beginning to be persuaded by him, until he exploded that cat-howl and startled me almost out of my clothes. But he never could be in earnest. He didn't know what it was. He had pictured a distinct and perfectly rational and feasible improvement upon constitutional monarchy, but he was too feather-headed to know it, or care. . . .

From Mark Twain's *Notebook* : What a funny thing is monarchy. . . . It assumes that a wrong maintained for a dozen or a thousand years becomes a right. It assumes that the wronged parties will presently give up and take the same view. . . . Now, by an effort one can imagine a family of bears taking pride in the historic fact that an ancestor of theirs took violent possession of a bee tree some centuries ago, and that the family have had a right to it ever since . . . but there the allegory fails; for the bees would attack the bears every day for a thousand years. You can make a man understand how time turns a wrong into a right, but you can't make a bee understand—in his present undeveloped stage.

THE OVERRATED ANT

This selection comes from *A Tramp Abroad*; "abroad," in this case, meant Germany and Switzerland. Here Mark Twain is resting by the road in the Black Forest, one of the few places in Germany where he really tramped.

Now and then, while we rested, we watched the laborious ant at his work. I found nothing new in him—certainly nothing to change my opinion of him. It seems to me that in the matter of intellect the ant must be a strangely overrated bird. During many summers now I have watched him, when I ought to have been in better business, and I have not yet come across a living ant that seemed to have any more sense than a dead one. I refer to the ordinary ant, of course; I have had no experience of those wonderful Swiss and African ones which vote, keep drilled armies, hold slaves, and dispute about religion. Those particular ants may be all that the naturalist paints them, but I am persuaded that the average ant is a sham. I admit his industry, of course; he is the hardest-working creature in the world—when anybody is looking—but his leather-headedness is the point I make against him. He goes out foraging, he makes a capture, and then what does he do? Go home? No; he goes anywhere but home. He doesn't know where home is. His home may be only three feet away; no matter, he can't find it. He makes his capture, as I have said; it is generally something which can be of no sort of use to himself or anybody else; it is usually seven times bigger than it ought to be; he hunts out the awkwardest place to take hold of it; he lifts it bodily up in the air by main force, and starts—not toward home, but in the opposite direction; not calmly and wisely, but with a frantic haste which is wasteful of his strength; he fetches up against a pebble, and, instead of going around it, he climbs over it backwards, dragging his booty after him, tumbles down on the other side, jumps up in a passion, kicks the dust off his clothes, moistens his hands, grabs his

property viciously, yanks it this way, then that, shoves it ahead
of him a moment, turns tail and lugs it after him another moment, gets madder and madder, then presently hoists it into the
air and goes tearing away in an entirely new direction; comes to
a weed; it never occurs to him to go around it. No; he must
climb it, and he does climb it, dragging his worthless property to
the top—which is as bright a thing to do as it would be for me to
carry a sack of flour from Heidelberg to Paris by way of
Strasbourg steeple. When he gets up there he finds that that is
not the place; takes a cursory glance at the scenery, and either
climbs down again or tumbles down, and starts off once more—
as usual, in a new direction. At the end of half an hour he
fetches up within six inches of the place he started from, and
lays his burden down. Meantime, he has been over all the
ground for two yards around, and climbed all the weeds and
pebbles he came across. Now he wipes the sweat from his brow,
strokes his limbs, and then marches aimlessly off, in as violent a
hurry as ever. He traverses a good deal of zigzag country, and by
and by stumbles on his same booty again. He does not remember to have ever seen it before; he looks around to see which is
not the way home, grabs his bundle, and starts. He goes through
the same adventures he had before; finally stops to rest, and a
friend comes along. Evidently the friend remarks that a last
year's grasshopper leg is a very noble acquisition, and inquires
where he got it. Evidently the proprietor does not remember exactly where he did get it, but thinks he got it "around here somewhere." Evidently the friend contracts to help him freight it
home. Then, with a judgment peculiarly antic (pun not inten-
tional), they take hold of opposite ends of that grasshopper leg
and begin to tug with all their might in opposite directions. Presently they take a rest, and confer together. They decide that
something is wrong, they can't make out what. Then they go at it
again, just as before. Same result. Mutual recriminations follow.
Evidently each accuses the other of being an obstructionist.
They warm up, and the dispute ends in a fight. They lock themselves together and chew each other's jaws for a while; then they
roll and tumble on the ground till one loses a horn or a leg and
has to haul off for repairs. They make up and go to work again
in the same old insane way, but the crippled ant is at a disadvan-
tage; tug as he may, the other one drags off the booty and him at

the end of it. Instead of giving up, he hangs on, and gets his shins bruised against every obstruction that comes in the way. By and by, when that grasshopper leg has been dragged all over the same old ground once more, it is finally dumped at about the spot where it originally lay. The two perspiring ants inspect it thoughtfully and decide that dried grasshopper legs are a poor sort of property after all, and then each starts off in a different direction to see if he can't find an old nail or something else that is heavy enough to afford entertainment and at the same time valueless enough to make an ant want to own it.

There in the Black Forest, on the mountain side, I saw an ant go through with such a performance as this with a dead spider of fully ten times his own weight. The spider was not quite dead, but too far gone to resist. He had a round body the size of a pea. The little ant—observing that I was noticing—turned him on his back, sunk his fangs into his throat, lifted him into the air, and started vigorously off with him, stumbling over little pebbles, stepping on the spider's legs and tripping himself up, dragging him backwards, shoving him bodily ahead, dragging him up stones six inches high instead of going around them, climbing weeds twenty times his own height and jumping from their summits—and finally leaving him in the middle of the road to be confiscated by any other fool of an ant that wanted him. I measured the ground which this ass traversed, and arrived at the conclusion that what he had accomplished inside of twenty minutes would constitute some such job as this—relatively speaking—for a man; to wit: to strap two eight-hundred-pound horses together, carry them eighteen hundred feet, mainly over (not around) boulders averaging six feet high, and in the course of the journey climb up and jump from the top of one precipice like Niagara, and three steeples, each a hundred and twenty feet high; and then put the horses down, in an exposed place, without anybody to watch them, and go off to indulge in some other idiotic miracle for vanity's sake.

Science has recently discovered that the ant does not lay up anything for winter use. This will knock him out of literature to some extent. He does not work, except when people are looking, and only then when the observer has a green, naturalistic look, and seems to be taking notes. This amounts to deception, and will injure him for the Sunday schools. He has not judgment enough to know what is good to eat from what isn't. This amounts to ignorance, and will impair the world's respect for him. He cannot stroll around a stump and find his way home again. This amounts to idiocy, and once the damaging fact is established, thoughtful people will cease to look up to him, the sentimental will cease to fondle him. His vaunted industry is but a vanity and of no effect, since he never gets home with anything he starts with. This disposes of the last remnant of his reputation, and wholly destroys his main usefulness as a moral agent, since it will make the sluggard hesitate to go to him any more.

From A Tramp Abroad : The two [ravens] sat side by side on the limb and discussed me as freely and offensively as two great naturalists might discuss a new kind of bug.

THE LOW-MINDED ANT

All over the world Mark Twain observed the conversion of the heathen and made his comments. Only in Hawaii was he of two minds about the missionaries. Theologically, he could not approve. "How sad it is," he observed acidly, "to think of the multitudes who have gone to their graves in this beautiful island and never knew there was a hell." On the other hand, he did wholeheartedly admire the improvements the missionaries had wrought in the everyday lives of the people by medical and educational services and by releasing them from the tyranny of the king and the chiefs.

Otherwise Mark Twain was anti-missionary. He reduced the American Board of Foreign Missions to impotent fury by exposing to the world their brutal treatment of Chinese peasants. He commented pointedly on the bitter "self-reproach" many a missionary must feel "when he beguiles . . . children from the religion [their] parents love and honor." And the end of it was that he stopped trying to spread his own gospel of godlessness. "I have found it pretty hard," he said at sixty-seven, in his *Autobiography*, "to give up missionarying—that last excusable of all human trades—but I was obliged to do it because I could not continue to exercise it without private shame while publicly and privately deriding and blaspheming the other missionaries."

Sir John Lubbock was the great English entymologist whose work Mark Twain read at sea on his way from Australia to India in 1896. Clemens was again at sea, in the same year, on his way from India to England, when he wrote up the following experiments in his *Notebook*. But as I have said (on pp. 149–150) I suspect these experiments were less profoundly influenced by Sir John Lubbock than by an American slave, Jerry, who lectured Sam Clemens in his childhood on "corn-pone opinions."

> In Jeypoor [Jaipur, India] I tried several of Sir John Lubbock's experiments, and got results similar to his. Then I tried some experiments of my own. These latter proved that the ant is peculiarly intelligent in the higher concerns of life. I constructed four miniature houses of worship—a Mohammedan mosque, a Hindu temple, a Jewish synagogue, and a Christian cathedral, and placed them in a row. I then marked fifteen ants with red paint and turned them loose. They made several trips to and fro, glancing in at the several places of worship, but not entering. I turned loose fifteen more, painted blue. They acted just as the red ones had done. I now gilded fifteen and turned them loose. No change in result: the forty-five traveled back and forth in an eager hurry, persistently and continuously, visiting each fane but never entering. This satisfied me that these ants were without religious prejudices—just what I wished; for under no other condition would my next and greater experiment be valuable.
>
> I now placed a small square of white paper within the door of each fane; upon the mosque paper I put a pinch of putty, upon the temple paper a dab of tar, upon the synagogue paper a trifle of turpentine, and upon the cathedral paper a small cube of sugar. First I liberated the red ants. They examined and rejected the putty, the tar, and the turpentine, and then took to the sugar with zeal and apparently sincere conviction. I next liberated the blue ants, they did exactly as the red ones had done. The gilded ants followed. The preceding results were precisely repeated. This seemed to prove beyond question that ants destitute of religious prejudices will always prefer Christianity to any of the other great creeds.
>
> However, to make sure I removed the ants and put putty in the cathedral and sugar in the mosque. I now liberated the ants in a body and they rushed tumultuously to the cathedral. I was

very much touched and gratified and went in the back room to write down the event; but when I came back the ants had all apostatized and gone over to the Mohammedan communion. I said that I had been too hasty in my conclusions, and naturally felt rebuked and humbled. With diminished confidence I went on with the test to the finish. I placed the sugar first in one house of worship, then another, till I had tried them all. With this result: that whatever church I put the sugar in, that was the one that the ants straightway joined. This was true, beyond shadow of a doubt, that in religious matters the ant is the opposite of man: for man cares for but one thing, to find the Only True Church; whereas the ant hunts for the one with the sugar in it.

Mark Twain, quoted by Paine in his biography: "What a fine boy that prehistoric man must have been—the very first one! Think of the gaudy style of him, how he must have lorded it over those other creatures, walking on his hind legs, waving his arms, practicing and getting ready for the pulpit."

Swinks and Sooflaskies

What thing is little?—
   The aphis hid
In a house of spittle?
   The hinge of the lid

Of the spider's eye
   At the spider's birth?
"Greater am I
   By the earth's girth

"Than Mighty Death!"
   All creatures cry
That can summon breath;—
   And speak no lie.

—Edna St. Vincent Millay, "Moriturus"

When he was seventy Mark Twain had the time of his life writing what must surely be the most fascinating science-fiction in the language. It's called *3,000 Years Among the Microbes* and it's the story of an American scientist whom some fool of a magician has accidentally changed into a cholera germ and found a home for in a body of a tramp named Blitzowski. There he lives three thousand years microbe time, or three weeks human time.

Modestly, Mark Twain claimed to be only the translator of this remarkable tale, which was written in "microbic." This is his "translator's" preface:

> I have translated the author's style and construction, as well as his matter. I began by reforming these, but gave it up. It amounted to putting evening dress on a stevedore and making him stand up in the college and lecture. He was trim, but he was stiff; he delivered strict English, polished English, but it seemed strained and artificial, coming from such a source and was not pleasant, not satisfactory. Elegant, but cold and unsympathetic. In fact, corpsy. It seemed best to put him back into his shirtsleeves and overalls, and let him flounder around after the fashion that he was used to.
>
> His style is loose and wandering and garrulous and self-contented beyond anything I have ever encountered before, and his grammar breaks the heart. But there is no remedy: let it go.
>
> The Translator

Perhaps by coincidence, most of the microbe's literary faults have also been found in Mark Twain's own style, but so far no remedy has been found, although one earnest attempt has been made: in 1970 Professor John Seelye rewrote *Huckleberry Finn*, to show how it should have been done.[1]

The microbe author's name is Bkshp, for he is not of the microbe nobility, who are born with vowels in their name. Bkshp is "three clucks and a belch" so he calls himself "Huck, an abbreviation of my American middle name, Huxley."

Mark Twain died before the humble bacteria provided antibiotics and before the atom was split, corroborating some guesses in this selection. But guessing alone could not have kept *3,000 Years Among the Microbes* looking so fresh and young after half a century. For this miracle its author also needed an unusually profound layman's knowledge of scientific developments in his own time.

Detailed records of Mark Twain's massive reading have always been available—in letters, notebooks, published work, and in his biography by A. B. Paine. Despite this fact, the literary rumor arose after his death that Mark Twain knew nothing, that he'd "sat down," as critic Ludwig Lewisohn put it, "to develop out of his own head, like an adolescent, like a child, a theory to fit the facts as he seemed to see them." [2] One result of all this was a surge of Mark Twain scholarship. According to the most thorough investigation of Mark Twain's scientific background—by H. H. Waggoner, who could not possibly have known that the microbe's middle name was Huxley—the scientific philosophy closest to Mark Twain's was Thomas Huxley's, Darwin's friend.[3]

Unfortunately, in the case of Mark Twain literary critics have never been unduly influenced by scholarly spadework. Years later, according to Floyd Stovall, Mark Twain was still "a representative American of his time . . . ignorant, cynical and crude." [4]

3,000 Years Among the Microbes, from which this selection comes, was first released in 1967 by The Mark Twain Papers in a volume of hitherto unpublished Mark Twain called *Which Was the Dream?* [5] Mark Twain considered it unfinished—it's halfway between a story and a book. He had stopped, as he always did, when his "think tank" ran out, and never got back to the story. But he stopped at what seems like a splendid ending.

IN BLITZOWSKI

Here the newly made microbe, Bkshp-Huck, is describing his new home.

The erring magician introduced me into the blood of a hoary and moldering old bald-headed tramp. His name is Blitzowski— if that isn't an alias—and he was shipped to America by Hungary because Hungary was tired of him. He tramps in the summer and sleeps in the fields; in the winter he passes the hat in cities, and sleeps in the jails when the gutter is too cold; he was sober once, but does not remember when it was; he never shaves, never washes, never combs his tangled fringe of hair; he is wonderfully ragged, incredibly dirty; he is malicious, malignant, vengeful, treacherous; he was born a thief, and will die one; he is unspeakably profane, his body is a sewer, a reek of decay, a charnel house, and contains swarming nations of all the different kinds of germ-vermin that have been invented for the contentment of man. He is their world, their globe, lord of their universe, its jewel, its marvel, its miracle, its masterpiece. They are as proud of their world as is any earthling of his. When the soul of the cholera germ possesses me I am proud of him: I shout for him, I would die for him; but when the man-nature invades me I hold my nose. At such times it is impossible for me to respect this pulpy old sepulchre. . . .

Our world [the tramp] is as large and grand and awe-compelling to us microscopic creatures as is man's world to man. Our tramp is mountainous, there are vast oceans in him, and lakes that are sea-like for size, there are many rivers (veins and arteries) which are fifteen miles across, and of a length so stupendous as to make the Mississippi and the Amazon trifling little Rhode Island brooks by comparison. As for our minor rivers, they are multitudinous, and the dutiable commerce of disease which they carry is rich beyond the dreams of the American custom-house. . . .

Take a man like Sir Oliver Lodge, and what secret of Nature can be hidden from him? He says: "A billion, that is a million millions, of atoms is truly an immense number, but the resulting aggregate is still excessively minute. A portion of substance consisting of a billion atoms is only barely visible with the *highest* power of a microscope; and a speck or granule, in order to be visible to the naked eye, like a grain of lycopodium-dust, *must be a million times bigger still.*"

The human eye could see it then—that dainty little speck. But with my microbe-eye I could see *every individual* of the whirling billions of *atoms* that *compose* the speck. *Nothing is ever at rest—* wood, iron, water, everything is alive, everything is raging, whirling, whizzing, day and night and night and day, nothing is dead, *there is no such thing as death,* everything is full of bristling life, tremendous life, even the bones of the crusader that perished before Jerusalem eight centuries ago. There are no vegetables, *all things are* ANIMAL; each electron is an animal, each molecule is a collection of animals, and each has an appointed duty to perform and a soul to be saved. Heaven was not made for man alone, and oblivion and neglect reserved for the rest of His creatures. He gave them life, He gave them humble services to perform, they have performed them, and they will not be forgotten, they will have their reward. Man—always vain, windy, conceited—thinks he will be in the majority there. He will be disappointed. Let him humble himself. But for the despised microbe and the persecuted bacillus, who needed a home and nourishment, he would not have been created. He has a mission, therefore—a reason for existing: let him do the service he was made for, and keep quiet.

From a letter to his brother: If I were a heathen, I would rear a statue to Energy, and fall down and worship it!

MONARCHIES

Political organizations in Blitzowski are strangely like those on our planet. This is a Mark Twain's-eye-view of the monarchies, with savage attention to England. (Nevertheless, in many moods Mark Twain loved and admired the English.)

There are upwards of a thousand republics in our planet, and as many as thirty thousand monarchies. Several of these monarchies have a venerable history behind them. . . . In one case *the same dynasty* holds the throne today that established it twenty-five hundred thousand years ago. This is the Pus family—Pus being the family name, just as Romanoff is the family name of the Czars; the official title is His August Majesty Henry, D.G. Staphylococcus Pyogenes Aureus* CMX—that is to say, he is the One Hundred and Ten Thousandth monarch of the Pus lineage that has occupied that throne. They have all used the one name, HENRY. . . .

The English monarchy—the *real* English monarchy—has

---

* Latin, "D.G." (Deus gratias) means *by the grace of God.* The long word means *pus-tank.* The next word—when used in a scientific sense—means *principal;* politically it means *imperial;* in the slang of the common people it means *brick,* and is a term of admiration. Aureus means *gold.* Hence the title, when occurring in a State paper, could be translated *Henry by the grace of God Imperial Pus-Tank,* while in the endearing speech of the common people it would be shortened to *Henry the Gold Brick.*

been in existence about 840 years; its 36 reigns have averaged about 23 years each. Pretty nearly the same average obtains here. At least it is so with the great monarchy of which I have been speaking—the greatest, in population, and the most ambitious, in all Blitzowski. . . . It is a stern and noble race, and by diplomacy and arms has pushed its frontiers far. Wherever it has deprived a conquered nation of its liberties and its religion it has replaced these with something better. It is justly claimed for this great House that it has carried the blessings of civilization further than has any other imperial power. In honor of this good work many of our microbe nations have come to speak of pus and civilization as being substantially the same thing.

From *Following the Equator*—on England: It is made up of very simple details—just grass, and trees, and shrubs, and roads, and hedges, and gardens, and houses, and vines, and churches, and castles, and here and there a ruin—and over it all a mellow dream-haze of history. But its beauty is incomparable, and all its own.

THE GREAT REPUBLIC AND OTHER MATTERS

Catherine, who chatters on here, is a sort of stenographer—that is, Bkshp-Huck directs his thoughts into a wonderful "thought-recorder" machine and she works the machine. But Catherine is an unusual character. For the microbe population, Bkshp-Huck says, is divided into two parts. There are a few Malignants—Cholera, Typhoid, Sleeping Sickness, Yellow Fever, Diphtheria—who make up the nobility and upper classes. The rest of the microbes are Benevolents, who are not only harmless but do the world's work. They labor at everything from saving the planet from "denudation and irremediable sterility" to fermenting bread and liquors and dairy products and curing tobacco. And Mark Twain, who was perpetually fuming at the meekness of working people, found out that in Blitzowski the Benevolents were born stupid. Catherine was "an ass by right of birth" since she was "a daughter of the people, the masses, the humble hard-workers, the ill-paid, the oppressed, the despised, the unthanked" but she was an exception because, thanks to some "ancestral adventure," "part of a drop of cancer-blood had trickled down to her" and improved her brains. In one of the more terrible sentences in the book its author observes, "The other aristocracies breed a bright specimen now and then, but with the cancers, and with the cancers only, brightness is the rule."

Getrichquick, the microbe says elsewhere, is the only country in Blitzowski where foreigners are not regarded as inferior. On the contrary, there "a third-rate foreign microbic celebrity easily outranks a first-rate native one, and . . . gets more champagne than he gets beer at home."

Here Catherine is chattering about her friend the countess. And Mark Twain is preaching one of the greatest sermons of his old age.

"She's a foreigner—the countess. She's a GRQ, and—"

"What's a GRQ?"

"Getrichquick—and she was a lady there; though here, people of her family's condition, being SBE's would have to stick to their proper place, and so—"

"What's an SBE?"

"Soiled-Bread Eater."

"Why *soiled* bread?"

"Because it's earned."

"Because it's *earned?*"

"Yes."

"Does the act of earning it soil it?"

. . . My question made her laugh. She repeated it—apparently to taste again the refreshing ignorance of it:

" 'Does the act of earning it soil it?' Why, don't you know—"

"I don't. I give you my word."

She looked [me] straight in the eye, and said—

"If you are joking, I shall see it. Now I will ask you in earnest . . . Have you ever heard of a nation—a *large* nation—where earning the bread didn't soil it?"

It was my turn to laugh! I started to do it, but—something moved me to wait a minute . . . Great nations began to drift past my mind's eye—habitants of both the planets—and I soon reached a decision, and said—

"I thought it was a foolish question, Catherine, but really it isn't, when a body examines it. I reckon we are pretty full of notions which we got at second hand . . . I know of a country— through talking with natives of it—where the dignity of labor is a phrase which is in everybody's mouth . . . where everybody says it is an honor to a person that he works for the bread he

eats; that earned bread is noble bread, and lifts the earner to the
level of the highest in the land; that unearned bread, the bread
of idleness, is tainted with discredit; a land where the sayers of
these things say them with strong emotion, and think they believe what they say, and are proud of their land because it is the
sole land where the bread-earners are the only acknowledged aristocracy. And yet I do see, that when you come to examine into
it—"

"I know the land you mean! It's GRQ! Honest—isn't it
GRQ?"

"Yes, it is."

"I recognized it in a minute! The countess is always talking
about it. . . . she told me about the dignity-of-labor gospeling,
and says it's all sham. She says a mechanic is the same there as
anywhere. They don't ask him to dinner—plumber, carpenter,
blacksmith, cobbler, butler, coachman, sailor, soldier, stevedore,
it's all the same all around, they don't ask *any* of them. The professionals and merchants and preachers don't, and the idle rich
don't invite *them*—not by a damn sight, she says, and—"

". . . You *must* stop this habit of picking up and fetching
home every dreadful word you—" . . .

"The rest that she said was, that if the banker's daughter married the plumber, and if the multimillionaire's daughter married
the editor, and if the bishop's daughter married the horse-doc-
tor, and if the governor's daughter married the coachman, there
was hell to pay!"

"Now *there* you go, again! I—" . . .

"And she said there's families that are so awful high-up and
swell, that they won't let their daughters marry any native at all,
if they can help it. They save them up till a foreign bacillus with
a title comes along; then if they can agree on the price they
make the trade. But they don't have auctions, she says. Not public ones. She's as nice as she can be, and it's most interesting to
hear her talk. . . .

"So you see, there *isn't* any big nation, after all, where it
doesn't soil the bread to earn it. . . .

"The countess says it's all a sham, in GRQ, and of course if
there was a big nation anywhere where it *wasn't* a sham, it would
be there, which is a republic and a democracy, and the greatest

one on the planet, and everybody letting on to be equal and some of them succeeding, God only knows which ones, *she* says! . . . and there isn't a person in the land that can see it. That's what *she* says—all blind-fuddled with bogus sentiment.

". . . Mesalliances! why, she says it's just the natural native home of them, on account of there being so many more ranks and aristocracies there than anywhere else. She says there's families that the very President isn't good enough to marry into—at least *until* he's President. They're nearly always SBE's—tanners, or rail-splitters, or tailors, or prohibitionists, or some other low trade, and they've got to climb *away* up above that before they can crowd into those families . . . *They* consider it climbing, she says, and everybody does. They admire him—admire him immensely—for what he is *now,* don't you know—admire him for the respectability he's climbed up to. They don't say, with swelling pride and noble emotion, 'Look at him, the splendid SBE— he's a rail-splitter!' No, they say, with swelling pride and noble emotion, 'Look at him—*away up there!*—and just think, he used to wasn't anything but a rail-splitter!' . . .

"So there 'tis, and I reckon you've got to come down . . . and acknowledge it."

"Acknowledge what?"

"That *earned* bread is soiled bread—everywhere on the planet of Blitzowski, republics and all. It's the soiled bread that *makes* a nation; makes it great, makes it honored, makes it strong, props up its throne and saves it from the junk-shop, makes its waving flag a beautiful thing to see and bring the proud tears to your eyes to look at it . . . keeps its Grand Dukes out of the hog-wallow, the jail and the alms-house—if you sh'd sweep the SBE's and their dirty bread away there wouldn't be a solitary valuable thing left in the land! and yet, by God—"

Thank heaven there was a knock on the door! It was the good Brother, the impressive Sleeping Sickness germ.

He had a gentle way with him, and a kind and winning face, for he was a Malignant; that is to say, a noble of the loftiest rank and the deadliest, and the gentle bearing and the kind face are theirs by nature and old heredity.

From "The New Dynasty": Many a time, when I have seen a man abusing a horse, I have wished I knew that horse's language, so that I could whisper in his ear, "Fool, you are master here, if you but knew it. Launch out with your heels!" The working millions, in all the ages, have been horses. . . .

THE SWINKS' RUSSIA

Once Bkshp-Huck learns that germs have germs—"wee creatures" which infest them and which are called swinks—he is, as he says, "in a fever to see them!" Here he does so and finds out that the swinks' Russia is simply a minute duplicate of the human one. And so it goes.

In the microbe story, which was Mark Twain's *Gulliver's Travels,* class and national and biological relationships are infinitely and infinitesimally repeated. So are attitudes. This is Mark Twain's attempt to define the microbe word "sooflasky":

> The microbe's name for himself is not Microbe, it is *Sooflasky.*
> . . . Straitly translated, it means in Blitzowski what the word Man—as chief creature in the scheme of Creation—means in the human World: that is to say, The Pet, The Chosen One, The Wonderful One, The Grand Razzledazzle, The Whole Thing, The Lord of Creation, The Drum Major, The Head of the Procession. The word Sooflasky means all that, includes all those shades. To construct an English equivalent that would hold them all and not leak was exceedingly difficult, for me, but I believe Bullyboywithaglasseye came nearest. I often applied it to my fellow microbes, from the very first, and they liked it. Partly because it was long and fine-sounding and foreign, and partly because of the modified translation I furnished along with it. I told them it . . . meant "the Deity's Delight." On these terms I worked it into universal use among the grateful clergy, the poets, the great orators, and the rest of our best people. Quaintly and prettily accented, and delivered lingeringly and lovingly and impressively in a sermon, or with fire and thunder and gush in a great oration, it is certainly one of the nobbiest things I know of.

The microbe Duke is an expert on swinks and explains to Bkshp-Huck that, among swinks, only the upper classes are deadly. But neither the Duke nor anyone else in Blitzowski, except the once-human Bkshp-Huck, realizes that this situation is the same among sooflaskies and of course (though this is never spelled out) among humans.

This glance at the swinks' imperial Russia was influenced by the fact that Mark Twain wrote it during the Russo-Japanese war.

We rigged a microscope for an exhibition at once, and put a drop of my blood under it, which got mashed flat when the lens got shut down upon it. The result was beyond my dreams. The field stretched miles away, green and undulating, threaded with streams and roads, and bordered all down the mellowing distances with picturesque hills. And there was a great white city of tents; and everywhere were parks of artillery, and divisions of cavalry and infantry—waiting. We had hit a lucky moment; evidently there was going to be a march-past, or something like that. At the front where the chief banner flew, there was a large and showy tent, with showy guards on duty, and about it were some other tents of a swell kind.

The warriors—particularly the officers—were lovely to look at, they were so trim-built and so graceful and so handsomely uniformed. They were quite distinct, vividly distinct, for it was a fine day, and they were so immensely magnified that they looked to be fully finger-nail high.*

Everywhere you could see officers moving smartly about, and they looked gay, but the common soldiers looked sad. Many wife-swinks and daughter-swinks and sweetheart-swinks were about—crying, mainly. It seemed to indicate that this was a case of war, not a summer-camp for exercise, and that the poor labor-swinks were being torn from their planet-saving industries to go and distribute civilization and other forms of suffering among the feeble benighted, somewhere; else why should the swinkesses cry?

The cavalry was very fine; shiny black horses, shapely and

* My own expression, and a quite happy one. I said to the Duke—
"Your grace, they're just about finger-nailers!"
"How do you mean, m'lord?"
"This. You notice the stately General standing there with his hand resting upon the muzzle of a cannon? Well, if you could stick your little finger down against the ground alongside of him, his plumes would just reach up to where your nail joins the flesh."
The Duke said "finger-nailers was good"—good and exact; and he afterward used it several times himself. In about a minute a mounted General rode up alongside of the other one and saluted, and the Duke said—
"There, now—with the horse to help, this one's nearly a nail and a third high."

spirited; and presently when a flash of light struck a lifted bugle delivering a command which we couldn't hear and a division came tearing down on a gallop it was a stirring and gallant sight, until the dust rose an inch—the Duke thought more—and swallowed it up in a rolling and tumbling long gray cloud, with bright weapons glinting and sparking in it.

Before long the real business of the occasion began. A battalion of priests arrived, carrying sacred pictures. That settled it: this was war; these far-stretching masses of troops were bound for the front. Their little monarch came out now, the sweetest little thing that ever travestied the human shape, I think; and he lifted up his hands and blessed the passing armies, and they looked as grateful as they could, and made signs of humble and real reverence as they drifted by the holy pictures.

It was beautiful—the whole thing; and wonderful, too, when those serried masses swung into line and went marching down the valley under the long array of fluttering flags.

Evidently they were going somewhere to fight for their country, which was the little manny that blessed them; and to preserve him and his brethren that occupied the other swell tents; and to civilize and grab a valuable little unwatched country for them somewhere. But the little fellow and his brethren didn't fall in—that was a noticeable particular. But the Duke said it was without doubt a case of Henry and Family on a minute scale— *they* didn't fight; they stayed at home, where it was safe, and waited for the swag.

Very well, then—what ought *we* to do? Had we no moral duty to perform? Ought we to allow this war to begin? Was it not our duty to stop it, in the name of right and righteousness? Was it not our duty to administer a rebuke to this selfish and heartless Family?

The Duke was struck by that, and greatly moved. He felt as I did about it, and was ready to do whatever was right, and thought we ought to pour boiling water on the Family and extinguish it, which we did.

It extinguished the armies, too, which was not intended. We both regretted this, but the Duke said that these people were nothing to us, and deserved extinction anyway for being so poor-spirited as to serve such a Family. He was loyally doing the like himself, and so was I, but I don't think we thought of that.

And it wasn't just the same, anyway, because we were sooflaskies; and they were only swinks.

From "The Czar's Soliloquy": We and our uncles are a family of cobras set over a hundred and forty million rabbits, whom we torture and murder and feed upon all our days; yet the moralist urges that to kill us is a crime, not a duty.

AFTERLIFE

Franklin realizes that no atom is destructible; that it has always existed and will exist forever; but he thinks all atoms will go out of this world someday and continue their life in a happier one. Old Tolliver thinks no atom's life will ever end, but he also thinks Blitzowski is the only world it will ever see, and that at no time in its eternity will it be either worse off or better off than it is now and always has been. Of course he thinks the planet Blitzowski is itself eternal and indestructible—at any rate he says he thinks that. It could make me sad, only I know better. D. T. will fetch Blitzy yet, one of these days.

But these are alien thoughts, human thoughts, and they falsely indicate that I do not want this tramp to go on living. What would become of me if he should disintegrate? My molecules would scatter all around and take up new quarters in hundreds of plants and animals; each would carry its special feelings along with it, each would be content in its new estate, but where should *I* be? I should not have a rag of a feeling left, after my disintegration—with his—was complete. Nothing to think with, nothing to grieve or rejoice with, nothing to hope or despair with. There would be no more *me*. I should be musing and thinking and dreaming somewhere else—in some distant animal, maybe—perhaps a cat; by proxy of my oxygen I should be raging and fuming in some other creature—a rat, perhaps; I should be smiling and hoping in still another child of Nature—heir to my hydrogen—a weed, or a cabbage, or something; my carbonic acid (ambition) would be dreaming dreams in some lowly wood-violet that was longing for a showy career; thus my details would be doing as much feeling as ever, but I should not be aware of it, it would all be going on for the benefit of those others, and I not in it at all. I should be gradually wasting away, atom by atom, molecule by molecule, as the years went on, and at last I should be all distributed, and nothing left of what had once been Me. It is curious, and not without impressiveness: I should still be alive, intensely alive, but so scattered that I would not know it. I should not be dead—no, one cannot call it that— but I should be the next thing to it. And to think what centuries and ages and eons would drift over Me before the disintegration was finished, the last bone turned to gas and blown away! I wish I knew what it is going to feel like, to lie helpless such a weary, weary time, and see my faculties decay and depart, one by one, like lights which burn low, and flicker, and perish, until the ever-deepening gloom and darkness which—oh, away, away with these horrors, and let me think of something wholesomer!

My tramp is only eighty-five; there is good hope that he will live ten years longer—five hundred thousand of my microbe years. So may it be.

From Mark Twain's *Notebook*: The Bible of Nature . . . is not intended as a message to us, any more than the scientist intends a message to surviving microbes when he boils the life out of a billion of them in a thimble. The microbes discover a message in it; this is certain—if they have a pulpit.

BLASPHEMY

God appears & God is Light
To those poor Souls who dwell in Night,
But does a Human Form Display
To those who Dwell in Realms of day.

—WILLIAM BLAKE, "Auguries of Innocence"

An honest God is the noblest work of man.

—ROBERT INGERSOLL, *The Gods*

One man's blasphemy may be another man's truism, but in Mark Twain there is blasphemy for all. "Noah's Ark" is blasphemy for atheists, no doubt because Mark Twain, far from denying God, insists upon him, hunts him down, and reviles him.

To Mark Twain, the denial of a supreme being was the truism. Robert Ingersoll, fed "a hungry place" in him only because he was so bold and eloquent in denying God. Ingersoll's thinking was not so unusual in the United States; elsewhere in the world thoroughgoing atheists and agnostics were almost nonexistent, but here, especially on the frontier where churches were few, many people made do with a moral code instead of God. It was Ingersoll's daring and lucidity that made him so remarkable. When he publicly defied God to strike him dead, millions were thrilled, shocked, or frightened. That, in its time, was great blasphemy. And of course, to millions it would be still. So would the denial of that very human God of so many Jews and Christians, the one who sits, in Mark Twain's work, "on his throne, attended by his four and twenty elders and some other dignitaries pertaining to his court, and looks out over his miles and miles of tempestuous worshipers, and smiles, and purrs, and nods his satisfaction."

"Noah's Ark" was based partly on direct observation in the East, where so much religion was born. According to Mark Twain, it was easy to see "that the inventor of the heaven did not originate the idea, but copied it from the show-ceremonies of some sorry little sovereign State up in the back settlements of the Orient somewhere." But that is not Mark Twain speaking; it is an archangel and his favorite: the fallen one, Satan. (He is not to be confused with the Satan in "This Friend of Satan" [pp. 218–230], who was a perfectly respectable person in Paradise, and merely happened to be named for an unfortunate uncle.) Nor, strictly, is Satan speaking; he is writing "Letters from the Earth," of which "Noah's Ark" is an excerpt. He has fallen because he uttered some "sarcasms" about the Creator of Heaven and earth; they were intended for archangels only, but were overheard by some ordinary angels and reported to headquarters. Consequently he was banished from Heaven for a "celestial day" and, bored with flapping through space, he decided to investigate what he had ridiculed: the Creator's human race experiment. His letters are a confidential report on it to some archangel friends.

"Letters from the Earth" is Satan's, and Mark Twain's, defense of man. It is the last word from Mark Twain, written, not for posterity, but for his own pleasure, in his last few months of life. For he believed, with excellent reason, that it could never be published. Publication would be a felony, he wrote a friend—and so it would have been then. Nowhere else did he so completely ignore all literary precedents for the handling of religious and sexual matters.

It's man's heaven that first fascinates Satan, and his description of it is interlarded with pleas to be believed: "It consists—utterly and entirely—of diversions which he cares next to nothing about, here in the earth, yet is quite sure he will like in heaven. Isn't it curious? Isn't it interesting? You must not think I am exaggerating, for it is not so. I will give you details." He then reports that most men can't sing or play musical instruments and don't want to; that few like to pray and all find the Sabbath "a dreary, dreary bore." As to what they do like: All—even "the urchin who is his comrade's superior in games"—enjoy exercising their mental faculties, for which there is no chance in heaven. But, above all, "like the immortals" the human being "naturally places sexual intercourse far and away above all other joys." Of course he is pitifully limited: "At its very best and longest the act is brief beyond imagination—the imagination of an immortal, I mean. In the matter of repetition the man is limited—oh, quite beyond im-

mortal conception. We who continue the act and its supremest ecstasies unbroken and without withdrawal for centuries, will never be
able to understand or adequately pity the awful poverty of these people in that rich gift which, possessed as we possess it, makes all other
possessions trivial and not worth the trouble of invoicing."

Nevertheless, man loves his poor sexual pleasures as even the immortals their great ones: "opportunity sets him wild; in this state he
will risk life, reputation, everything—even his queer heaven itself—to
make good that opportunity and ride it to the overwhelming climax."
And yet "it is not in their heaven; prayer takes its place." Prayer,
music, and singing—merciless, hideous, uninterrupted noise. (Satan,
like Mark Twain, is abnormally sensitive to noise.)

Finally: "Here in the earth all nations hate each other, and every
one of them hates the Jew"; "All white nations despise all colored nations, of whatever hue, and oppress them when they can"; "White
men will not associate with 'niggers,' nor marry them." And yet: "The
inventor of their heaven empties into it all the nations of the earth, in
one common jumble . . . they have to be 'brothers'; they have to mix
together, pray together, harp together, hosannah together" and man
"thinks he thinks that if he were only there he would take all the populace to his heart, and hug, and hug, and hug!"

"He is a marvel—man is! I would I knew who invented him."

And that is the question: who is responsible for the poor thing? Not
the wicked thing. In Mark Twain only an "aggressive and pitiless mi-
nority" of men are wicked. But where to put the blame for the suffering and the idiocy?

And, after a lifetime of raging at his fellow idiots, Mark Twain took
his stand with them. Illogically but brilliantly, he reversed the doctrine
of original sin, and transferred the guilt from man to God. This is the
root of his God-hatred; but, even for Satan, it was a difficult decision
to make. "What shall we do?" he inquired of his friends, Saints Mi-
chael and Gabriel, after explaining to them man's terrible Bible: the
Old Testament was "interested mainly in blood and sensuality" and
the New Testament in "Salvation by fire."

"What shall we do? If we believe, with these people, that their God
invented these cruel things, we slander him; if we believe that the people invented them themselves, we slander them. It is an unpleasant di-
lemma in either case . . . for neither of these parties has done *us* any
harm." But: "For the sake of tranquillity, let us take a side. Let us join
forces with the people and put the whole ungracious burden upon

him—heaven, hell, Bible, and all. It does not seem right, it does not seem fair; and yet . . ."

Yet such was Mark Twain's decision. He—or Satan—justified it cleverly: when you consider that heaven so full of everything repugnant to man, you realize man could *not* have invented it. But this is sophistry. The truth was that Mark Twain belonged to the damned race himself and he never forgot it. "In myself," he wrote, "I find in big or little porportion every quality and every defect that is findable in the mass of the race." And so he took his last stand with his fellow fools, which meant, in his final work, that he stood for man against all his gods.

If he stood for Satan too—which has never been proved—it may be that he inherited the tendency. It was of his mother that he said, "This friend of Satan was a most gentle spirit." And he told how the friendship, such as it was, commenced:

> She was the natural ally and friend of the friendless. It was believed that, Presbyterian as she was, she could be beguiled into saying a soft word for the Devil himself, and so the experiment was tried. The abuse of Satan began; one conspirator after another added his bitter word, his malign reproach, his pitiless censure, till at last, sure enough, the unsuspecting subject of the trick walked into the trap. She admitted that the indictment was sound, that Satan was utterly wicked and abandoned . . . *but* would any claim that he had been treated fairly? A sinner was but a sinner, Satan was just that like the rest. What saves the rest?—their own efforts alone? No . . . appealing, imploring prayers . . . out of all the churches in Christendom. . . . But who prays for Satan?

His mother's soft spot for the Devil has never been psychoanalyzed, but Mark Twain's has, along with other tendencies that are obvious in "The Brutes." Coleman O. Parsons has found that Clemens' sympathy for Satan as well as for "the black man, the witch, the misbeliever, the weaker vessel [women]" came from "psychic malaise induced by a sense of guilt." [1]

"Letters from the Earth" is not to be confused with the book of that title, in which it appears. The book, an anthology of unpublished Mark Twain, was prepared for publication in 1939, by Bernard DeVoto, then editor of The Mark Twain Papers. But Mark Twain's daughter Clara, a Christian Scientist, objected to publication and did not withdraw her objections until 1962; then the book appeared.

THE GOAT AND THE TORTOISE

Every man's temperament, according to Mark Twain, is born in him, and "nothing can modify it—except temporarily." Adam's temperament "was the first command the Deity ever issued to a human being . . . the only command Adam would *never* be able to disobey." It said, "Be weak, be water, be characterless, be cheaply persuadable." And no son of Adam, Mark Twain maintained, ever disobeyed.

Animals are equally helpless before God's degrees. "In the Animals' Court" describes how the lion is given a dukedom for his courage, while, for "having deserted in the face of the enemy," the rabbit is "marched to the scaffold, bearing a placard marked 'Coward' and hanged." The rabbit's only defense is "The law of God, which denies courage to the rabbit."

"The Goat and the Tortoise" is a variation on this theme which was long unpublishable. It comes from the book *Letters from the Earth.*

Take two extremes of temperament—the goat and the tortoise.

Neither of these creatures makes its own temperament, but is born with it, like man, and can no more change it than can man.

Temperament is the law of God written in the heart of every creature by God's own hand, and *must* be obeyed, and will be obeyed in spite of all restricting or forbidding statutes, let them emanate whence they may.

Very well, lust is the dominant feature of the goat's temperament, the law of God in its heart, and it must obey it and *will* obey it the whole day long in the rutting season, without stopping to eat or drink. If the Bible said to the goat, "Thou shalt not fornicate, thou shalt not commit adultery," even Man—sapheaded man—would recognize the foolishness of the prohibition, and would grant that the goat ought not to be punished for obeying the law of his Maker. Yet he thinks it right and just that man should be put under the prohibition. All men. All alike.

On its face this is stupid, for, by temperament, which is the *real* law of God, many men are goats and can't help committing adultery when they get a chance; whereas there are numbers of men who, by temperament, can keep their purity and let an opportunity go by if the woman lacks in attractiveness. But the Bible doesn't allow adultery at all, whether a person can help it or not. It allows no distinction between goat and tortoise—the excitable goat, the emotional goat, that has to have some adultery every day or fade and die; and the tortoise, that cold calm puritan, that takes a treat only once in two years and then goes to sleep in the midst of it and doesn't wake up for sixty days. No lady goat is safe from criminal assault, even on the Sabbath Day, when there is a gentleman goat within three miles to leeward of her and nothing in the way but a fence fourteen feet high, whereas neither the gentleman tortoise nor the lady tortoise is ever hungry enough for the solemn joys of fornication to be willing to break the Sabbath to get them. Now according to man's curious reasoning, the goat has earned punishment, and the tortoise praise.

From *Following the Equator* : Man is the only animal that blushes. Or needs to.

THIS FRIEND OF SATAN

Many Mark Twain readers are acquainted with *The Mysterious Stranger*—a tale of Satan come to earth, from which this selection comes. But in 1970 The Mark Twain Papers published three unfinished stories of Satan come to earth, and editor William Gibson revealed that the book known as *The Mysterious Stranger*—the one published six years after Mark Twain's death—was created by his literary executor, A. B. Paine, who welded together two Mark Twain manuscripts (the bulk of the book and an ending) and changed them somewhat.[1] Two of the unfinished tales are very unlike *The Mysterious Stranger*; the third is the story that Paine altered and published. All are good reading but probably what we now know as *The Mysterious Stranger* will always be the best loved, partly because it is simplest and swiftest, partly because it is finished. Certainly, despite Paine's changes, it comes the closest to fulfilling Mark Twain's purpose, as he described it in a letter to Howells:

> What I have been wanting is a chance to write a book . . . which should say my say, right out of my heart, in the plainest language and without a limitation of any sort. . . .
> It is under way, now, and it *is* a luxury! an intellectual drunk. . . . I believe I can make it tell what I think of Man, and how he is constructed, and what a shabby poor ridiculous thing he is, and how mistaken he is in his estimate of his character and powers and qualities and his place among the animals.

The Mysterious Stranger goes this way: an angel who is the namesake of his fallen uncle Satan, makes himself visible, during the Middle Ages, to three teen-aged boys in an Austrian village named Eseldorf—German for Jackassville.

Satan takes the form of a young man nobody can resist. The boys adore him, although he teaches him what no boys could really accept: that life is a tale told by an idiot, signifying nothing, "a grotesque and foolish dream." His other message—on many points he sees eye to eye with Mark Twain—is that only man can do wrong, for only he has the Moral Sense; the other animals, who have it not, are like the angels.

The story is told by Theodor Fischer, one of the favored boys. Seppi is another. Ursula is the housekeeper of Marget and her uncle, Father Peter. They are a very poor family, especially at this point in the story when Father Peter is in jail for witchcraft. But this is not surprising, for Father Peter, popular though he was, always had a bad reputation professionally. According to Theodor, some people even "charged him with talking around in conversation that God was all goodness and would find a way to save all his poor human children. It was a horrible thing to say, but there was never any absolute proof that Father Peter said it; and it was out of character for him to say it, too, for he was always good and gentle and truthful. He wasn't charged with saying it in the pulpit . . . but only outside, in talk; and it was easy for enemies to manufacture *that*."

When Mark Twain showed the first chapters of this book to his wife, she said, as so he wrote Howells, "It is perfectly horrible—and perfectly beautiful!" He added, "Within the due limits of modesty, that is what *I* think." It is what a great many people have thought.

Satan not only reads minds; when necessary, his magic even extends to preventing the boys, who are about Tom Sawyer's age, from uttering indiscretions. That is what he is up to in "Agnes the Lucky Cat."

AGNES THE LUCKY CAT

I was walking along the path, feeling very down-hearted, when a most cheery and tingling freshening-up sensation went rippling through me, and I was too glad for any words, for I knew by that sign that Satan was by. I had noticed it before. Next moment he was alongside of me and I was telling him all my trouble and what had been happening to Marget and her uncle. While we were talking we turned a curve and saw old Ursula resting in the shade of a tree, and she had a lean stray kitten in her lap and was petting it. I asked her where she got it, and she said it came out of the woods and followed her; and she said it probably hadn't any mother or any friends and she was going to take it home and take care of it. Satan said:

"I understand you are very poor. Why do you want to add another mouth to feed? Why don't you give it to some rich person?"

Ursula bridled at this and said: "Perhaps you would like to have it. You must be rich, with your fine clothes and quality airs." Then she sniffed and said: "Give it to the rich—the idea! The rich don't care for anybody but themselves; it's only the poor that have feeling for the poor, and help them. The poor and God. God will provide for this kitten."

"What makes you think so?"

Ursula's eyes snapped with anger. "Because I know it!" she said. "Not a sparrow falls to the ground without His seeing it."

"But it falls, just the same. What good is seeing it fall?"

Old Ursula's jaws worked, but she could not get any word out for the moment, she was so horrified. When she got her tongue she stormed out, "Go about your business, you puppy, or I will take a stick to you!"

I could not speak, I was so scared. I knew that with his notions about the human race Satan would consider it a matter of no consequence to strike her dead, there being "plenty more"; but my tongue stood still, I could give her no warning. But nothing happened; Satan remained tranquil—tranquil and indifferent. I suppose he could not be insulted by Ursula any more than the king could be insulted by a tumble-bug. The old woman jumped to her feet when she made her remark, and did it as briskly as a young girl. It had been many years since she had done the like of that. That was Satan's influence; he was a fresh breeze to the weak and the sick, wherever he came. His presence affected even the lean kitten, and it skipped to the ground and began to chase a leaf. This surprised Ursula, and she stood looking at the creature and nodding her head wonderingly, her anger quite forgotten.

"What's come over it?" she said. "A while ago it could hardly walk."

"You have not seen a kitten of that breed before," said Satan.

Ursula was not proposing to be friendly with the mocking stranger, and she gave him an ungentle look and retorted: "Who asked you to come here and pester me, I'd like to know? And what do you know about what I've seen and what I haven't seen?"

"You haven't seen a kitten with the hair-spines on its tongue pointing to the front, have you?"

"No—nor you, either."

"Well, examine this one and see."

Ursula was become pretty spry, but the kitten was spryer, and she could not catch it, and had to give it up. Then Satan said:

"Give it a name, and maybe it will come."

Ursula tried several names, but the kitten was not interested.

"Call it Agnes. Try that."

The creature answered to the name and came. Ursula examined its tongue. "Upon my word, it's true!" she said. "I have not seen this kind of a cat before. Is it yours?"

"No."

"Then how did you know its name so pat?"

"Because all cats of that breed are named Agnes; they will not answer to any other."

Ursula was impressed. "It is the most wonderful thing!" Then a shadow of trouble came into her face, for her superstitions were aroused, and she reluctantly put the creature down, saying: "I suppose I must let it go; I am not afraid—no, not exactly that, though the priest—well, I've heard people—indeed, many people . . . And, besides, it is quite well now and can take care of itself." She sighed, and turned to go, murmuring: "It is such a pretty one, too, and would be such company—and the house is so sad and lonesome these troubled days . . . Miss Marget so mournful and just a shadow, and the old master shut up in jail."

"It seems a pity not to keep it," said Satan.

Ursula turned quickly—just as if she were hoping some one would encourage her.

"Why?" she asked, wistfully.

"Because this breed brings luck."

"Does it? Is it true? Young man, do you know it to be true? How does it bring luck?"

"Well, it brings money, anyway."

Ursula looked disappointed. "Money? A cat bring money? The idea! You could never sell it here; people do not buy cats here; one can't even give them away." She turned to go.

"I don't mean sell it. I mean have an income from it. This kind is called the Lucky Cat. Its owner finds four silver groschen in his pocket every morning."

I saw the indignation rising in the old woman's face. She was insulted. This boy was making fun of her. That was her thought. She thrust her hands into her pockets and straightened up to give him a piece of her mind. Her temper was all up, and hot. Her mouth came open and let out three words of a bitter sentence . . . then it fell silent, and the anger in her face turned to surprise or wonder or fear, or something, and she slowly brought out her hands from her pockets and opened them and held them so. In one was my piece of money, in the other lay four silver groschen. She gazed a little while, perhaps to see if the groschen would vanish away; then she said, fervently:

"It's true—it's true—and I'm ashamed and beg forgiveness, O dear master and benefactor!" And she ran to Satan and kissed his hand, over and over again, according to the Austrian custom.

In her heart she probably believed it was a witch-cat and an agent of the Devil; but no matter, it was all the more certain to be able to keep its contract and furnish a daily good living for the family, for in matters of finance even the piousest of our peasants would have more confidence in an arrangment with the Devil than with an archangel. Ursula started homeward, with

Agnes in her arms, and I said I wished I had her privilege of
seeing Marget.

Then I caught my breath, for we were there. There in the parlor, and Marget standing looking at us, astonished. She was feeble and pale, but I knew that those conditions would not last in
Satan's atmosphere, and it turned out so. I introduced Satan—
that is, Philip Traum*—and we sat down and talked. There was
no constraint. We were simple folk, in our village, and when a
stranger was a pleasant person we were soon friends. Marget
wondered how we got in without her hearing us. Traum said the
door was open, and we walked in and waited until she should
turn around and greet us. This was not true; no door was open;
we entered through the walls or the roof or down the chimney,
or somehow; but no matter, what Satan wished a person to believe, the person was sure to believe . . . Ursula put her head in
at the door now and said:

"Supper's ready, miss." Then she saw us and looked frightened, and motioned me to come to her, which I did, and she
asked if we had told about the cat. I said no, and she was re-
lieved, and said please don't; for if Miss Marget knew, she
would think it was an unholy cat and would send for a priest
and have its gifts all purified out of it, and then there wouldn't
be any more dividends. So I said we wouldn't tell, and she was
satisfied. Then I was beginning to say good-by to Marget, but
Satan interrupted and said, ever so politely—well, I don't remember just the words, but anyway he as good as invited himself to supper, and me, too. Of course Marget was miserably em-
barrassed, for she had no reason to suppose there would be half
enough for a sick bird. Ursula heard him, and she came straight
into the room, not a bit pleased. At first she was astonished to
see Marget looking so fresh and rosy, and said so; then she
spoke up in her native tongue, which was Bohemian, and said—
as I learned afterward—"Send him away, Miss Marget; there's
not victuals enough."

Before Marget could speak, Satan had the word, and was talking back to Ursula in her own language—which was a surprise
to her, and for her mistress, too. He said, "Didn't I see you down
the road a while ago?"

* *Traum* is German for dream—ED.

"Yes, sir."

"Ah, that pleases me; I see you remember me." He stepped to her and whispered: "I told you it is a Lucky Cat. Don't be troubled; it will provide."

That sponged the slate of Ursula's feelings clean of its anxieties, and a deep, financial joy shone in her eyes. . . .

We had supper in the kitchen, and Ursula waited at table. A small fish was in the frying pan, crisp and brown and tempting, and one could see that Marget was not expecting such respectable food as this. Ursula brought it, and Marget divided it between Satan and me, declining to take any of it herself; and was beginning to say she did not care for fish today, but she did not finish the remark. It was because she noticed that another fish had appeared in the pan. She looked surprised, but did not say anything. She probably meant to inquire of Ursula about this later. There were other surprises: flesh and game and wines and fruits—things which had been strangers in that house lately; but Marget made no exclamations, and now even looked unsurprised, which was Satan's influence, of course. Satan talked right along, and was entertaining, and made the time pass pleasantly and cheerfully; and although he told a good many lies, it was no harm in him, for he was only an angel and did not know any better. They do not know right from wrong; I knew this, because I remembered what he had said about it. He got on the good side of Ursula. He praised her to Marget, confidentially but speaking just loud enough for Ursula to hear. He said she was a fine woman, and he hoped some day to bring her and his uncle together. Very soon Ursula was mincing and simpering around in a ridiculous girly way, and smoothing out her gown and prinking at herself like a foolish old hen, and all the time pretending she was not hearing what Satan was saying. I was ashamed, for it showed us to be what Satan considered us, a silly race and trivial. Satan said his uncle entertained a great deal, and to have a clever woman presiding over the festivities would double the attractions of the place.

"But your uncle is a gentleman, isn't he?" asked Marget.

"Yes," said Satan indifferently; "some even call him a Prince, out of compliment, but he is not bigoted; to him personal merit is everything, rank nothing."

My hand was hanging down by my chair; Agnes came along

and licked it; by this act a secret was revealed. I started to say, "It is all a mistake; this is just a common, ordinary cat; the hairneedles on her tongue point inward, not outward." But the words did not come, because they couldn't. Satan smiled upon me, and I understood.

From "Concerning the Jews": We may not pay [Satan] reverence, for that would be indiscreet, but we can at least respect his talents. A person who has for untold centuries maintained the imposing position of spiritual head of four-fifths of the human race, and political head of the whole of it, must be granted the possession of executive abilities of the loftiest order.

THE BRUTES

Seppi . . . was full of the last new mystery, now—the disappearance of Hans Oppert, the village loafer. . . . No one had seen Hans for a couple of days.

"Not since he did that brutal thing, you know," he said.

"What brutal thing?" It was Satan that asked.

"Well, he is always clubbing his dog, which is a good dog, and his only friend, and is faithful, and loves him, and does no one any harm; and two days ago he was at it again, just for nothing —just for pleasure—and the dog was howling and begging, and Theodor and I begged, too, but he threatened us, and struck the dog again with all his might and knocked one of his eyes out, and he said to us, 'There, I hope you are satisfied now; that's what you have got for him by your damned meddling'—and he laughed, the heartless brute." Seppi's voice trembled with pity and anger. I guessed what Satan would say, and he said it.

"There is that misused word again—that shabby slander. Brutes do not act like that, but only men."

"Well, it was inhuman, anyway."

"No, it wasn't, Seppi; it was human—quite distinctly human. It is not pleasant to hear you libel the higher animals by attributing to them dispositions which they are free from, and which are found nowhere but in the human heart. None of the higher animals is tainted with the disease called the Moral Sense. Purify your language, Seppi; drop those lying phrases out of it."

He spoke pretty sternly—for him—and I was sorry I hadn't

warned Seppi to be more particular about the word he used. I
knew how he was feeling. He would not want to offend Satan;
he would rather offend all his kin. There was an uncomfortable
silence, but relief soon came, for that poor dog came along now,
with his eye hanging down, and went straight to Satan, and
began to moan and mutter brokenly, and Satan began to answer
in the same way, and it was plain that they were talking together
in the dog language. We all sat down in the grass, in the moonlight, for the clouds were breaking away now, and Satan took
the dog's head in his lap and put the eye back in its place, and
the dog was comfortable, and he wagged his tail and licked Satan's hand, and looked thankful and said the same; I knew he
was saying it, though I did not understand the words. Then the
two talked together a bit, and Satan said:

"He says his master was drunk."

"Yes, he was," said we.

"And an hour later he fell over the precipice there beyond the
Cliff Pasture."

"We know the place; it is three miles from here."

"And the dog has been often to the village, begging people to
go there, but he was only driven away and not listened to."

We remembered it, but hadn't understood what he wanted.

"He only wanted help for the man who had misused him, and
he thought only of that, and has had no food nor sought any. He
has watched by his master two nights. What do you think of
your race? Is heaven reserved for it, and this dog ruled out, as
your teachers tell you? Can your race add anything to this dog's
stock of morals and magnanimities?" He spoke to the creature,
who jumped up, eager and happy, and apparently ready for orders and impatient to execute them. "Get some men; go with the
dog—he will show you that carrion; and take a priest along to
arrange about insurance, for death is near."

With the last word he vanished, to our sorrow and disappointment. We got the men and Father Adolf, and we saw the man
die. Nobody cared but the dog; he mourned and grieved, and
licked the dead face, and could not be comforted. We buried
him where he was, and without a coffin, for he had no money,
and no friend but the dog. If we had been an hour earlier, the
priest would have been in time to send that poor creature to
heaven, but now he was gone down into the awful fires, to burn

forever. It seemed such a pity that in a world where so many
people have difficulty to put in their time, one little hour could
not have been spared for this poor creature who needed it so
much, and to whom it would have made the difference between
eternal joy and eternal pain. It gave an appalling idea of the
value of an hour, and I thought I could never waste one again
without remorse and terror. Seppi was depressed and grieved,
and said it must be so much better to be a dog and not run such
awful risks. We took this one home with us and kept him for our
own. Seppi had a very good thought as we were walking along,
and it cheered us up and made us feel much better. He said the
dog had forgiven the man that had wronged him so, and maybe
God would accept that absolution.

There was a very dull week, now, for Satan did not come,
nothing much was going on . . . But we came across Ursula a
couple of times taking a walk in the meadows beyond the river
to air the cat, and we learned from her that things were going
well. She had natty new clothes on and bore a prosperous look.
The four groschen a day were arriving without a break, but were
not being spent for food and wine and such things—the cat attended to all that. . . .

Ursula gave us a small item of information: money being
plenty now, she had taken on a servant to help about the house
and run errands. She tried to tell it in a commonplace, matter-
of-course way, but she was so set up by it and so vain of it that
her pride in it leaked out pretty plainly. It was beautiful to see
her veiled delight in this grandeur, poor old thing, but when we
heard the name of the servant we wondered if she had been altogether wise; for although we were young, and often thoughtless,
we had fairly good perception on some matters. This boy was
Gottfried Narr, a dull, good creature, with no harm in him and
nothing against him personally; still, he was under a cloud, and
properly so, for it had not been six months since a social blight
had mildewed the family—his grandmother had been burned as
a witch. When that kind of a malady is in the blood it does not
always come out with just one burning. Just now was not a good
time for Ursula and Marget to be having dealings with a member of such a family, for the witch-terror had risen higher during
the past year than it had ever reached in the memory of the
oldest villagers. The mere mention of a witch was almost enough

to frighten us out of our wits. This was natural enough, because of late years there were more kinds of witches than there used to be; in old times it had been only old women, but of late years they were of all ages—even children of eight and nine; it was getting so that anybody might turn out to be a familiar of the Devil—age and sex hadn't anything to do with it. In our little region we had tried to extirpate the witches, but the more of them we burned, the more of the breed rose up in their places.

Once, in a school for girls only ten miles away, the teachers found that the back of one of the girls was all red and inflamed, and they were greatly frightened, believing it to be the Devil's marks. The girl was scared, and begged them not to denounce her, and said it was only fleas; but of course it would not do to let the matter rest there. All the girls were examined, and eleven out of the fifty were badly marked, the rest less so. A commission was appointed, but the eleven only cried for their mothers and would not confess. Then they were shut up, each by herself, in the dark, and put on black bread and water for ten days and nights; and by that time they were haggard and wild, and their eyes were dry and they did not cry any more, but only sat and mumbled, and would not take the food. Then one of them confessed, and said they had often ridden through the air on broomsticks to the witches' Sabbath, and in a bleak place high up in the mountains had danced and drunk and caroused with several hundred other witches and the Evil One, and all had conducted themselves in a scandalous way and had reviled the priests and blasphemed God. That is what she said—not in narrative form, for she was not able to remember any of the details without having them called to her mind one after the other; but the commission did that, for they knew just what questions to ask, they being all written down for the use of witch-commissioners two centuries before. They asked, "Did you do so and so?" and she always said yes, and looked weary and tired, and took no interest in it. And so when the other ten heard that this one confessed, they confessed, too, and answered yes to the questions. Then they were burned at the stake all together, which was just and right; and everybody went from all the countryside to see it. I went, too; but when I saw that one of them was a bonny, sweet girl I used to play with, and looked so pitiful there chained to the stake, and her mother crying over her and devouring her with kisses and clinging around her neck, and saying, "Oh, my God! oh, my God!" it was too dreadful, and I went away.

It was bitter cold weather when Gottfried's grandmother was burned. It was charged that she had cured bad headaches by kneading the person's head and neck with her fingers—as she said—but really by the Devil's help, as everybody knew. They were going to examine her, but she stopped them, and confessed straight off that her power was from the Devil. So they appointed to burn her next morning, early, in our market-square. The officer who was to prepare the fire was there first, and prepared it. She was there next—brought by the constables, who left her and went to fetch another witch. Her family did not come with her. They might be reviled, maybe stoned, if the people were excited. I came, and gave her an apple. She was squatting at the fire, warming herself and waiting; and her old lips and hands were blue with the cold. A stranger came next. He was a traveler, passing through; and he spoke to her gently, and, seeing nobody but me there to hear, said he was sorry for her. And he asked if what she confessed was true, and she said no. He looked surprised and still more sorry then, and asked her:

"Then why did you confess?"

"I am old and very poor," she said, "and I work for my living. There was no way but to confess. If I hadn't, they might have set me free. That would ruin me, for no one would forget that I had been suspected of being a witch, and so I would get no more work, and wherever I went they would set the dogs on me. In a little while I would starve. The fire is best; it is soon over. You have been good to me, you two, and I thank you."

She snuggled closer to the fire, and put out her hands to warm them, the snowflakes descending soft and still on her old gray head and making it white and whiter. The crowd was gathering now, and an egg came flying and struck her in the eye, and broke and ran down her face. There was a laugh at that.

I told Satan all about the eleven girls and the old woman, once, but it did not affect him. He only said it was the human race, and what the human race did was of no consequence. And he said he had seen it made; and it was not made of clay; it was made of mud—part of it was, anyway. I knew what he meant by that—the Moral Sense. He saw the thought in my head, and it tickled him and made him laugh. Then he called a bullock out of a pasture and petted it and talked with it, and said:

"There—he wouldn't drive children mad with hunger and fright and loneliness, and then burn them for confessing to things invented for them which had never happened. And neither would he break the hearts of innocent, poor old women and make them afraid to trust themselves among their own race; and he would not insult them in their death-agony. For he is not besmirched with the Moral Sense, but is as the angels are, and knows no wrong, and never does it."

Lovely as he was, Satan could be cruelly offensive when he chose; and he always chose when the human race was brought to his attention.

From a letter to W. D. Howells: Is [man] really fit for anything but to be stood up on the street corner as a convenience for dogs?

DOG STORY

This bit of a letter, witten in Florence in 1892, was found in Mark Twain's *Notebook*. Joe was his good friend the Reverend Joseph Twitchell of Hartford, Connecticut.

Dear Joe:
. . . The dogs of the Campagna (they watch sheep without human assistance) are big and warlike, and are terrible creatures to meet in those lonely expanses. Two young Englishmen—one of them a friend of mine—were away out there yesterday, with a peasant guide of the region who is a simple-hearted and very devout Roman Catholic. At one point the guide stopped, and said they were now approaching a spot where two especially ferocious dogs were accustomed to herd sheep: that it would be well to go cautiously and be prepared to retreat if they saw the dogs. So then they started on, but presently came suddenly upon the dogs. The immense brutes came straight for them, with death in their eyes. The guide said in a voice of horror, "Turn your backs, but for

God's sake don't stir—I will pray—I will pray the Virgin to do a miracle and save us; she will hear me, oh, my God, she surely will."
And straightway he began to pray. The Englishmen stood quaking with fright, and wholly without faith in the man's prayer. But all at once the furious snarling of the dogs ceased—at three steps distant—and there was dead silence. After a moment my friend, who could no longer endure the awful suspense, turned—and there was the miracle, sure enough: the gentleman dog had mounted the lady dog and both had forgotten their solemn duty in the ecstasy of a higher interest!

The strangers were saved, and they retired from that place with thankful hearts. The guide was in a frenzy of pious gratitude and exultation, and praised and glorified the Virgin without stint; and finally wound up with "But you—you are Protestants; she would not have done it for you; she did it for me—only me—praised be she forevermore! and I will hang a picture of it in the church and it shall be another proof that her loving care is still with her children who humbly believe and adore."

By the time the dogs got unattached the men were five miles from there.

Mark Twain's note in his copy of Alexander Winchell's *Sketches of Creation* : Theology seems to be an ass.

NOAH'S ARK

This selection, from "Letters from the Earth" is the satanic version of the Noah's Ark story; Satan wrote it for the amusement and instruction of his archangel friends.

THE PLAN AND THE PASSENGERS

. . . the population grew and grew until it numbered several millions. But it was a disappointment to the Deity. He was dissatisfied with its morals; which in some respects were not any better than his own. Indeed they were an unflatteringly close imitation of his own. They were a very bad people, and as he knew of no way to reform them, he wisely concluded to abolish them.

This is the only really enlightened and superior idea his Bible has credited him with, and it would have made his reputation for all time if he could only have kept to it and carried it out. But he was always unstable—except in his advertisements—and his good resolution broke down. He took a pride in man; man was his finest invention; man was his pet, after the housefly, and he could not bear to lose him wholly; so he finally decided to save a sample of him and drown the rest.

Nothing could be more characteristic of him. He created all those infamous people, and he alone was responsible for their conduct. Not one of them deserved death, yet it was certainly good policy to extinguish them; especially since in creating them the master crime had already been committed, and to allow them to go on procreating would be a distinct addition to the crime. But at the same time there could be no justice, no fairness, in any favoritism—all should be drowned or none.

No, he would not have it so; he would save half a dozen and try the race over again. He was not able to foresee that it would go rotten again, for he is only the Far-Sighted One in his advertisements.

He saved out Noah and his family, and arranged to exterminate the rest. He planned an Ark, and Noah built it. Neither of them had ever built an Ark before, nor knew anything about Arks; and so something out of the common was to be expected. It happened. Noah was a farmer, and although he knew what was required of the Ark he was quite incompetent to say whether this one would be large enough to meet the requirements or not (which it wasn't), so he ventured no advice. The Deity did not know it wasn't large enough, but took the chances and made no adequate measurements. In the end the ship fell far short of the necessities, and to this day the world still suffers for it.

Noah built the Ark. He built it the best he could, but left out most of the essentials. It had no rudder, it had no sails, it had no compass, it had no pumps, it had no charts, no lead-lines, no anchors, no log, no light, no ventilation, and as for cargo room—which was the main thing—the less said about that the better. . . .

For not only was a sample of man to be saved, but business samples of the other animals, too. . . .

Noah began to collect animals. There was to be one couple of each and every sort of creature that walked or crawled, or swam or flew, in the world of animated nature. We have to guess at how long it took to collect the creatures and how much it cost, for there is no record of these details. When Symmachus made preparation to introduce his young son to grown-up life in imperial Rome, he sent men to Asia, Africa, and everywhere to collect wild animals for the arena-fights. It took the men three years to accumulate the animals and fetch them to Rome. Merely quadrupeds and alligators, you understand—no birds, no snakes, no frogs, no worms, no lice, no rats, no fleas, no ticks, no caterpillars, no spiders, no houseflies, no mosquitoes—nothing but just plain simple quadrupeds and alligators: and no quadrupeds except fighting ones. Yet it was as I have said: it took three years to collect them, and the cost of animals and transportation and the men's wages footed up $4,500,000.

How many animals? We do not know. But it was under five thousand, for that was the largest number *ever* gathered for those Roman shows, and it was Titus, not Symmachus, who made that collection.[1] Those were mere baby museums, compared to Noah's contract. Of birds and beasts and fresh-water creatures he had to collect 146,000 kinds; and of insects upwards of two million species.

Thousands and thousands of those things are very difficult to catch, and if Noah had not given up and resigned, he would be on the job yet, as Leviticus used to say.[2] . . .

If he had known all the requirements in the beginning, he would have been aware that what was needed was a fleet of Arks. But he did not know how many kinds of creatures there were, neither did his Chief. So he had no kangaroo, and no 'possum, and no Gila monster, and no ornithorhynchus, and lacked a multitude of other indispensable blessings which a loving Creator had provided for man and forgotten about, they having long ago wandered to a side of this world which he had never seen and with whose affairs he was not acquainted. And so everyone of them came within a hair of getting drowned.

They only escaped by an accident. There was not water enough to go around. Only enough was provided to flood one small corner of the globe—the rest of the globe was not then known, and was supposed to be nonexistent.

However, the thing that really and finally and definitely determined Noah to stop with enough species for purely business purposes and let the rest become extinct, was an incident of the last days: an excited stranger arrived with some most alarming news. He said he had been camping among some mountains and valleys about six hundred miles away, and he had seen a wonderful thing there: he stood upon a precipice overlooking a wide valley, and up the valley he saw a billowy black sea of strange animal life coming. Presently the creatures passed by, struggling, fighting, scrambling, screeching, snorting—horrible vast masses of tumultuous flesh! Sloths as big as an elephant; frogs as big as a cow; a megatherium and his harem huge beyond belief; saurians and saurians and saurians, group after group, family after family, species after species—a hundred feet long, thirty feet high, and twice as quarrelsome; one of them hit a perfectly blameless Durham bull a thump with its tail and sent it whizzing three hundred feet into the air and it fell at the man's feet with a sigh and was no more. The man said that these prodigious animals had heard about the Ark and were coming. Coming to get saved from the flood. And not coming in pairs, they were *all* coming: they did not know the passengers were restricted to pairs, the man said, and wouldn't care a rap for the regulations, anyway—they would sail in that Ark or know the reason why. The man said the Ark would not hold the half of them; and moreover they were coming hungry, and would eat up everything there was, including the menagerie and the family.

All these facts were suppressed, in the Biblical account. You find not a hint of them there. The whole thing is hushed up. Not even the names of those vast creatures are mentioned. It shows you that when people have left a reproachful vacancy in a contract they can be as shady about it in Bibles as elsewhere. Those powerful animals would be of inestimable value to man now, when transportation is so hard-pressed and expensive, but they are all lost to him. All lost, and by Noah's fault. They all got drowned. Some of them as much as eight million years ago.

Very well, the stranger told his tale, and Noah saw that he must get away before the monsters arrived. He would have sailed at once, but the upholsterers and decorators of the housefly's drawing room still had some finishing touches to put on, and that lost him a day. Another day was lost in getting the flies aboard, there being sixty-eight billions of them and the Deity still afraid there might not be enough. Another day was lost in stowing forty tons of selected filth for the flies' sustenance.

Then at last, Noah sailed; and none too soon, for the Ark was only just sinking out of sight on the horizon when the monsters arrived, and added their lamentations to those of the multitude of weeping fathers and mothers and frightened little children who were clinging to the wave-washed rocks in the pouring rain and lifting imploring prayers to an All-Just and All-Forgiving and All-Pitying Being who had never answered a prayer since those crags were builded, grain by grain out of the sands, and would still not have answered one when the ages should have crumbled them to sand again.

From Mark Twain's *Autobiography*—on his brother: He was always honest and honorable. But in light matters—matters of small consequence, like religion and politics and such things—he never acquired a conviction that could survive a disapproving remark from a cat.

HOUSEFLY FORGOTTEN

On the third day, about noon, it was found that a fly had been left behind. The return voyage turned out to be long and difficult, on account of the lack of chart and compass, and because of the changed aspects of all coasts, the steadily rising water having submerged some of the lower landmarks and given to higher ones an unfamiliar look; but after sixteen days of earnest and faithful seeking, the fly was found at last, and received on board with hymns of praise and gratitude, the Family standing meanwhile uncovered, out of reverence for its divine origin. It was weary and worn, and had suffered somewhat from the weather, but was otherwise in good estate. Men and their families had died of hunger on barren mountain tops, but it had not lacked for food, the multitudinous corpses furnishing it in rank and rotten richness. Thus was the sacred bird providentially preserved.

Providentially. That is the word. For the fly had not been left behind by accident. No, the hand of Providence was in it. There are no accidents. All things that happen, happen for a purpose. They are foreseen from the beginning of time, they are ordained from the beginning of time. From the dawn of Creation the Lord had foreseen that Noah, being alarmed and confused by the invasion of the prodigious brevet fossils, would prematurely fly to sea unprovided with a certain invaluable disease. He would have all the other diseases, and could distribute them among the new races of men as they appeared in the world, but he would lack one of the very best—typhoid fever; a malady which, when the circumstances are especially favorable, is able to utterly wreck a patient without killing him; for it can restore him to his feet with a long life in him, and yet deaf, dumb, blind, crippled, and idiotic. The housefly is its main disseminator, and is more competent and more calamitously effective than all the other distributors of the dreaded scourge put together. And so, by foreordination from the beginning of time, this fly was left behind to seek out a typhoid corpse and feed upon its corruptions and gaum its legs with the germs and transmit them to the re-peopled world for permanent business. From that one housefly, in the ages that have since elapsed, billions of sickbeds have been stocked, billions of wrecked bodies sent tottering about the earth, and billions of cemeteries recruited with the dead.

From *The Innocents Abroad*—In Palestine: Yesterday we met a woman riding on a little jackass, and she had a little child in her arms; honestly, I thought the child had goggles on as we approached. . . . But when we drew nearer, we saw that the goggles were nothing but a camp-meeting of flies assembled around each of the child's eyes.

MICROBES

The Family consisted of Noah, his wife, their three sons, and their three daughters-in-law.

Noah and his family were saved—if that could be called an advantage. I throw in the *if* for the reason that there has never been an intelligent person of the age of sixty who would consent to live his life over again. His or anyone else's. The Family were saved, yes, but they were not comfortable, for they were full of microbes. Full to the eyebrows; fat with them, obese with them; distended like balloons. It was a disagreeable condition, but it could not be helped, because enough microbes had to be saved to supply the future races of men with desolating diseases, and there were but eight persons on board to serve as hotels for them. The microbes were by far the most important part of the Ark's cargo, and the part the Creator was most anxious about and most infatuated with. They had to have good nourishment and pleasant accommodations. There were typhoid germs, and cholera germs, and hydrophobia germs, and lockjaw germs, and consumption germs, and black plague germs, and some hundreds of other aristocrats, specially precious creations, golden bearers of God's love to man, blessed gifts of the infatuated Father to his children—all of which had to be sumptuously housed and richly entertained; these were located in the choicest places the interiors of the Family could furnish: in the lungs, in the heart, in the brain, in the kidneys, in the blood, in the guts. In the guts particularly. The great intestine was the favorite resort. There they gathered, by countless billions, and worked, and fed, and squirmed, and sang hymns of praise and thanksgiving; and at night when it was quiet you could hear the soft murmur of it. The large intestine was in effect their heaven. They stuffed it solid; they made it as rigid as a coil of gaspipe. They took a pride in this. Their principal hymn made gratified reference to it:

> Constipation, O constipation,
> The joyful sound proclaim
> Till man's remotest entrail
> Shall praise its Maker's name.

From an unpublished Mark Twain notebook: There being 22 billion microbes in each man, and feeding upon him, we now perceive who the whole outfit was made for.

SHEM'S HOOKWORM

Shem was the eldest son of Noah. Hookworm was the special disease of the people Mark Twain grew up among—poor Southerners. In a Tennessee village, in his *The Gilded Age*, there stand the men— hands in their pockets except to readjust the angle of their dilapidated straw hats—who were typical hookworm victims, though nobody knew that then. The picture is precise, from their blue or yellow jeans and the "thick jungle of hair under the chin" to the home-made tobacco all chewed or smoked. Above all, their apathy, so typical of hookworm victims, still lives in Mark Twain's picture:

The long-legged youth who carried the mail tarried an hour to talk . . . and in a little while the male population of the village assembled to help. . . . These neighbors stood a few moments looking at the mail-carrier reflectively while he talked; but fatigue soon began to show itself, and one after another they climbed up and occupied the top rail of the fence, hump-shouldered and grave, like a company of buzzards assembled for supper and listening for the death-rattle.

These words were written thirty-six years before Dr. Charles Wardell Stiles discovered the American hookworm, and Mark Twain, remembering—always remembering—wrote "Shem's Hookworm."

Stiles, still an unsung hero, was a medical zoologist with the United States Public Health Service. Chief among "his helpers" was John D. Rockefeller the first, who financed the Sanitary Commission that eradicated the disease in this country.

Mark Twain's favorable mention of Rockefeller here would have been, had it been published last century, the final blasphemy; at the time many Americans might more easily have forgiven all his attacks on God. For Rockefeller—more than any of the other rich men of his day—was once so hysterically hated that even the churches dared not accept his "tainted money."

Science has not yet conquered the African sleeping sickness, though it is sometimes kept under control by cutting the brush and spraying with insecticide.

Shem was full of hookworms. It is wonderful, the thorough and comprehensive study which the Creator devoted to the great work of making man miserable. I have said he devised a special affliction-agent for each and every detail of man's structure, overlooking not a single one, and I said the truth. Many poor people have to go barefoot, because they cannot afford shoes. The Creator saw his opportunity. I will remark, in passing, that he always has his eye on the poor. Nine-tenths of his disease-inventions were intended for the poor, and they *get* them. The well-to-do get only what is left over. Do not suspect me of speaking unheedfully, for it is not so: the vast bulk of the Creator's affliction-inventions *are* specially designed for the persecution of the poor. You could guess this by the fact that one of the pulpit's finest and commonest names for the Creator is "The Friend of the Poor." Under no circumstances does the pulpit ever pay the Creator a compliment that has a vestige of truth in it. The poor's most inplacable and unwearying enemy is their Father in Heaven. The poor's only real friend is their fellow man. He is sorry for them, he pities them, and he shows it by his deeds. He does much to relieve their distresses; and in every case their Father in Heaven gets the credit of it.

Just so with diseases. If science exterminates a disease which has been working for God, it is God that gets the credit, and all the pulpits break into grateful advertising raptures and call attention to how good he is! Yes, *he* has done it. Perhaps he has waited a thousand years before doing it. That is nothing; the pulpit says he was thinking about it all the time. When exasperated men rise up and sweep away an age-long tyranny and set a nation free, the first thing the delighted pulpit does is to advertise it as God's work, and invite the people to get down on their knees and pour out their thanks to him for it. And the pulpit says with admiring emotion, "Let tyrants understand that the Eye that never sleeps is upon them; and let them remember that the Lord our God will not always be patient, but will loose the whirlwinds of his wrath upon them in his appointed day."

They forget to mention that he is the slowest mover in the universe . . .

Very well, six thousand years ago Shem was full of hookworms. Microscopic in size, invisible to the unaided eye. All of the Creator's specially deadly disease-producers are invisible. It is an ingenious idea. For thousands of years it kept man from getting at the roots of his maladies, and defeated his attempts to master them. It is only very recently that science has succeeded in exposing some of these treacheries.

The very latest of these blessed triumphs of science is the discovery and identification of the ambuscaded assassin which goes by the name of the hookworm. Its special prey is the barefooted poor. It lies in wait in warm regions and sandy places and digs its way into their unprotected feet.

The hookworm was discovered two or three years ago by a physician, who had been patiently studying its victims for a long time. The disease induced by the hookworm had been doing its evil work here and there in the earth ever since Shem landed on Ararat, but it was never suspected to *be* a disease at all. The people who had it were merely supposed to be *lazy,* and were therefore despised and made fun of, when they should have been pitied. The hookworm is a peculiarly sneaking and underhand invention, and has done its surreptitious work unmolested for ages; but that physician and his helpers will exterminate it now.

God is back of this. He has been thinking about it for six thousand years, and making up his mind. The idea of exterminating the hookworm was his. He came very near doing it before Dr. Charles Wardell Stiles did. But he is in time to get the credit of it. He always is.

It is going to cost a million dollars. He was probably just in the act of contributing that sum when a man pushed in ahead of him—as usual. Mr. Rockefeller. He furnishes the million, but the credit will go elsewhere—as usual. This morning's journals tell us something about the hookworm's operations:

> The hookworm parasites often so lower the vitality of those who are affected as to retard their physical and mental development . . . It has been shown that the lowered vitality of multitudes, long attributed to malaria and climate and seriously affecting economic development, is in fact due in some districts to this parasite. . . . It is a conservative estimate that two millions of our people are affected by this parasite. The disease is more common and more serious in children of school age than in other persons. . . .

The poor children are under the Eye that never sleeps, you see. They have had that ill luck in all the ages. They and "the Lord's poor"—as the sarcastic phrase goes—have never been able to get away from that Eye's attentions.

Yes, the poor, the humble, the ignorant—they are the ones that catch it. Take the "Sleeping Sickness," of Africa. This atrocious cruelty has for its victims a race of ignorant and unoffending blacks whom God placed in a remote wilderness, and bent his parental Eye upon them—the one that never sleeps when there is a chance to breed sorrow for somebody. He arranged for these people before the Flood. The chosen agent was a fly, related to the tsetse; the tsetse is a fly which has command of the Zambezi country and stings cattle and horses to death, thus rendering that region uninhabitable by man. The tsetse's awful relative deposits a microbe which produces the Sleeping Sickness. Ham was full of these microbes, and when the voyage was over he discharged them in Africa and the havoc began, never to find amelioration until six thousand years should go by and science should pry into the mystery and hunt out the cause of the disease. The pious nations are now thanking God, and praising him for coming to the rescue of his poor blacks. The pulpit says the praise is due to him, for the reason that the scientists got their inspiration from him. He is surely a curious Being. He commits a fearful crime, continues that crime unbroken for six thousand years, and is then entitled to praise because he suggests to somebody else to modify its severities. He is called patient, and he certainly must be patient, or he would have sunk the pulpit in perdition ages ago for the ghastly compliments it pays him.

Science has this to say about the Sleeping Sickness, otherwise called the Negro Lethargy:

> It is characterized by periods of sleep recurring at intervals. The disease lasts from four months to four years, and is always fatal. The victim appears at first languid, weak, pallid, and stupid. His eyelids become puffy, an eruption appears on his skin. He falls asleep while talking, eating, or working. As the disease progresses he is fed with difficulty and becomes much emaciated. The failure of nutrition and the appearance of bedsores are followed by convulsions and death. Some patients become insane.

It is he whom Church and people call Our Father in Heaven who has invented the fly and sent him to inflict this dreary long misery and melancholy and wretchedness, and decay of body and mind, upon a poor savage who has done the Great Criminal no harm. There isn't a man in the world who doesn't pity that poor black sufferer, and there isn't a man that wouldn't make him whole if he could. To find the one person who has no pity for him you must go to Heaven. . . .

Mark Twain's note in his copy of Rufus K. Noyes's *Views of Religion*: The wise Fiji chief said to a missionary, "We do not pray to the Good Spirit to spare us, but to the other one; a *good* spirit is not going to hurt us."

"THE LAST POSSIBILITY
OF THE BEAUTIFUL"

The Child's Toys & the Old Man's Reasons
Are the Fruits of the Two seasons.

—WILLIAM BLAKE, "Auguries of Innocence"

Mark Twain was one of the most heavily pedigreed Americans we know about. His father's line has been traced, by Dixon Wecter, through generations of southern Quakers—many of them slaveholders and many revolutionary soldiers—to a sixteenth-century English tradesman whose grandson settled in Virginia. His mother was descended, on the one hand, through some famous Indian-fighters, to an Irishman who settled in Virginia in 1779; and on the other hand to some landed English gentry.

Mainly, Mark Twain was like his mother, who "thought in epigrams" and could "see seven sides to a cube." [1] His red hair, tricks of speech, charm, and passion for animals he got from her. But beautiful, lively Jane Clemens was ancestor-proud and nonbookish. From his austere father, Judge John Marshall Clemens, who died when he was twelve, Sam Clemens inherited or imitated bookishness, godlessness, and a truly extreme "horror of boasting." This went so far in the Judge, that a favorite family story is about the Monday he invited an acquaintance home for "a washday dinner." As told by his grandson: "By some strange freak, there was a turkey dinner. My grandfather was terribly mortified. 'What will that man think of me—pretending that a turkey dinner was only a washday dinner?'" [2]

Mark Twain makes a character obviously based on his father long to "lie down in the peace and the quiet and be an ancestor, I do get so tired of being posterity." [3] He did not investigate his own ancestors, he said in his *Autobiography,* because he was "so busy polishing up this

end of the line and trying to make it showy." The only one he claimed
with pride was a Gregory Clement who helped sentence Charles I to
death. It is possible that Clemens was descended from Clement, although the only evidence Mark Twain adduced was a certain instinc-
tive feeling about kings, and, "Whenever we have a strong and persistent and uneradicable instinct, we may be sure it is not original with us
but inherited."

On this theory, all that his children certainly inherited was a passion
for animals—especially cats—which clearly began with Mark Twain's
mother. Even that turkey dinner was attributable to it. A boy had
come to the door, according to her biographer, dragging a poor little
turkey, "its head down, and gasping" and offered to sell it for fifty
cents. "I wanted to get it out of its misery," said Jane.[4]

And then there were the cats. Judge Clemens' advice to his daughter Pamela was wistful: to be a good housekeeper, see that her husband was comfortable, and not have too many cats in the house. But
Jane Clemens' feeling for cats was very different from her son's and
her cats were not like his. "By some subtle sign," he said, "the homeless, hunted, bedraggled and disreputable cat recognized her at a
glance as the born refuge and champion of his sort—and followed her
home. His instinct was right, he was as welcome as the prodigal son.
We had nineteen cats at one time in 1845. And there wasn't one in the
lot that had any character, not one that had any merit, except the
cheap and tawdry merit of being unfortunate. They were a vast burden to us all—including my mother—but they were out of luck, and
that was enough; they had to stay."

If he sounded bitter, he had reason. For in a poor family the cat
burden sometimes became unbearable, and "If a cat was to be
drowned or shot," wrote his older brother Orion, "Sam (though un-
willing yet firm) was selected for the work." [5]

Yet cat-executioner Sam was also the cat-worshiper of the family,
and had always been, even as "a pale, sickly boy" who "teased girls
with green garter snakes" and always had at least three pet cats. The
cousin who so remembered him, belonged to the relatively rich branch
of the family, at whose farm the Clemenses often summered, and she
also remembered how it was when Sam arrived: ". . . father would
lift his big carpet bag out of the wagon and then would come Sam
with a basket in his hand. The basket he would allow no one except
himself to carry. In the basket would be his pet cat. This he had

trained to sit beside himself at the table. He would play contentedly with a cat for hours." [6]

The names of the cats his own children played with feature more largely even than Mark Twain's name in the delightful childish biography his daughter Susy wrote of her father when she was thirteen, and which he treasured and reread and quoted from through the many years that were left to him after she died at twenty-four. He and the children named the cats: Motley, Fraulein, Tammany, Danbury, Satan, Sin, Buffalo Bill, Pestilence, Blatherskite, Famine, Stray Kit, Minnie-Cat, Abner, Soapy Sal, Cleveland, Billiards, Sinbad, Sour Mash . . .

Mainly it was cats in the Clemens family. But in their summers at Quarry Farm, near Elmira, New York, there was a rich assortment of other animals, including dogs. "By what right," Mark Twain once inquired, "has the dog come to be regarded as a 'noble' animal? The more brutal and cruel and unjust you are to him the more your fawning and adoring slave he becomes; whereas, if you shamefully misuse a cat once she will always maintain dignified reserve toward you afterward." But even when he wrote that, according to Paine, he was on such terms with a hound named Bones that he was caught embracing him.

Jane Clemens, armed only with her tongue, could stop a Missouri cartman beating his horse. It was a long jump from that to Mark Twain's daughters in Paris where, armed with the blue cards of the French SPCA, they strove manfully to prevent the cabdrivers from beating their horses. The drivers laughed at them, and sometimes crowds collected, and once, reported Clara, her father was "rabid" against her for making herself conspicuous. Moreover, he was not a patient man, and when the girls, invoking the majesty of the French law, did prevent the driver from using his whip, the horse stopped. Once Mark Twain jumped out of the carriage: "Girls, you can drive the other two blocks alone; I wouldn't go to hell at such a pace." [7]

In Jean Clemens, the baby of the family, a cycle was tragically completed, for Jean became a neurotic. Toward the end of her short life (she died at twenty-nine a few months before her father), she held herself increasingly aloof from people and became more and more passionately devoted to the other creatures. Jean was a sick exaggeration of her father. He admired the human species least but was nevertheless deeply attached to many people. Pale, beautiful Jean became something of a recluse, somewhat obsessed with creating a good world for animals, and apparently far more attached to them than to people.

Those were the lonely years, with Susy and Mrs. Clemens dead, and Jean so ill with epilepsy and emotional problems, and Mark Twain's other daughter, Clara, so often in sanitariums or abroad, and Mark Twain, near Redding, Connecticut, so often alone in the loveliest of his houses, Stormfield. But there were friends, including his young biographer, Albert Bigelow Paine, who lived nearby and came daily. And the cats. "The cats really owned Stormfield," says Paine, "anyone could tell that from their deportment. Mark Twain held the title deeds, but it was Danbury and Sinbad and the others that possessed the premises. . . . Mark Twain might be proccupied and indifferent to . . . other members of the household; but no matter what he was doing, let Danbury appear in the offing and he was observed and greeted with due deference, and complimented and made comfortable. Clemens would arise from the table and carry certain choice food out on the terrace to Tammany and be satisfied with almost no acknowledgement by way of appreciation." [8]

"Sour Mash and Others" was written during those years, about the happy times that lived in Susy's biography and in her father's memory.

SOUR MASH AND OTHERS

"Our various occupations, wrote thirteen-year-old Susy in her biography of her father, "are as follows. Papa rises about $\frac{1}{2}$ past 7 in the morning, breakfasts at eight, writes, plays tennis with Clara and me and tries to make the donkey go. . . . in the evenings plays tennis with Clara and me and amuses Jean and the donkey." [1]

But that was a Susy's-eye view of the matter. Summers at Quarry Farm, Mark Twain spent most of his days writing in his "study on the hill." This was an octangular cottage, high enough for him to see for many miles, wreathed with wild flowers outside and tobacco smoke inside.

The most beautiful Clemens' cat must have been either Tammany "much the handsomest cat on this planet" or "Stray Kit, the slender, the graceful, the sociable, the beautiful, the incomparable, cat of cats, the tortoise-shell." But Sour Mash had most of the kind of character Mark Twain liked most. She was "just to her friends and unjust to her enemies" and "righteously entitled" to the compliment of a neighboring farmer: " 'Other Christians is always worrying about other people's opinions, but Sour Mash don't give a damn.' " And Mark Twain adds: "Indeed, she was just that independent of criticism and I think it was her supreme grace." [2]

This selection comes from the section of Mark Twain's *Autobiography* published in *The North American Review,* April 5, 1907.

FROM SUSY'S BIOGRAPHY OF ME

Papa says that if the collera comes here he will take Sour Mash to the mountains.

This remark about the cat is followed by various entries . . . then Susy drops this remark . . . :

Sour Mash is a constant source of anxiety, care, and pleasure to papa.

I did, in truth, think a great deal of that old tortoise-shell harlot; but I haven't a doubt that in order to impress Susy I was pretending agonies of solicitude which I didn't honestly feel. Sour Mash never gave me any real anxiety; she was always able to take care of herself, and she was ostentatiously vain of the fact; vain of it to a degree which often made me ashamed of her, much as I esteemed her.

Many persons would like to have the society of cats during the summer vacation in the country, but they deny themselves this pleasure because they think they must either take the cats along when they return to the city, where they would be a trouble and an encumbrance, or leave them in the country, houseless and homeless. These people have no ingenuity, no invention, no wisdom; or it would occur to them to do as I do: rent cats by the month for the summer and return them to their good homes at the end of it. Early last May I rented a kitten of a farmer's wife, by the month; then I got a discount by taking three. They have been good company for about five months now, and are still kittens—at least they have not grown much, and to all intents and purposes are still kittens, and as full of romping energy and enthusiasm as they were in the beginning. This is remarkable. I am an expert in cats, but I have not seen a kitten keep its kittenhood nearly so long before.

These are beautiful creatures—these triplets. Two of them wear the blackest and shiniest and thickest of sealskin vestments all over their bodies except the lower half of their faces and the terminations of their paws. The black masks reach down below the eyes, therefore when the eyes are closed they are not visible; the rest of the face, and the gloves and stockings, are snow-white. These markings are just the same on both cats—so exactly the same that when you call one the other is likely to answer, because they cannot tell each other apart. Since the cats are precisely alike, and can't be told apart by any of us, they do not need two names, so they have but one between them. We call both of them Sackcloth, and we call the gray one Ashes. I believe I have never seen such intelligent cats as these before. They are full of the nicest discriminations. When I read German aloud they weep; you can see the tears run down. It shows what pathos there is in the German tongue. I had not noticed before that all German is pathetic, no matter what the subject is nor how it is treated. It was these humble observers that brought the knowledge to me. I have tried all kinds of German on these cats; romance, poetry, philosophy, theology, market reports; and the result has always been the same—the cats sob, and let the tears run down, which shows that all German is pathetic.[3] . . . Hardly any cats are affected by music, but these are; when I sing they go reverently away, showing how deeply they feel it. Sour Mash never cared for these things. She had many noble qualities, but at bottom she was not refined, and cared little or nothing for theology and the arts.

It is a pity to say it, but these cats are not above the grade of human beings, for I know by certain signs that they are not sincere in their exhibitions of emotion, but exhibit them merely to show off and attract attention—conduct which is distinctly human, yet with a difference: they do not know enough to conceal their desire to show off, but the grown human being does. What is ambition? It is only the desire to be conspicuous. The desire for fame is only the desire to be continuously conspicuous and attract attention and be talked about. . . .

These cats are like human beings in another way: when Ashes began to work his fictitious emotions, and show off, the other members of the firm followed suit, in order to be in the fashion.

From **Pudd'nhead Wilson**: When there was room on the ledge . . . for a cat, the cat was there—in sunny weather—stretched at full length, asleep and blissful, with her furry belly to the sun and a paw curled over her nose. Then that house was complete, and its contentment and peace were made manifest to the world by this symbol, whose testimony is infallible. A home without a cat—and a well-fed, well-petted, and properly revered cat—may be a perfect home, perhaps, but how can it prove title?

THE ADMIRAL AND THE CAT

This bit—I think it is a poem and not a story—comes from "The Refuge of the Derelicts," a Mark Twain story that was not published until 1972, when it appeared in *Mark Twain's Fables of Man.*[1] The background for this selection is that there is a poet whose name is George and who, for good reasons of his own, wants the friendship of a gentleman whose courtesy title is Admiral.

THE MEETING

George makes the worst possible first impression. Even his eye the Admiral considers "malignant." But then:

The cat came loafing in—just at the right time; the fortunate time. George forgot all about the Admiral, and cut his sentence off in the middle; for by birth and heredity he was a worshiper of cats, and when a fine animal of that species strays into the cat-lover's field of vision it is the one and only object the cat-lover is conscious of for one while; he can't take his eyes off it, nor his mind. The Admiral noted the admiration and the welcome in George's face, and . . . his own face relaxed, softened, sweetened, and became as the face of a mother whose child is being praised. George made a swift step, gathered the cat up in his arms, gave him a hug or two, then sat down and spread him out across his lap, and began to caress his silken body with lingering long strokes, murmuring, "Beautiful creature . . . wonderful creature!" and such things as that, the Admiral watching him with grateful eyes and a conquered heart. . . .

The caressing of the purring cat went on, its flexile body hanging over at both ends, its amber eyes blinking slowly and contentedly, its strong claws working in and out of the gloved paws in unutterable satisfaction, the pearl-lined ears taking in the murmured ecstasies of the stranger and understanding them perfectly and deeply approving them, the Admiral looking on enchanted, moist-eyed, soaked to the bone with happiness.

From Mark Twain's *Notebook* : Of all God's creatures there is only one that cannot be made the slave of the lash. That one is the cat. If man could be crossed with the cat, it would improve man, but it would deteriorate the cat.

LITERARY TRIBUTE

When Rudyard Kipling was still unknown, and only twenty-four, he made a pilgrimage to Elmira, New York, especially to meet Mark Twain. They talked for more than two hours, and Kipling reported every detail to his friends in India:

"Once, indeed, he put his hand on my shoulder. It was an investiture of the Star of India, blue silk, trumpets, and diamond-studded jewel, all complete. If hereafter, in the changes and chances of this mortal life, I fall to cureless ruin, I will tell the superintendent of the workhouse that Mark Twain once put his hand on my shoulder; and he shall give me a room to myself and a double allowance of paupers' tobacco." [2]

The Admiral's homage to Kipling is not so fine as that, but Kipling might also have preferred it to the Star of India. For the cat is called Bags. That's short for Bagheera, the Admiral tells the poet. And goes on:

"Here she is," he said, "Kipling. Volume VII. Collected Works. Immortal?"

"It's the right word, Admiral, in my opinion."

"You bet you! It'll outlast the rocks. Now I'm going to read to you out of this book. You look at the cat and listen: 'A black shadow dropped down into the circle. It was Bagheera the Black

Panther, inky black all over'—*now notice, keep your eye on the cat*—'inky black all over, but with the panther markings showing up in certain lights like the pattern of watered silk.' There . . . ain't he watered silk? Look at his highlights—look at his twilights—look at his deep glooms! Now you listen again: 'He had a voice as soft as wild honey dripping from a tree, and a skin softer than down.' *Bags!*"

The cat raised a sleepy head, and delivered an inquiring look from a blinking eye.

"Speak!"

The cat uttered a quivery-silvery mew.

"You hear that? Is it soft as wild honey dripping from a tree?"

Mark Twain, in his old age, writing to his daughter Jean: This morning I saw a splendid blue-and-white shuttle sail across the sunny air, and guessed it was one of my favorites, the blue jay. Danbury [a Clemens cat] saw it too, and started indolently away with an air intended to make me think he was going to church, but I am used to that look of his, and know all about it. If he comes back with feathers in his mouth, he will be bound over for trial till you come.

TO BAGS

Cat-worship continues to everybody's satisfaction, including Bags's, until the Admiral produces pictures of his idol. Then Bags is bored, and "flirts" them off the table with his paw. The Admiral cheerfully returns to talk. It is not his intention to teach the poet about poetry, but this is what he says:

". . . look at him! *Ain't* he the very blackest object that ever cast a gloom in the daytime? Do you know, he's just solid midnight-black all over, from cutwater to tip-end of spanker-boom. Except that he's got a faint and delicate little fringe of white hairs on his breast, which you can't find at all except when the light strikes them just right. . . . Black? Why, you know, Satan looks faded alongside of Bags."

"Is that—"

"Look at him *now!* Velvet—satin—sealskin; can't you pick them out on him? Notice that brilliant sheen all down his for-rard starboard paw, and a flesh of it in the hollow of his side,

and another one on his flank: is it satin or *ain't* it?—just you answer me that!"

"It *is.* . . ."

"Right you are. Now then, look at that port shoulder, where
the light don't strike direct—sort of twilight as you may say:
does it precisely counterfeit imperial Lyons velvet, forty dollars
a yard, or *don't* it; come!"

"It does. . . ."

"The thickest fur and the softest you ever s— there! catch it in
the shadow! in the deep shadow, under his chin—ain't it sealskin, *ain't* it?. . . . *Say!* look at him now. He's just perfect now;
wait till he gets through with that comfortable long summer-
Sunday-afternoon stretch and curls his paw around his nose,
then you'll see something. You'll *never* know how black he is,
nor how big and splendid and trim-built he is till he puts on his
accent. . . . Th-there it is—just the wee tip of his pink tongue
showing between his lips—now he's *all* there—sheen and gloom
and twilight—satin, sealskin, velvet—! and the tip of his tongue
like a fire-coal to accent him, just the blackest black outlay this
side of the sub-cellars of perdition—now I ask you honest, *ain't*
he?"

The poet granted it, and poured out . . . rapture upon rapture, from his sincere soul, closing with—

"He *is* the last possibility of the beautiful!"

From No. 44, *The Mysterious Stranger* : In her triumph and delight
[the cat] tried to clap her hands, but it was a failure, they wouldn't clap
any more than mushrooms.

A Cat-Tale

Not even Mark Twain could have told this story impromptu, to his
children or to anyone else; in fact, we have his notes for the written
version. But he may have begun one like it a thousand times. For on
the shelf next to the mantelpiece, in the Hartford house, there was a
painting of a cat's head. And the children's rules for storytelling were
strict: Papa had to begin with the cat picture and then include in the

story all fifteen pieces of bric-a-brac and three pictures that were on the shelves and mantelpiece in that room in order: "It was not permissible to introduce a bric-a-brac ornament into the story out of its place in the procession."

He had other problems: "In Paris, when my day's writing, on the 6th floor, was done, I used to slip quietly into our parlor on the 2nd floor, hoping to have a rest and a smoke on the sofa before dinner." But the children usually discovered him. If it was Clara, she would call: " 'Susy, come!—going to have a story!' Without any remark to me, she would go and get a magazine, perch herself on the chair-arm, seek out a suggestive picture (Susy taking perch on the other arm, meantime) . . . .

"The tough part of it was, that every detail of the story . . . must *fit the picture*. . . . Their selections were pretty odd, too, sometimes. For instance, in the back part of a 'Scribner's Monthly' they once found an outline figure . . . of the human frame. . . . The chances of getting anything romantic, adventurous, and heroic out of so sterile a text as that, seemed so remote, that I tried to divert them to a more promising picture; but no, none but this one would answer. So I bent myself to my task; and made such a thrilling and rattling success of it that I was rewarded with the privilege of digging a brand-new story out of that barren text during the next *five ensuing evenings*."

Still further: "In all my inventions for the children . . . any villains *must not lie*. This hampered me a good deal. The blacker and bloodier and viler I painted the villain . . . the more the children delighted in him, until he made the mistake of telling a lie—then . . . he simply ad to pack up and go; his character was damaged beyond help, the ildren wouldn't have him around. . . .

"They did not get this prejudice from me." [1]

They got good children's stories, though. That unfortunate outline re, Mark Twain said, was drowned and hanged and fed to the cats 's and "pitted against giants and genii" and "adventure under- h fairyland."

e really tell his children "A Cat-Tale"? Could any njoy it? If he'd told it, would results have been any r Clara remembered the real storytelling?—in t d house, where she sat on his lap with Susy (Jea the colored butler, George, interrupted the tale or a meal . . . our hearts sank and did not ri the tales." [2]

He said that he told it. But he also said that he could remember anything, "whether it happened or not."

A "Cat-Tale" first appeared in 1962, in the book *Letters from the Earth,* a collection of hitherto unpublished Mark Twain.

My little girls—Susy, aged eight, and Clara, six—often require me to help them go to sleep, nights, by telling them original tales. They think my tales are better than paregoric, and quicker. While I talk, they make comments and ask questions, and we have a pretty good time. I thought maybe other little people might like to try one of my narcotics—so I offer this one.

—M.T.

Once there was a noble big cat, whose Christian name was Cata-sauqua—because she lived in that region—but she did not have any surname, because she was a short-tailed cat—being a Manx—and did not need one. It is very just and becoming in a long-tailed cat to have a surname, but it would be very ostentatious, and even dishonorable, in a Manx. Well, Catasauqua had a beautiful family of catlings; and they were of different colors, to harmonize with their characters. Cattaraugus, the eldest, was white, and he had high impulses and a pure heart; Catiline, the youngest, was black, and he had a self-seeking nature, his motives were nearly always base, he was truculent and insincere. He was vain and foolish, and often said he would rather be what he was, and live like a bandit, yet have none above him, than be a cat-o'-nine-tails and eat with the King. He hated his harmless and unoffending little catercousins, and frequently drove them from his presence with imprecations, and at times even resorted to violence.

Susy: What are catercousins, Papa?

Quarter-cousins—it is so set down in the big dictionary. You observe I refer to it every now and then. This is because I do wish to make any mistakes, my purpose being to instruct as as entertain. Whenever I use a word which you do not stand, speak up and I will look and find out what it me do not interrupt me except for cause, for I am alway when I am erecting history, and want to get on. W Catasauqua met with a misfortune; her house bu was the very day after it had been insured for able it too—how singular! Yes, and how lucky! This often happens. It teaches us that mere loading a house down with insurance isn't going to save it. Very well, Catasauqua took the insurance money and built a new house; and a much better one, too; and what is more, she had money left to add a gaudy concatenation of extra improvements with. Oh, I tell you! What she didn't know about catallactics no other cat need ever try to acquire.

CLARA: What is catallactics, Papa?

The dictionary intimates, in a nebulous way, that it is a sort of demi-synonym for the science commonly called political economy.

CLARA: Thank you, Papa.

Yes, behind the house she constructed a splendid large catadrome, and enclosed it with a caterwaul about nine feet high, and in the center was a spacious grass plot where—

CLARA: What is a catadrome, Papa?

I will look. Ah, it is a race course; I thought it was a ten-pin alley. But no matter; in fact, it is all the better; for cats do not play ten-pins, when they are feeling well, but they *do* run races, you know; and the spacious grass plot was for cat fights, and other free exhibitions; and for ball games—three-cornered cat, and all that sort of thing; a lovely spot, lovely. Yes, indeed; it had a hedge of dainty little catkins around it, and right in the center was a splendid great categorematic in full leaf, and—

SUSY: What is a categorematic, Papa?

I think it's a kind of a shade tree, but I'll look. No—I was mistaken; it is a *word:* "a word which is capable of being employed by itself as a term."

SUSY: Thank you, Papa.

Don't mention it. Yes, you see, it wasn't a shade tree; the good Catasauqua didn't know that, else she wouldn't have planted it right there in the way; you can't run over a word like that, you know, and not cripple yourself more or less. Now don't forget that definition, it may come handy to you someday— there is no telling—life is full of vicissitudes. Always remember, a categorematic is a word which a cat can use by herself as a term; but she mustn't try to use it along with another cat, for that is not the idea. Far from it. We have authority for it, you see—Mr. Webster; and he is dead, too, besides. It would be a noble good thing if his dictionary was, too. But that is too much to expect. Yes; well, Catasauqua filled her house with internal improvements—catcalls in every room, and they are Oh, ever so much handier than bells; and catamounts to mount the stairs with, instead of those troublesome elevators which are always getting out of order; and civet cats in the kitchen, in place of the ordinary sieves, which you can't ever sift anything with, in a satisfactory way; and a couple of tidy ash cats to clean out the stove and keep it in order; and—catenated on the roof—an alert and cultivated polecat to watch the flagpole and keep the banner a-flying. Ah, yes—such was Catasauqua's country residence; and she named it Kamscatka—after her dear native land far away.

CLARA: What is catenated, Papa?

Chained, my child. The polecat was attached by a chain to some object upon the roof contiguous to the flagpole. This was to retain him in his position.

CLARA: Thank you, Papa.

The front garden was a spectacle of sublime and bewildering magnificence. A stately row of flowering catalpas stretched from the front door clear to the gate, wreathed from stem to stern with the delicate tendrils and shining scales of the cat's-foot ivy, whilst ever and anon the enchanted eye wandered from congeries of lordly cattails and kindred catapetalous blooms too deep for utterance, only to encounter the still more entrancing vision of catnip without number and without price, and swoon away in ecstasy unutterable, under the blissful intoxication of its too, too fragrant breath!

BOTH CHILDREN: Oh, how lovely!

You may well say it. Few there be that shall look upon the like again. Yet was not this all; for hither to the north boiled the majestic cataract in unimaginable grandiloquence, and thither to the south sparkled the gentle catadupe in serene and incandescent tranquillity, whilst far and near the halcyon brooklet flowed between!

BOTH CHILDREN: Oh, how sweet! What is a catadupe, Papa?

Small waterfall, my darlings. Such is Webster's belief. All things being in readiness for the housewarming, the widow sent out her invitations, and then proceeded with her usual avocations. For Catasauqua was a widow—sorrow cometh to us all. The husband-cat—Catullus was his name—was no more. He was of a lofty character, brave to rashness, and almost incredibly unselfish. He gave eight of his lives for his country, reserving only one for himself. Yes, the banquet having been ordered, the good Catasauqua tuned up for the customary morning-song, accompanying herself on the catarrh, and her little ones joined in. These were the words:

> There was a little cat,
> And she caught a little rat,
> Which she dutifully rendered to her mother,
> Who said "Bake him in a pie,
> For his flavor's rather high—
> Or confer him on the poor, if you'd druther."

Catasauqua sang soprano, Catiline sang tenor, Cattaraugus sang bass. It was exquisite melody; it would make your hair stand right up.

SUSY: Why, Papa, I didn't know cats could sing.

Oh, can't they, though! Well, these could. Cats are packed full of music—just as full as they can hold; and when they die, people remove it from them and sell it to the fiddle-makers. Oh, yes indeed. Such is Life.

SUSY: Oh, here is a picture! Is it a picture of the music, Papa?

Only the eye of prejudice could doubt it, my child.

SUSY: Did you draw it, Papa?

I am indeed the author of it.

SUSY: How wonderful! What is a picture like this called, Papa?

A work of art, my child. There—do not hold it so close; prop it up on the chair, *three steps away;* now then—that is right; you see how much better and stronger the expression is than when it is close by. It is because some of this picture is drawn in perspective.

CLARA: Did you always know how to draw, Papa?

Yes. I was born so. But of course I could not draw at first as well as I can now. These things require study—and practice. Mere talent is not sufficient. It takes a person a long time to get so he can draw a picture like this. [See following page—ED.]

CLARA: How long did it take you, Papa?

Many years—thirty years, I reckon. Off and on—for I did not devote myself exclusively to art. Still, I have had a great deal of

practice. Ah, practice is the great thing! It accomplishes wonders. Before I was twenty-five, I had got so I could draw a cork
as well as anybody that ever was. And many a time I have
drawn a blank in a lottery. Once I drew a check that wouldn't
go; and after the war I tried to draw a pension, but this was too
ambitious. However, the most gifted must fail sometimes. Do
you observe those things that are sticking up, in this picture?
They are not bones, they are paws; it is very hard to express the
difference between bones and paws, in a picture.

SUSY: Which is Cattaraugus, Papa?

The little pale one that almost has the end of his mother's tail
in his mouth.

SUSY: But, Papa, that tail is not right. You know Catasauqua
was a Manx, and had a short one.

It is a just remark, my child; but a long tail was necessary,
here, to express a certain passion, the passion of joy. Therefore
the insertion of a long tail is permissible; it is called a poetic li-
cense. You cannot express the passion of joy with a short tail.
Nor even extraordinary excitement. You notice that Cattaraugus
is brilliantly excited; now nearly all of that verve, spirit, e´lan, is
owing to his tail; yet if I had been false to art to be true to Nature, you would see there nothing but a poor little stiff and emo-

tionless stump on that cat that would have cast a coldness over the whole scene; yet Cattaraugus was a Manx, like his mother, and had hardly any more tail than a rabbit. Yes, in art, the office of the tail is to express feeling; so, if you wish to portray a cat in repose, you will always succeed better by leaving out the tail. Now here is a striking illustration of the very truth which I am trying to impress upon you. I proposed to draw a cat recumbent and in repose; but just as I had finished the front end of her, she got up and began to gaze passionately at a bird and wriggle her tail in a most expressively wistful way. I had to finish her with that end standing, and the other end lying. It greatly injures the picture. For, you see, it confuses two passions together—the passion of standing up, and the passion of lying down. These are incompatible; and they convey a bad effect to the picture by rendering it unrestful to the eye. In my opinion a cat in a picture ought to be doing one thing or the other, lying down or standing up, but not both. I ought to have laid this one down again, and put a brick or something on her; but I did not think of it at the time. Let us now separate these conflicting passions in this cat, so that you can see each by itself, and the more easily study it. Lay your hand on the picture, to where I have made those dots, and cover the rear half of it from sight—now you observe how reposeful the front end is. Very well; now lay your hand on the front end and cover *it* from sight—do you observe the eager wriggle in that tail? It is a wriggle which only the presence of a bird can inspire.

Susy: You must know a wonderful deal, Papa.

I have that reputation—in Europe; but here the best minds think I am superficial. However, I am content; I make no defense; my pictures show what I am.

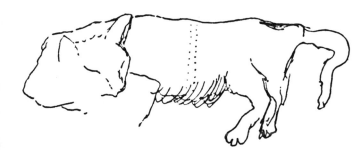

SUSY: Papa, I should think you would take pupils.

No, I have no desire for riches. Honest poverty and a conscience torpid through virtuous inaction are more to me than corner lots and praise.

But to resume. The morning-song being over, Catasauqua told Catiline and Cattaraugus to fetch their little books, and she would teach them how to spell.

BOTH CHILDREN: Why, Papa! Do cats have books?

Yes, catechisms. Just so. Facts are stubborn things. After the lesson, Catasauqua gave Catiline and Cattaraugus some rushes, so that they could earn a little circus-money by building cat's cradles, and at the same time amuse themselves and not miss her; then she went to the kitchen and dining room to inspect the preparations for the banquet.

The moment her back was turned, Catiline put down his work and got out his catpipe for a smoke.

SUSY: Why, how naughty!

Thou hast well spoken. It was disobedience; and disobedience is the flagship of the fleet of sin. The gentle Cattaraugus sighed and said: "For shame, Catiline! How often has our dear mother told you not to do that! Ah, how can you thus disregard the commandments of the author of your being?"

SUSY: Why, what beautiful language, for such a little thing, *wasn't* it, Papa?

Ah, yes, indeed. That was the kind of cat he was—cultivated, you see. He had sat at the feet of Rollo's mother; and in the able "Franconia Series" * he had not failed to observe how harmoniously gigantic language and a microscopic topic go together. Catiline heard his brother through, and then replied with the contemptuous ejaculation: "S'scat!"

It means the same that Shakespeare means when he says, "Go to." Nevertheless, Catiline's conscience was not at rest. He murmured something about where was the harm, since his mother would never know? But Cattaraugus said, sweetly but sadly, "Alas, if we but do the right under restaint of authoritative observance, where then is the merit?"

SUSY: How *good* he was!

* The Franconia and Rollo Series, improving children's books by Jacob Abbott, were read to the children by their mother—ED.

Monumentally so. The more we contemplate his character, the more sublime it appears. But Catiline, who was coarse and worldly, hated all lofty sentiments, and especially such as were stated in choice and lofty terms; he wished to resent this one, yet compelled himself to hold his peace; but when Cattaraugus said it over again, partly to enjoy the sound of it, but mainly for his brother's good, Catiline lost his patience, and said, "Oh, take a walk!"

Yet he still felt badly; for he knew he was doing wrong. He began to pretend he did not know it was against the rule to smoke his catpipe; but Cattaraugus, without an utterance, lifted an accusing paw toward the wall, where, among the illuminated mottoes, hung this one:

NO SMOKING. STRICTLY PROHIBITED.

Catiline turned pale; and, murmuring in a broken voice, "I am undone—forgive me, Brother," laid the fatal catpipe aside and burst into tears.

CLARA: Poor thing! It was cruel, *wasn't* it, Papa?

SUSY: Well, but he oughtn't to done so, in the first place. Cattaraugus wasn't to blame.

CLARA: Why, *Susy!* If Catiline didn't *know* he wasn't allowed—

SUSY: Catiline did know it—Cattaraugus told him so; and besides, Catiline—

CLARA: Cattaraugus only told Catiline that if—

SUSY: Why, *Clara!* Catiline didn't *need* for Cattaraugus to say one single—

Oh, hold on! It's all a mistake! Come to look in the dictionary, we are proceeding from false premises. The Unabridged says a catpipe is "a squeaking instrument used in play-houses to condemn plays." So you see it wasn't a pipe to smoke, after all; Catiline *couldn't* smoke it; therefore it follows that he was simply pretending to smoke it, to stir up his brother, that's all.

SUSY: But, Papa, Catiline might as well smoke as stir up his brother.

CLARA: Susy, you don't like Catiline, and so whatever he does, it don't suit you, it ain't right; and he is only a little fellow, anyway.

SUSY: I don't *approve* of Catiline, but I *like* him well enough; I only say—

CLARA: What is approve?

SUSY: Why, it's as if you did something, and I said it was all right. So *I* think he might as well smoke as stir up his brother. Isn't it so, Papa?

Looked at from a strictly mathematical point of view, I don't know, but it *is* a case of six-in-one-and-half-a-dozen-in-the-other. Still, *our* business is mainly with the historical facts; if we only get *them* right, we can leave posterity to take care of the moral aspects of the matter. To resume the thread of the narrative, when Cattaraugus saw that Catiline had not been smoking at all, but had only been making believe, and this too with the avowed object of fraternal aggravation, he was deeply hurt; and by his heat was beguiled into recourse to that bitter weapon, sarcasm; saying, "The Roman Catiline would have betrayed his foe; it was left to the Catasauquian to refine upon the model and betray his friend."

"Oh, a gaudy speech!—and very erudite and swell!" retorted Catiline, derisively, "but just a *little* catachrestic."

SUSY: What is catachrestic, Papa?

"Farfetched," the dictionary says. The remark stung Cattaraugus to the quick, and he called Catiline a catapult; this infuriated Catiline beyond endurance, and he threw down the gauntlet and called Cattaraugus a catso. No cat will stand that; so at it they went. They spat and clawed and fought until they dimmed away and finally disappeared in a flying fog of cat fur.

CLARA: What is a catso, Papa?

"A base fellow, a rogue, a cheat," says the dictionary. When the weather cleared, Cattaraugus, ever ready to acknowledge a fault, whether committed by himself or another, said, "I was wrong, brother—forgive me. A cat may err—to err is cattish; but toward even a foreigner, even a wildcat, a catacaustic remark is in ill taste; how much more so, then, when a brother is the target! Yes, Catiline, I was wrong; I deeply regret the circumstance. Here is my hand—let us forget the dark o'erclouded past in the bright welkin of the present, consecrating ourselves anew to its nobler lessons, and sacrificing ourselves yet again, and forever if need be, to the thrice-armed beacon that binds them in one!"

SUSY: He was a splendid talker, *wasn't* he, Papa? Papa, what is catacaustic?

Well, a catacaustic remark is a bitter, malicious remark—a

sort of a—sort of—or a kind of a—well, let's look in the dictionary; that is cheaper. Oh, yes, here it is: "CATACAUSTIC, *n.*, a caustic curve formed by reflection of light." Oh, yes, that's it.

SUSY: Well, Papa, what does *that* mean?

From "A Horse's Tale": Dogmatics is quite beyond me, quite; so I am not competing.

CHRONOLOGY OF MARK TWAIN'S LIFE

I have not tried to include in this outline the dates on which Mark Twain published all the various items of the massive literature he left us. Nor have I included dates on all his wanderings, for he shuttled freely across the ocean, visited every continent except South America, and spent more than a third of his life abroad.

November 30, 1835   Samuel Langhorne Clemens, who is to become Mark Twain, is born in Florida, Missouri.

1839   The Clemenses move to Hannibal, Missouri, a town on the Mississippi where Samuel Clemens is raised, and which he is to use repeatedly as literary material.

1847   Sam's father, Judge John Marshall Clemens, dies; Sam quits school.

1848   Becomes apprenticed to a local printer.

1851   Goes to work for his older brother, Orion Clemens, who has bought a local newspaper that does not thrive.

1853   Leaves home and works as a traveling printer in New York, Philadelphia, and St. Louis.

1855   Rejoins Orion in Keokuk, Iowa, to work on another failing newspaper.

1856   More wandering as a printer; meets Macfarlane in Cincinnati.

1856   Finds a fifty-dollar bill on the street and sets off with it to make his fortune in cocoa, on the upper Amazon.

1857   Bound for the Amazon, on a steamboat to New Orleans, decides to become a steamboat pilot. Pilot Horace Bixby agrees to teach him piloting for five hundred dollars, which Clemens borrows.

1857–58   Works as an apprentice pilot.

1859–60   Is a crack Mississippi pilot.

1861   The Civil War breaks out and Clemens is uncertain in his allegiance; finally joins some Hannibal boys to form a Confederate battalion; deserts that after two weeks.

1861   Accompanies Orion, on a mail coach, to Carson City, Nevada; Orion, an abolitionist, has been appointed Territorial Secretary there by the Lincoln administration. Out West collects material for *Roughing It*, which is written in 1871 and published in 1872.

1861–62   Prospects for gold and silver; writes unsolicited and unpaid material for Nevada's chief newspaper, the *Territorial Enterprise*.

1862   Fails as a prospector; goes to work for the *Territorial Enterprise* for twenty-five dollars a week.

1862–64   Works happily as a feature writer on the *Enterprise*; acquires fame in the West and the name Mark Twain.

1864   Illegally challenges another newspaperman to a duel and has to leave the state. Goes to work as a reporter for the San Francisco *Morning Call*; dislikes work.

1864–65   Becomes involved in a feud with the San Francisco police and hides from them in Jackass Hill, California, with Jim Gillis and a colony of other pocket-miners. There he hears the "Jumping Frog" and "Blue Jay" stories.

1866   Is sent to Hawaii to write "travel letters" for the Sacramento *Union*. On his return "lectures" successfully on Hawaii. Thereafter "lectures" intermittently all his life.

1867   Sent by the *Alta California* to cover the "pleasure cruise" of the *Quaker City*, bound for Europe and the Holy Land. Sends back "travel letters."

1868   Acts as correspondent in Washington for various newspapers.

1869   Publishes *The Innocents Abroad*, his first international best-seller, which is based on his "travel letters" much changed and expanded.

1870   Marries Olivia Langdon of Elmira, New York; sets up housekeeping in Buffalo; buys into and edits the Buffalo *Express*. Son, Langdon, prematurely born.

1871   Moves to Hartford, Connecticut; eventually builds his own house there.

1872   Langdon Clemens dies and a daughter, Susan Olivia, is born.

1874   Daughter Clara is born.

1880   Daughter Jean is born.

1881   Ex-printer Clemens begins to become emotionally, intellectually, and financially involved with a mechanical typesetter invented by James W. Paige, an obsessive genius who spends years improving on it. In the ten years before Mark Twain gives up the machine, he loses $190,000 on it.

1884   Starts his own publishing house, Webster & Co., with his nephew, Charles Webster, in charge. Among other things it publishes *Huckleberry Finn* (1884) and Grant's *Personal Memoirs* (1885).

1893   National economic depression and the beginning of Mark Twain's financial troubles.

1894   Meets Standard Oil executive, Henry H. Rogers, who begins straightening out his financial affairs.

1896   Rather than go into bankruptcy, sets off on a paying lecture tour around the world. The trip is a financial success and provides material for *Following the Equator*, which is published in 1897. He is still in London when his daughter Susy dies of spinal meningitis in Hartford.

1903   Doctors recommend that Mrs. Clemens go to Italy for her health; the family moves to Florence.

1904   Death of Mrs. Clemens.
1909   Death of Jean Clemens.
April 21, 1910   Mark Twain dies of heart disease in Stormfield, his home
near Redding, Connecticut.

NOTES AND REFERENCES

EXPLANATION OF REFERENCES

The Mark Twain material quoted in my notes is generally not referenced—primarily, because to have done so would have been to pockmark my pages so that the reader would have been more distracted than helped. In addition, Mark Twain's work is available in so many editions that it is difficult to give helpful pages references. I have made some exceptions, referencing Mark Twain material where the source was especially obscure or when I needed to credit other scholars.

About three-fourths of Mark Twain's *Autobiography* has, at one time or another, been in print, although it is not so now. The complete manuscript will in time be released by The Mark Twain Papers. I have quoted from the following out-of-print sources:

Sections of Mark Twain's *Autobiography*, which he published before his death, in the *North American Review*.

Mark Twain's Autobiography, the sections edited by Albert Bigelow Paine, P. F. Collier and Son Co., New York, 1925.

Mark Twain in Eruption—sections edited by Bernard DeVoto, Harper & Brothers, New York and London, 1940.

Another version, *The Autobiography of Mark Twain*, edited by Charles Neider and published by Harper & Brothers in 1959, has not been used. This version attempted to arrange pieces of his *Autobiography* chronologically—in violation of Mark Twain's instructions.

Other abbreviations are:

Letters–Mark Twain's Letters, edited by A. B. Paine, Harper & Brothers, New York and London, 1917.

Notebook–Mark Twain's Notebook, edited by A. B. Paine, Harper & Brothers, New York and London, 1935.

Brooks, original—This is Van Wyck Brooks's *The Ordeal of Mark Twain* as it originally appeared in 1920 and made its impact on Mark Twain criticism. The text was substantially changed in 1933, when Bernard DeVoto's *Mark Twain's America*, which exposed many misstatements in Brooks, was known to be forthcoming.

Brooks—Van Wyck Brooks, *The Ordeal of Mark Twain*, Meridian Books, New York, 1955.

When critical material quoted is available in an anthology of critical essays, I have added that reference. Abbreviations for the anthologies are:

Scott—Mark Twain: Selected Criticism, edited by Arthur L. Scott, Southern Methodist University Press, Dallas, 1955.

Leary—Mark Twain's Wound, edited by Lewis Leary, Thomas Y. Crowell Co., New York, 1962.

Smith—Mark Twain: A Collection of Critical Essays, edited by Henry Nash Smith, Prentice-Hall, Englewood Cliffs, New Jersey, 1963.

The source to which I am most indebted is Albert Bigelow Paine's great three-volume *Mark Twain: A Biography,* published by Harper & Brothers, 1912, and referred to as *Paine.* I am also indebted to numerous modern scholars who have enlarged or amended Paine's work, although not all of them could be mentioned in my notes. I owe a special debt to Caroline Thomas Harnsberger, whose *Mark Twain's Views of Religion,* published by the Schori Press in 1961, supplied many of the marginal notes that Mark Twain made in his books, some of which I have quoted.

NOTES ON THE SELECTIONS

INTRODUCTION

1. W. D. Howells, *My Mark Twain* (New York and London, Harper & Brothers, 1910), p. 181.
2. The attack began January 18, 1967, in *The New York Review of Books,* with Lewis Mumford's criticism of the scholarly edition of Emerson. Edmund Wilson then took up the theme in the same publication and various critics wrote letters in his support. In 1968 Wilson's articles were republished, with slight changes, by *The New York Review of Books* in a pamphlet entitled *The Fruits of the MLA* by Edmund Wilson. The pamphlet is the source I'm using.
   The other eight people who endorsed Mr. Wilson's views were Marius Bewley, Van Wyck Brooks, Alfred Kazin, Norman Holmes Pearson, John Crowe Ransom, Allen Tate, Lionel Trilling, and Robert Penn Warren. The lone dissenter was the late Perry Miller, a professor of American literature at Harvard.
3. Edmund Wilson, *The Fruits of the MLA,* p. 35.
4. Edmund Wilson, *The Fruits of the MLA,* p. 25.
5. Alfred Kazin, *On Native Grounds* (New York, Reynal & Hitchcock, 1942), pp. 400–401.
6. Granville Hicks, *The Great Tradition* (New York, The Macmillan Co., 1933), p. 43; *Scott,* p. 218.
7. Charles Compton, *Who Reads What?* (New York, The H. W. Wilson Co., 1934). This work is based on a survey conducted in five geographically scattered public libraries.

8. An exception is critic Maxwell Geismar's *Mark Twain: An American Prophet* (Boston, Houghton Mifflin Co., 1970). Although I do not agree with many of the judgments and theories in this book, it does include warm appreciation of much of Mark Twain's work.
9. Edmund Wilson, *The Fruits of the MLA*, p. 33.
10. Van Wyck Brooks, *America's Coming of Age* (New York, Doubleday Anchor Books, 1958), p. 154.
11. "The Function of Criticism at the Present Time," *Matthew Arnold's Essays* (London and New York, J. M. Dent and Sons, Ltd., 1954).
12. Katherine Buxbaum, "Mark Twain and the American Dialect," *American Speech*, February, 1927.
13. Harvey O'Higgins and Edward H. Reede, *The American Mind in Action* (New York and London, Harper & Brothers, 1924), p. 284.
14. Lewis Mumford, *The Golden Day* (New York, Boni & Liveright, 1926), p. 176; *Scott*, p. 186.
15. Theodore Dreiser, "Mark the Double Twain," *English Journal*, October, 1935; *Leary*, p. 155.
16. Leslie Fiedler, *Love and Death in the American Novel* (New York, Criterion Books, 1960), p. 560; *Leary*, p. 284.
17. Dwight Macdonald, "Mark Twain: An Unsentimental Journey," *The New Yorker*, April 6, 1960, p. 177.
18. Lewis Leary, *Mark Twain's Wound* (New York, Thomas Y. Crowell Co., 1962), p. 19.
19. Alfred Kazin, *On Native Grounds* (New York, Reynal & Hitchcock, 1942), p. 284; *Leary*, p. 19. "The Gilded Age" was Mark Twain's name for his own times and the title of a novel he wrote in collaboration with Charles Dudley Warner. The term is still widely used by historians and literary men. Clemens' second literary executor, the scholarly Bernard DeVoto, proved in *Mark Twain's America* (Boston, Little, Brown & Co., 1932) that Brooks's picture of those times was wildly inaccurate; this is now conceded even by critics who still find Brooks's "legend" valuable.
20. V. S. Pritchett, "Books in General," *New Statesman and Nation*, August 2, 1941.

FRIENDS AND RELATIONS

1. W. D. Howells, *My Mark Twain* (New York and Boston, Harper & Brothers, 1910), p. 7.
2. W. D. Howells, *My Mark Twain*, p. 4.
3. According to his biographer, Albert Bigelow Paine, Mark Twain said years later that in 1866 he put a loaded gun to his head but lacked courage to squeeze the trigger (*Paine*, p. 291). However, this despair came at the end of his Western and Hawaiian adventures, when he thought he was doomed forever to be a San Francisco newspaperman. For details see my preface to "Hawaiian Holiday," pp. 88–89.

4. *Brooks, original edition,* p. 73.
5. Mark Twain's letter to his sister-in-law, on his brother's death, quoted by DeLancey Ferguson in *Mark Twain: Man and Legend* (Indianapolis and New York, Bobbs-Merrill Co., 1943), Charter edition, p. 276.
6. *Brooks,* p. 139.
7. W. D. Howells, *My Mark Twain,* p. 169.

Bird of Birds

1. Quoted in Ralph Holmes, "Mark Twain and Music," *Century,* October, 1922.

The Tarantulas and the Brigade

1. *Paine,* p. 177.

Sailor Dog

1. *Which Was the Dream?,* edited by John S. Tuckey (Berkeley and Los Angeles, University of California Press, 1967). Originally published by the University of California Press; reprinted by permission of The Regents of the University of California.

Baker's Blue Jays

1. So Mark Twain's biographer, A. B. Paine, was told when he went out West to investigate (*Paine,* p. 264).
2. Paine, p. 264.

The Celebrated Jumping Frog of Calaveras County

The American Frog
1. Mark Twain's comments on the Greek frog mystery all come from *The Jumping Frog* (New York and London, Harper & Brothers, 1903).
The French Frog
1. Marie-Thérèse Blanc, "Les Humoristes Américains: I. Mark Twain," *Revue des Deux-Mondes,* July 15, 1872. (Blanc was the pen name for Madame Thérèse Bentzon.)
2. Madame Blanc in *Revue des Deux-Mondes,* July 15, 1872.
3. Eugène Forgues, "Les Caravanes d'un Humoriste: Mark Twain," *Revue des Deux-Mondes,* February 15, 1886.

Mule Race

1. Partly because of the attacks on Scott, there is a venerable critical tradition that the second volume of *Life on the Mississippi* is vulgar. But in 1960, when Scott was going out of style, critic Leslie Fiedler supplied a new twist; he said that Mark Twain only "affected to despise" Scott, but really imitated him. (Leslie Fiedler, *Love and Death in the American Novel* [New York, Criterion Books, 1960], p. 558; *Leary,* p. 282.)

2. George Harrison Orians, "Walter Scott, Mark Twain and the Civil War," *South Atlantic Quarterly,* October, 1941.

Camping Out

1. *Paine,* p. 184–185.
2. Mrs. Partington was the creation of B. P. Shillaber and is the American version of Mrs. Malaprop.

"My Dear Mother"

1. Jane Clemens' instructions quoted in Sam Clemens' reply to her letter. (*Letters,* p. 53.)
2. *Paine,* p. 185.
3. Billy C. and Gus were, respectively, lawyers Billy Clagget and A. W. Oliver. Fillon was the blacksmith, Mr. Ballou, in "Camping Out."
4. Kinnikinick was something the Indians smoked. Chief ingredients: dried sumach and dogwood bark. Mark Twain could smoke anything, although his preference, always, was for the cheapest cigars that money could buy. The *Carmina Sacra* was an American hymn book.
5. The two lawyers, according to Paine, really did as described. The Captain and the Colonel refer to Mr. Fillon, the blacksmith, and a Mr. Pfersdoff, who was going their way, and whom Paine describes as "a fat-witted, arrogant Prussian." (*Paine,* p. 186.) He appears as Ollendorf in other parts of *Roughing It.*

Adam and Eve and Kangaroorum Adamiensis

1. Howells to J. M. Comly; quoted in *Mark Twain—Howells Letters,* edited by Henry Nash Smith and William M. Gibson with the assistance of Frederick Anderson (Cambridge, Mass., Harvard University Press, 1960), Vol. I, p. 16.

AUTHORITIES

1. "Dr. Loeb's Incredible Discovery," *Europe and Elsewhere,* edited by A. B. Paine (New York and London, Harper & Brothers, 1923), pp. 305–306.
2. "A Horse's Tale," first published in *Harper's Magazine,* 1906.
3. "A Dog's Tale" first published in *Harper's Magazine,* 1903.
4. Darwin, *The Descent of Man,* Chapter 3.
5. *Brooks,* p. 35.
6. Tony Tanner, "The Lost America—The Despair of Henry Adams and Mark Twain," *Modern Age,* Summer, 1961; *Smith,* p. 171.
7. The occasion for this remark arose at a program of Authors' Readings in 1887. There Charles E. Norton, when introducing Mark Twain, said that Darwin had told him that "during those sleepless nights of weariness which followed his days of hard research he had always been accustomed to

amuse himself with the books of Mr. Clemens, and always kept them on a table by his bedside." Norton added a reference to Mark Twain's "syrup" and said, "Children cry for it." According to Howells, who was there, the introduction was not altogether happy and "a sort of blank ensued which Clemens filled in the only possible way." Clemens said that "some might shrink from accepting the anecdote as a compliment, but it had always struck him as a great one. If he had helped to put that great brain when weary to sleep, he was glad of it." *Mark Twain—Howells Letters*, edited by Henry Nash Smith and William M. Gibson with the assistance of Frederick Anderson (Cambridge, Mass., Harvard University Press, 1960), Vol. II, p. 589–590.

The Naturalist and the Ornithorhyncus

1. *The Galaxy,* November, 1870. This was a New York magazine for which Mark Twain conducted a department for about a year, beginning in May, 1870. There he invited readers to contribute samples of "hog-wash" and printed only the finest.
2. Quoted by Mark Twain in Chapter XXXVI of *Following the Equator.* It was his favorite Mrs. Moore.

Edison and the Animals

1. Justin Kaplan, *Mr. Clemens and Mark Twain* (New York, Simon and Schuster, 1966). On p. 340 Kaplan argues that Mark Twain's real motive for writing *What Is Man?* was "simple self-exoneration." On p. 347 he elaborates this thesis.

The President and the Nature Fakir

1. All quotations from the Roosevelt-Long battle come from William Henry Harbaugh, *Power and Responsibility, The Life and Times of Theodore Roosevelt* (New York, Farrar, Straus and Cudahy, 1961), pp. 308–309.
2. *The World of Mr. Dooley,* edited by Louis Filler (New York, Collier Books, 1962), "T.R." pp. 81–82.
3. In the Russo-Japanese War, when the Japanese destroyed the Russian fleet in 1905.
4. Mark Twain, writing in May, 1907, was mistaken. Roosevelt did not accept defeat, but reopened hostilities the following September.

THE JOY OF KILLING

1. Theodore Roosevelt, *The Strenuous Life* (New York, New York Review of Reviews Co., 1910).
2. Quoted in Howard K. Beale, *Theodore Roosevelt and the Rise of America to World Power* (New York, Collier Books, 1962), p. 48.
3. Quoted from Mark Twain's unpublished "A Family Sketch" in Caroline

Thomas Harnsberger, *Mark Twain, Family Man* (New York, The Citadel Press, 1960), pp. 37–38.

The President and the Cow

1. Howard K. Beale, *Theodore Roosevelt and the Rise of America to World Power* (New York, Collier Books, 1956), p. 50.

SERMONS

1. Mark Twain on Jerry and his teachings is in "Corn-Pone Opinions," first published in *Europe and Elsewhere*, edited by A. B. Paine (New York and London, Harper & Brothers, 1923).
2. This is a pervading theme of Brooks's *The Ordeal of Mark Twain;* see especially the first and last chapters.

The Lowest Animal

1. *Brooks,* p. 48.
2. Quoted in Caroline Thomas Harnsberger, *Mark Twain: Family Man* (New York, The Citadel Press, 1960), p. 113.

Reptiles

1. D. W. Brogan, "Clio, a Muse," *The New York Times Book Review,* February 14, 1965.

The Ways of Righteousness

1. Justin Kaplan, *Mr. Clemens and Mark Twain* (New York, Simon and Schuster, 1966), p. 52.
2. Louis J. Budd, *Mark Twain: Social Philosopher* (Bloomington, Ind., Indiana University Press, 1962), p. 26. Professor Budd bases his conclusion as to Mark Twain's hard-heartedness even more on a similar breakfast during this trip, during which starving people watched the Americans eat. Professor Budd would have liked, he said, "to explain away this hardness as masking [Mark Twain's] dispair over misery" but the evidence allowed no such interpretation.

Arab Steeds

1. Constance Rourke, *American Humor: A Study of the National Character* (Garden City, N.Y., Doubleday Anchor Books, 1931), p. 171.
2. Douglas Grant, *Mark Twain* (New York, Grove Press, 1962), p. 41.

Bashful Boy

1. Alexander E. Jones, "Mark Twain and Sexuality," *Publications of the Modern Language Association,* September, 1956; *Leary,* pp. 252, 254.

Royal Cats

1. Allen Guttmann, "Mark Twain's *Connecticut Yankee:* Affirmation of the Vernacular Tradition?" *The New England Quarterly,* June, 1960.

Swinks and Sooflaskies

1. *The true adventures of Huckleberry Finn,* as told by John Seelye (Evanston, Ill., Northwestern University Press, 1970). Professor Seelye added a little sex and profanity and cut the story down to those few parts which critics have approved of. From the jacket copy: ". . . the majority of modern critics . . . have questioned the integrity and credibility of Huck's narrative and . . . have concurred in condemning Mark Twain's artistry and historical accuracy in recording it. . . . At long last, however, Huck has found an able champion in John Seelye, who has diligently and faithfully recorded the full account of Huck's epic journey the way Huck himself would have told it. . . ." Many critics—whom Huck, in this version, playfully calls "crickits"—approved Seelye's rewrite, although so far as I know only Leslie Fiedler has called it better than the original—this in a statement quoted in an advertisement for the book that appeared in *The American Scholar* shortly after the book's publication.
2. Ludwig Lewisohn, *Expression in America* (New York and London, Harper & Brothers, 1932), p. 225.
3. H. H. Waggoner, "Science in the Thought of Mark Twain," *American Literature,* January, 1937.
4. Floyd Stovall, *American Idealism* (Norman, Okla., University of Oklahoma Press, 1943), p. 114.
5. *Which Was the Dream?* edited by John S. Tuckey (Los Angeles and Berkeley, University of California Press, 1967). Originally published by the University of California Press; reprinted by permission of The Regents of the University of California.

BLASPHEMY

1. Coleman O. Parsons, "The Devil and Samuel Clemens," *The Virginia Quarterly Review,* Autumn, 1947; *Leary,* p. 202.

This Friend of Satan

1. The unfinished versions of the Satan stories are published in book form as *The Mysterious Stranger,* by Mark Twain, edited by William M. Gibson (Berkeley and Los Angeles, University of California Press, 1970).
   Probably the ethics of Paine's changes in Mark Twain's story will long be debated. Editor Gibson in his introduction found that Paine, along with Harper editor Frederick A. Duneka, was guilty of "editorial fraud" because he did not reveal that he had made changes. But Mr. Gibson has no objection to the act of rewriting Mark Twain, provided that act be ac-

knowledged. He suggests that other writers may "carry on," "flesh out," "condense," "rework," and "strengthen" any of the unfinished versions of Mark Twain's Satan stories, and that they may do a better job than Paine and Duneka.

Noah's Ark

1. Symmachus was a Roman prefect and Titus an emperor; only Mark Twain has ever known the details of their animal collecting.
2. Leviticus is the third book of Moses in the Old Testament.

"THE LAST POSSIBILITY OF THE BEAUTIFUL"

1. Rachel M. Varble, *Jane Clemens* (Garden City, N.Y., Doubleday and Co., 1964), pp. 187, 199.
2. Samuel Charles Webster, *Mark Twain, Business Man* (Boston, Little Brown and Co., 1946), p. 44.
3. Quoted in Dixon Wecter, *Sam Clemens of Hannibal* (Boston, Houghton Mifflin Co., 1952), p. 1.
4. Rachel M. Varble, *Jane Clemens,* p. 159.
5. "Letter from Orion Clemens," *Paine,* Appendix A, p. 1591.
6. Interview with Tabitha Quarles Greening, St. Louis *Post-Dispatch,* December 10, 1899, quoted by Dixon Wecter, *Sam Clemens of Hannibal,* pp. 81, 92.
7. Caroline Thomas Narnsberger, *Mark Twain, Family Man* (New York, The Citadel Press, 1960), p. 105.
8. *Paine,* p. 1462.

Sour Mash and Others

1. Quoted in Edith Colgate Salsbury, *Susy and Mark Twain* (New York, Harper & Row, 1965), p. 208.
2. From an unpublished Mark Twain dictation of September 3, 1906.
3. The cats must have taught Mark Twain about German twenty-seven years earlier. In his "The Awful German Language," published in 1880, he said that ". . . chiefly in those words which express pathos" the German language was "surpassingly rich and effective. There are German songs which can make a stranger to the language cry. That shows that the *sound* of the words is correct . . ."

The Admiral and the Cat

1. *Mark Twain's Fables of Man,* edited by John S. Tuckey with texts prepared by Kenneth Sanderson and Bernard Stein (Los Angeles and Berkeley, University of California Press, 1972). Originally published by the University of California Press; reprinted by permission of The Regents of the University of California. This is one of the books that the Modern Language Association helped finance.

2. Rudyard Kipling, *From Sea to Sea* (New York, Doubleday, Page and Company, 1909), Vol. II, p. 177.

A Cat-Tale

1. From Mark Twain's "A Record of the Small Foolishnesses of Bay and Susie Clemens," quoted in Edith Colgate Salsbury, *Susy and Mark Twain* (New York, Harper and Row, 1965), pp. 101–103.
2. Clara Clemens, *My Father Mark Twain* (New York and London, Harper & Brothers, 1931), p. 2.